The Word, Worship and the Work Week

A Monday to Friday Devotional
on
Every Chapter in the New Testament

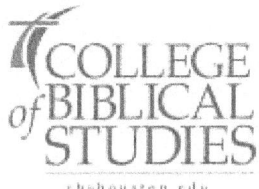

William Blocker, Editor

Israel Loken and Rick Kress, Associate Editors

From the faculty and staff of the College of Biblical Studies

Copyright © 2020 College of Biblical Studies

All rights reserved.

TRUTH. TRAINING. TRANSFORMATION

Scripture quotations taken from the New American Standard Bible® (NASB), Copyright © 1960, 1962, 1963, 1968, 1971, 1972, 1973, 1975, 1977, 1995 by The Lockman Foundation. Used by permission. www.Lockman.org

ISBN-13: 978-0-9979150-1-3

www.cbshouston.edu

DEDICATION

To the students, staff, faculty, and faithful supporters
of the
College of Biblical Studies.

CONTENTS

PREFACE xiii
WHY START WITH A GENEALOGY? 1
THREE KINGS? 2
WHY DID JESUS GET BAPTIZED? 3
MOUNTAINTOPS, VALLEYS, AND VICTORY IN JESUS 4
LOVE SO AMAZING, SO DIVINE 5
~~ANNUAL~~ DAILY EYE EXAM 6
ASK, SEEK, KNOCK—FOR WHAT? 7
WHAT KIND OF MAN IS THIS … 8
CALLING ALL SINNERS 9
THE ANSWER TO YOUR OWN PRAYER 10
FINDING REST 11
BLOOD OR BELIEF 12
WHEAT AND TARES 13
LITTLE FAITH 14
GREAT FAITH 15
WHEN FAITH IS NO LONGER EASY 16
THE KINGDOM BEYOND THE CROSS 17
THE PERILOUS SURGE FOR GREATNESS 18
MORE COMMITMENT THAN EXPECTED 19
REWARDS GO TO SERVANTS 20
LOOK WHO IS COMING! 21
TRICK QUESTIONS 22
TARGETING HYPOCRISY 23
THE ONLY SURE WAY TO BE READY 24
SEEING THE KING IN HIS PEOPLE 25
A WILLING SACRIFICE 26
WHEN ALL SEEMS LOST 27
THE KINGDOM IS STILL IN BUSINESS 28
LIFE CHANGE 29
LOAD SHARING 30
LOONEY TUNES 31
LISTENING, ACCEPTING, DOING 32
LEGION OF PROBLEMS 33
LEGACY 34
LISTS OF MEN 35
LESSONS FROM THE LOAVES 36
LAST IS FIRST 37
LASTING ROI 38
LORD HAS NEED OF YOU 39
LIVING NOT DEAD 40

LEARNING THE SEASONS	41
LIMITATIONS OF THE FLESH	42
LAID IN A TOMB	43
LOOKING FOR JESUS THE NAZARENE	44
PERSIST IN PRAYER	45
GOOD NEWS!	46
REPENT AND REFORM	47
ARE YOU MALNOURISHED?	48
SLIP AWAY TO PRAY	49
LOVE OTHERS WELL	50
SPIRITUAL MATHEMATICS	51
CULTIVATING GOOD SOIL	52
NO MORE EXCUSES	53
PRAYING WHILE GOING	54
SHAMELESS PERSISTENCE	55
WHEN PERSECUTION COMES	56
OF MUSTARD SEED AND LEAVEN	57
JESUS' FAMILY VALUES	58
3 PARABLES, 2 AUDIENCES, 1 THEME	59
WISDOM WITH TRUE RICHES	60
INCREASE YOUR FAITH	61
SPIRITUAL AND PHYSICAL BLINDNESS	62
THE THINGS WHICH MAKE FOR PEACE	63
RENDER UNTO CAESAR	64
PREPARING FOR A DIFFICULT FUTURE	65
BUT I HAVE PRAYED FOR YOU	66
CURIOSITY'S GOT YOUR TONGUE?	67
ONE ENDING MARKS A NEW BEGINNING	68
WAS JESUS HUMAN OR DIVINE? YES!	69
FAN OR FOLLOWER?	70
THE WITNESS	71
LIVING WATER	72
DISPLAYING HIS DIVINITY	73
PASS THE BREAD	74
GOD'S TIMING	75
DIVINE LIGHT	76
SPIRITUAL OPTOMETRY	77
THE DOOR & THE SHEPHERD	78
RESURRECTION AND LIFE	79
PREPARATIONS FOR DEATH	80
LESSONS OF HUMILITY	81
COMFORT FOR TROUBLED HEARTS	82
IS THERE A CONNECTION?	83

PEACE IN TROUBLESOME TIMES	84
TRUE INTERCESSORY PRAYER	85
MAKING THE RIGHT CHOICE	86
IS BLOOD REALLY THICKER THAN WATER?	87
THE POWER OF THE RESURRECTION	88
BOUNCING BACK FROM FAILURE	89
MARCHING ORDERS	90
PENTECOST	91
THE MAKING OF THE BEAUTIFUL	92
UNTRAINED MEN	93
OBEY GOD RATHER THAN MEN	94
ARE YOU WILLING TO BE USED?	95
THE SACRIFICE OF LIFE	96
PERSECUTION TO SALVATION	97
NURTURING NEW BELIEVERS	98
ALL ARE CLEAN	99
JEWS + GENTILES = THE CHURCH	100
EXPECTANT PRAYER	101
THE POWER OF THE WORD	102
PREACHING DESPITE PERSECUTION	103
GRACE ON TRIAL	104
FINDING DISCIPLES	105
THE UNKNOWN GOD	106
THE LORD IS WITH US	107
EFFECTIVE MINISTRY	108
A CHARGE FOR SHEPHERDS	109
TO GO OR NOT TO GO	110
SPIRITUAL TRANSFORMATION	111
DIVINE ENCOURAGEMENT	112
A GOOD CONSCIENCE	113
WHY DID PAUL APPEAL TO CAESAR?	114
WORDS OF SOBER TRUTH	115
PROVIDENTIAL CARE	116
THE GOSPEL REACHES ROME	117
THREE MOTIVATIONS FOR THE GOSPEL	118
IS A "GOOD" PERSON SAVED?	119
REDEMPTION AND PROPITIATION	120
THE SECURITY OF JUSTIFICATION	121
THE HOPE OF HIS GLORY	122
THE REALM OF GRACE	123
THE STRUGGLE WITH THE FLESH	124
GOD WILL WORK IT FOR GOOD	125
A HEART FOR THE LOST	126

BEAUTIFUL FEET	127
THE INFINITE PLAN OF GOD	128
A LIVING SACRIFICE TO GOD	129
THE DEBT OF LOVE	130
JUDGING ONE ANOTHER	131
THREE CHARACTERISTICS OF MATURITY	132
ESTABLISHED BY THE GOSPEL	133
SPIRITUAL UNITY	134
EMBRACING THE MIND OF CHRIST	135
PLANTERS AND WATERERS	136
FOR WHOM ARE YOU FAITHFUL?	137
COMPASSIONATE CONFRONTATION	138
SAINTS IN SECULAR COURTS?	139
SINGLE OR MARRIED, WALK IN THIS MANNER	140
LIBERTY AND LOVE	141
YOUR RIGHTS AND THE GOSPEL	142
WHICH CUP ARE YOU DRINKING?	143
THE LORD'S SUPPER	144
ONE BODY, ONE SPIRIT	145
LOVE NEVER FAILS	146
EDIFICATION OF THE BRETHREN	147
THE GOSPEL IN WHICH WE STAND	148
STAND FIRM	149
DIFFERENT ON PURPOSE?	150
LOVE EVEN WHEN IT HURTS!	151
FREE INDEED!	152
A GREAT TREASURE!	153
LIVING FOREVER	154
MINDFUL MINISTRY	155
WALKING IN HOLINESS	156
ABUNDANT GIVING	157
CHEERFUL GIVING	158
AUTHORITY UNDER GOD	159
PASTORAL PERSEVERANCE	160
APPRECIATION FOR AFFLICTION?	161
CARING CONFRONTATION	162
JESUS IS LORD	163
LIVING BY FAITH IN THE SON OF GOD	164
JESUS IS REDEEMER	165
AN HEIR THROUGH GOD	166
WALKING BY THE SPIRIT	167
DO NOT GROW WEARY	168
OUR HEAVENLY RICHES	169

FROM DEATH TO LIFE	170
BEYOND WHAT WE ASK OR THINK	171
AT PEACE WITH OTHERS	172
BEING AN IMITATOR OF GOD	173
PREPARING FOR BATTLE	174
REJOICING IN PRISON?	175
SELFISH OR SELFLESS?	176
THE GIFT OF RESURRECTION	177
THANKFUL SPIRIT = GENTLE SPIRIT	178
JESUS IS THE IMAGE OF GOD	179
MADE ALIVE WITH CHRIST	180
IMAGE RESTORATION	181
GRACIOUS SPEECH	182
THE POWER OF EXAMPLE	183
IMAGES OF SERVANT LEADERSHIP	184
COMFORT THROUGH COMMUNITY	185
A DIFFERENT KIND OF GRIEF	186
THE DAY OF THE LORD	187
DEFENDING THOSE WE LOVE	188
MAN OF LAWLESSNESS	189
RESPONSE AND RESPONSIBILITY	190
LEADING WITH A CLEAR CONSCIENCE	191
PEACE AND QUIET AIDS THE GOSPEL	192
IS YOUR LEADER(SHIP) SETTING A GOOD EXAMPLE?	193
THE ANTIDOTE TO FALSE TEACHING	194
KEEP CHURCH FINANCES PURE	195
HOW TO GET RICH OFF THE GOSPEL	196
ENTRUSTED WITH TREASURE	197
A SACRED TRUST	198
~~DEATH~~ PERSECUTION AND TAXES	199
LOOKING TO THE CROWN	200
CHOSEN OF GOD	201
ZEALOUS FOR GOOD DEEDS	202
FROM GRACE TO GODLINESS	203
THE COST OF BEING A LITTLE CHRIST	204
EVEN THE ANGELS WORSHIP HIM	205
DRIFTING AWAY	206
THE DANGER OF SIN'S DECEIT	207
THE COMPASSIONATE HIGH PRIEST	208
GROWN BABIES	209
SIMILAR SOIL, DISSIMILAR RESULTS	210
NEW LAW, NEW PRIEST	211
NEW COVENANT, SAME RECIPIENTS	212

BETTER BLOOD	213
EVERY SAINT IS PERFECT	214
THE GREAT REWARDER	215
THE FATHER'S LOVING DISCIPLINE	216
HONOR MARRIAGE	217
WORSHIP HIM BY ASKING FOR WISDOM	218
ARE YOU JUSTIFIED BY FAITH OR WORKS?	219
TEACH YOUR TONGUE SELF-CONTROL	220
TRUSTING IN TOMORROW	221
PERSPECTIVE, PERSEVERANCE, PRAYER	222
THIS WORLD IS NOT MY HOME	223
ACTING LIKE BABIES?	224
THE HOPE THAT IS IN YOU	225
SUFFERING, SUBMISSION, AND SERVICE	226
STAND FIRM AGAINST THE DEVIL	227
PERFECT PROVISION	228
NOAH … AND LOT?	229
LIVING IN LIGHT OF THE DAY OF THE LORD	230
FELLOWSHIP WITH GOD AND OTHERS	231
DILIGENT IN RIGHTEOUSNESS	232
GOD'S LOVE VERSUS SATAN'S HATRED	233
SECURE IN GOD'S LOVE	234
FAITH MAKES THE CHOICE EASY	235
JESUS UNDERSTANDS US	236
IMITATING THE GODLY	237
YOU ARE KEPT—SO KEEP ON KEEPING ON	238
READ AND HEED	239
THE ONE WHO KNOWS	240
THE ONE WHO EXHORTS	241
THE ONE WHO REIGNS	242
THE ONE WHO IS WORTHY	243
THE WRATH OF GOD	244
SEALED AND DELIVERED	245
SILENCE IN HEAVEN	246
DIVINE JUDGMENT	247
SWEET AND BITTER	248
GOD'S WITNESSES	249
DIVINE PROTECTION	250
THE UNHOLY TRINITY	251
PERSEVERANCE	252
THE SONG OF MOSES	253
THE BOWLS OF WRATH	254
THE BEST INTERPRETER	255

BABYLON THE ~~GREAT~~ GROTESQUE 256
HALLELUJAH! WORSHIP GOD! 257
THY KINGDOM COME, THY WILL BE DONE 258
ALL THINGS WILL BECOME NEW 259
HE IS COMING SOON 260
SCRIPTURE INDEX 261
SUBJECT INDEX 275
CONTRIBUTING AUTHORS 278

PREFACE

There are 260 chapters in the New Testament, and in God's providence there are just over 260 weekdays in a year (depending on how the calendar falls in any given year). By reading one chapter a day during your work week, you can read the entire New Testament in one year.

Starting in Matthew and ending in Revelation, the short devotions in this book follow the chapter order of the New Testament. Each devotion features expository thoughts to help you better grasp and apply the message from that portion of God's Word.

The faculty and staff who contributed to this volume (25 contributors) love the Lord Jesus Christ and have a passion to know Him and make Him known. They are scholars with a heart for the Word of God, and the God of the Word.

It is our prayer that the Holy Spirit would bless you as you spend time in the Scriptures He inspired, and that you would grow in the grace and knowledge of our great God and Savior.

Monday

WHY START WITH A GENEALOGY?
Read Matthew 1

The record of the genealogy of Jesus the Messiah, the son of David, the son of Abraham. (1:1)

From beginning to end, Matthew's Gospel was written for a Jewish audience wrestling with questions about the messianic kingdom and the Person of Jesus Christ. If Jesus was the Messiah, why hadn't the kingdom come? Why was He rejected by the Jewish authorities? Why are sinners, outcasts, and even Gentiles acknowledging Him as Messiah and worshipping Him as Lord?

To help answer the questions surrounding the Person of Christ, Matthew began his Gospel with a genealogy, confirming that Jesus is indeed the Jewish Messiah. He is the heir of the Davidic covenant, having descended from Israel's greatest king. And as a descendant of Abraham He is the One who fulfills the Abrahamic covenant with its blessing for all nations (cf. 28:18-20).

Upon closer scrutiny, however, the genealogy is ironically dotted with sinners, outcasts, and Gentiles right alongside the expected Jewish patriarchs and pillars. One of Christ's ancestors had been a Canaanite prostitute (Rahab) and another a Moabitess (Ruth), both members of Gentile nations condemned and ostracized in the Old Testament (cf. Dt 23:3; Zec 14:21). Even His Jewish ancestors were marked by scandal, notably Judah, who fathered Perez and Zerah by his daughter-in-law Tamar (Gn 38), and David, who fathered Solomon "by Bathsheba *who had been the wife of Uriah*" (v. 1:6b).

Yet despite the scandals of His legal genealogy, Matthew reassures his readers that Jesus' sinlessness was preserved, as He was virgin-born, conceived by the Holy Spirit (vv. 18-20). Paradoxically, He would be a descendant of sinful humans—yet still Immanuel, meaning "God with us" (v. 23). As a result, the Messiah's human name would be Jesus, meaning "salvation", because "He will save His people from their sins" (v. 21).

Praise God today for Jesus the Messiah! He came to save us from our sins! And for those who are fully aware of their own scandalous sin—that is truly good news!

RK

Tuesday

THREE KINGS?
Read Matthew 2

... magi from the east arrived in Jerusalem, saying, "Where is He Who has been born King of the Jews? For we saw His star in the east and have come to worship Him." (2:1-2)

In spite of the famous Christmas hymn, Matthew does not call Jesus' childhood visitors "kings", but rather "magi" (i.e., wise men). These magi were from the east, most likely a reference to the region of Babylon or perhaps Persia. Magi were typically schooled in astronomy and ancient writings. The magi who visited Christ offered three gifts—"gold, frankincense, and myrrh" (v. 11). Thus, three persons may be implied, but the number is nowhere explicitly stated.

Matthew does, however, clearly contrast these foreigners' response to Jesus with that of Herod and the Jewish religious leaders. The magi probably traveled with a significant entourage, perhaps even with a small militia for protection. Although Jerusalem was a bustling international city with foreigners arriving all the time, the arrival of these magi surely caused a stir throughout the city.

These men, with their questions regarding One born King of the Jews, attracted the attention of the Roman-appointed King Herod and the rest of Jerusalem—and it troubled them (v. 3). Herod inquired of the experts in the Jewish Scriptures, the chief priests and scribes, as to where the Messiah was to be born. They replied, "Bethlehem of Judea," referencing a prophecy recorded in Micah 5:2.

Notice the varying responses to King Jesus. The magi came to worship, not knowing exactly where He was, but yet compelled to seek Him. The religious leaders knew the biblical answer, but they did not search Him out. Herod wanted to eliminate the Messiah (vv. 7-18), because the true King was a threat to Herod's sovereignty.

Were there three *kings*? Perhaps not. Maybe *three* magi, though we can't be sure. But there were at least *three responses* to King Jesus. It's the same today. Some are complacent. Some are contemptuous and even hostile. Some are compelled to worship Him.

What is your response to Jesus?

RK

Wednesday

WHY DID JESUS GET BAPTIZED?
Read Matthew 3

But John tried to prevent Him, saying, "I have need to be baptized by You, and do You come to me?" But Jesus answering said to him, "Permit it at this time; for in this way it is fitting for us to fulfill all righteousness." (3:14-15a)

Was Jesus baptized because He was burdened by sin? Perhaps that question sounds almost heretical. After all, Jesus was and is the *sinless* Son of God. But consider the scene that unfolds in Matthew three. John's water baptism was a visual demonstration of repentance from sin in anticipation of the coming of One Who would baptize *with the Holy Spirit and fire* (v. 11)—One with the divine authority to save, cleanse, and judge.

When Jesus came to be baptized, John was understandably confused and reluctant. God's prophet knew that Jesus was different—He was sinless and therefore needed no repentance. In fact, Christ was the anticipated Messiah, the One with the divine authority to save, cleanse, and judge.

Jesus said in essence: "It's OK. It's the right thing to do at this time." But His somewhat cryptic answer begs the question—why? After all, there was nothing in the Old Testament requiring baptism. The answer is found in the context of John's ministry. John was preparing a people for the coming of the Lord. The Lord had entered this world to save His people from their sins (1:21). To do that, God became a man (1:23) and would offer Himself as a ransom for sinners (20:28). Therefore, Jesus was baptized *to identify with those He came to save—sinners.* Yes, Jesus was baptized because of sin—our sin.

The arrival of the Holy Spirit (v. 16) and the testimony of the Father (v. 17) both demonstrate God's delight in His Son (v. 17). Jesus' baptism confirmed that God had come to personally identify with and redeem sinners.

Praise God for His beloved Son. Christ humbled Himself so as to identify with you, and to give His life as a ransom so that you could be saved from your sin—so that you could likewise be baptized with the Holy Spirit and experience God's delight.

RK

Thursday

MOUNTAINTOPS, VALLEYS, AND VICTORY IN JESUS
Read Matthew 4

Then Jesus was led up by the Spirit into the wilderness to be tempted by the devil. (4:1)

Someone has said, "After every mountaintop there is a valley". After Jesus' baptism, the affirmation of the Spirit, and the glorious testimony of the Father—the Messiah was led *by the Spirit* into the wilderness to be tempted by the devil. This valley was no accident or mistake (none are); rather this wilderness experience was a divine appointment for our Lord.

Just as Israel had come out of Egypt through the waters of the Red Sea to be divinely led in the wilderness as God's corporate son (cf. Ex 14:22; Ps 78:52), now God's beloved Son would come through the waters of baptism to be divinely led in the wilderness.

While Israel often failed their wilderness tests, Jesus did not. He proved to be what Israel was not—a faithful Son. Jesus faced the devil's onslaught by depending on the Word of God. He understood its context and how it applied to His situation.

God allowed Israel to be hungry so that they might learn that God is the source of life—not food. Jesus understood that truth from the Scriptures and trusted the Lord to provide (4:4; cf. Dt 8:3). Israel had questioned whether God was among them or not—putting God to the test (Ex 17:2). Although the devil tried to provoke Him, Jesus refused to test His Father, citing Scripture to admonish Satan (4:7; cf. Dt 6:16). Israel worshiped the golden calf in the wilderness (Ex 32). Jesus would worship the Lord God alone, because the Scriptures told Him so (4:10; cf. Dt 6:13; 10:20).

Worship God by trusting Him both when the Spirit confirms you on the mountaintop, *and* when He leads you into the valley. Seek to understand what the Scriptures mean and how they apply to the tests you face. And glory in the faithfulness of God's Son, Jesus Christ, our Savior! He passed every test. Through Him we overcome the world and the god of this world (2 Cor 4:4-6; 1 Jn 5:4-5).

RK

Friday

LOVE SO AMAZING, SO DIVINE
Read Matthew 5

But I say to you, love your enemies and pray for those who persecute you, so that you may be sons of your Father Who is in heaven. (5:44-45a)

Chapters 5-7 of Matthew contain what is famously titled: "The Sermon on the Mount". This passage essentially serves as an explanatory delineation of our Lord's message, "Repent, for the kingdom of heaven is at hand" (4:17). In other words, the sermon reveals how a kingdom citizen should think and live. As church-age believers destined to participate in the messianic kingdom, we should seek to live in light of these kingdom principles.

From the world's perspective, blessing is found in wealth, power, and control. But those destined for the kingdom know that the ones who are truly blessed understand their spiritual poverty, which makes them humble, merciful, and hungry for righteousness (vv. 3-7).

Likewise, the world's perspective on love is that it must be earned. But believers are called to love those who don't deserve it—*even their enemies* (v. 44). Why? Because the God Who rules in the kingdom loves even those who deny and rebel against Him (v. 45).

A kingdom-minded person has a perspective that turns the world's priorities upside down. No wonder Jesus called such people "the light of the world" (v. 14). This counterintuitive way of thinking and living glorifies our Father Who is in heaven (v. 16).

But who can perfectly reflect and live out the righteousness found in the Father? The beloved Son, in Whom the Father is well-pleased (3:17)! And those who trust in the Son are declared righteous in Him (Rom 4:5). And those who love Christ are compelled to live for the One Who died and rose again on their behalf (2 Cor 5:14-15).

Praise God for the righteousness of Christ! Worship Him by prayerfully and intentionally loving those around you—even those who oppose and persecute you. You will experience the joy and strength of God's Spirit as you serve as a light to the world around you.

RK

Monday

~~ANNUAL~~ DAILY EYE EXAM
Read Matthew 6

The eye is the lamp of the body; so then if your eye is clear, your whole body will be full of light. (6:22)

Continuing His famous sermon on kingdom thinking and living, the Lord turns to issues of the heart (i.e., motives) in chapter six. Spiritual disciplines like giving, prayer, and fasting should be Godward focused rather than viewed as opportunities for self-promotion. God rewards those who seek Him in private and serve Him because of their relationship with Him—not for some earthly recognition (vv. 1-18).

Jesus then transitions to a related topic, namely, the subject of what one truly values—heavenly treasures or earthly treasures (vv. 19-24). This is the context of the enigmatic phrase, "The eye is the lamp of the body" (v. 22). Christ's words serve as a somewhat cryptic illustration of a person's focus in regard to wealth, or what one values greatly.

If you are overly focused on earthly treasure your eye will be clouded with darkness. You will be plagued with vision that leaves you groping in the dark after things that do not last.

But if you focus on heavenly treasure, you will see clearly and your whole being will find eternal purpose. What you focus on will determine how well you see and how well you live. In fact, Jesus reveals that a Godward focus is the cure for daily anxiety (vv. 25-34). When you focus on heavenly things you will be content, and experience the peace of God (cf. Phil 4:6-7).

Jesus is calling for a spiritual eye exam—not annually, but daily. What is your focus in life? Is it God's rule and righteousness or your own advancement in this world? Worship God today by setting your eyes on and seeking His kingdom and His righteousness. God will take care of your temporal needs. As you focus on and trust Him, Jesus will shine His light in you and through you. You will have the light of life and be a light to the world (cf. 5:14; Jn 8:12).

RK

Tuesday

ASK, SEEK, KNOCK—FOR WHAT?
Read Matthew 7

For everyone who asks receives, and he who seeks finds, and to him who knocks it will be opened. (7:8)

Many have heard Jesus' famous promise of answered prayer in Matthew seven, but few have noted the context in which it was given. Was Jesus issuing an open-ended guarantee that if we pray hard enough we will receive whatever we are asking for?

In 7:1-5, the Lord described the kingdom perspective on relationships. He said in essence: "Stop *condemning* others ... deal with your own sin, then you can see how best to *help* your brother with his sin." Notably, Christ was not forbidding all judgment, but rather condemnation—which is God's divine right, not man's.

Then Jesus issued a rather enigmatic statement: "Do not give what is holy to dogs, and do not throw your pearls before swine" (v. 6a). What does this have to do with the preceding command to help a fellow sinner and the guarantee of answered prayer that follows?

Dogs and pigs were ritually unclean animals in Jewish society. They would have been associated with unbelievers. The thought here is that God's people should share kingdom truth wisely and judiciously. Although we are to be careful to love, and not unnecessarily judge or condemn others (7:1-5), we are not to share God's truth without a sensitivity or judgment as to the receptivity of audiences (7:6). Some people are simply not ready for kingdom truth. Rather, the best course of action may be to pray for them, and for discernment, and for love (7:7-12).

So how do you find the spiritual wisdom to deal with sin—your own and your brother's? Through persistent prayer: "Ask, and it will be given to you; seek, and you will find; knock, and it will be opened to you" (v. 7).

View your relationships as opportunities to worship God. Ask Him to give you the wisdom needed to first deal with your own sin, and then to lovingly help others with their sin. Seek God's counsel by meditating on His Word. Knock on the doors of heaven for relational love and insight. Jesus guarantees that such prayers will be answered. Praise the Lord for His amazing grace! RK

Wednesday

WHAT KIND OF MAN IS THIS ...
Read Matthew 8

What kind of a man is this, that even the winds and the sea obey Him? (8:27b)

When Jesus finished His "Sermon on the Mount" (Mt 5-7), "the crowds were amazed at His teaching; for He was teaching them as one having authority, and not as their scribes" (7:28-29). It is one thing to teach as one having authority, but quite another to actually possess that authority.

In chapter eight, Matthew recorded several miracles that demonstrated that the Lord did indeed possess the power and authority of God. Jesus cured leprosy (vv. 2-4). He delivered a paralyzed servant simply by speaking (vv. 5-13). He healed Peter's mother-in-law with a touch (vv. 14-15). He cast out evil spirits from those who were demon-possessed, and healed all who were ill (v. 16). He quieted a deadly storm on the sea (vv. 23-27), and cast a legion of demons into a herd of swine in the land of the Gadarenes (vv. 28-34).

In the midst of these scenes, Matthew recorded dialogue designed to reveal an important implication of recognizing Christ's authority (vv. 18-22). In response to one would-be follower who asked to delay his professed allegiance, the Lord startlingly said: "Follow Me, and allow the dead to bury their own dead" (v. 22). There is only one truly appropriate response to One Who has the power and authority of God—immediate and complete obedience.

Just as the disciples who saw Jesus calm the deadly storm asked, "What kind of a man is this, that even the winds and the sea obey Him?", so we too must answer that question. Jesus is the God-man, possessing divine power and authority. He can heal, protect, guide, and deliver you. He is sovereign over all—and over all circumstances in life. Don't delay. Get to know Him more and more by reading and meditating on His Word. And follow Him in faithful obedience.

RK

Thursday

CALLING ALL SINNERS
Read Matthew 9
... for I did not come to call the righteous, but sinners. (9:13)

Charles Spurgeon aptly said: "Our imaginary goodness is harder to conquer than our actual sin .... It is a sign of grace to know one's need of grace." In chapter nine of his Gospel, Matthew continued to highlight Jesus' authority and the proper response to it—with a particular emphasis on His authority to forgive sins.

The Lord forgave the sins of a paralyzed man, then healed him to demonstrate to the doubters that He had that authority (vv. 2-8). On His way to heal the daughter of a synagogue official (vv. 18-31), He recognized the faith of an outcast woman and recognized her as a "daughter" (v. 22). Whether religious or rejected, Jesus loved sinners and rewarded their faith.

When Jesus cast out a mute man's demon, some of the religious leaders attributed His power to the prince of demons (v. 34). But Jesus continued to heal the afflicted, "teaching in their synagogues and proclaiming the gospel of the kingdom" (v. 35). Those religious leaders should have known that the Hebrew Scriptures associated such miracles with the messianic kingdom (cf. Is 29:18-19; 35:5-6). The Old Testament further confirms that God desires compassion more than a strict adherence to religious rules (v. 13; cf. Hos 6:6).

In the middle of these events, Matthew records his own story. He was a tax collector for the Gentiles—one likely seen as a traitor to his own people. Upon hearing Jesus' words, "Follow Me!", Matthew immediately left his tax collector's booth and followed Him (v. 9).

On another occasion, Jesus dined with his disciples in a house, joined by various tax collectors and sinners. The self-righteous Pharisees were offended and questioned the disciples about their Master's behavior. But Jesus, overhearing their question, uttered the glorious words, "I did not come to call the righteous, but sinners" (v. 13). They didn't understand that everyone is a sinner—whether religious or rejected.

Trust in Jesus alone for your righteousness. Follow Him today. And tell other sinners about your Savior.

RK

Friday

THE ANSWER TO YOUR OWN PRAYER
Read Matthew 10

These twelve Jesus sent out after instructing them ... (10:5)

At the end of Matthew nine, Jesus said to His disciples: "Beseech the Lord of the harvest to send out workers into His harvest" (9:38). Surely the twelve apostles listed in 10:2-4 were among those who heard these words and obediently laid this request before God. Therefore, Jesus called them to be, at least in part, the answer to their own prayer. They were being sent out into the harvest themselves!

Authority to heal and deliver the oppressed was associated with the coming messianic kingdom (cf. Is 29:18-19; 35:5-6). The twelve apostles were given authority over unclean spirits along with the ability to heal every kind of sickness and disease, thus validating their message concerning the kingdom of heaven (vv. 1, 7).

The rest of the chapter records the instructions Jesus gave in equipping the Twelve for their future ministry. It was probably not what they expected. Jesus announced that they would face opposition, difficulty, and even betrayal. But there would also be eternal reward if they were faithful.

The language Jesus used indicates that the ministry of His disciples would extend beyond the immediate assignment recorded in this chapter (cf. vv. 17-20)—and in some measure beyond just the Twelve (cf. vv. 32-42). While the Twelve were granted unique authority, future disciples would share in the mission, the sufferings, and the eternal reward.

The Lord's paradoxical statement to His disciples in verse thirty-nine has eternal implications: "He who has found his life will lose it, and he who has lost his life for My sake will find it." Those who live for themselves will forfeit their future reward while those who give up their personal rights to follow Christ (even to the point of death) will be greatly rewarded.

Who are you living for, yourself or your Savior? What is the focus of your life, following Christ or seeking your own comfort? And what are you praying for? God's kingdom or your safety? Perhaps *you* are—at least in part—the answer to your own prayer.

RK

Monday

FINDING REST
Read Matthew 11

Come to Me, all who are weary and heavy-laden, and I will give you rest. (11:28)

Having announced the future rejection of the disciples in the previous chapter, here Matthew described the nation's rejection of John the Baptist and the divine judgment that would follow. John the Baptist, having heard reports concerning the extraordinary works being performed by Jesus, sent messengers to ask Him whether He was the expected Messiah. This same question was being pondered by the rest of the nation. The Lord responded by pointing to the numerous miracles that He and His disciples were performing. These miracles provided ample evidence that Jesus was indeed the Messiah.

Christ then addressed the crowds, explaining to them that John was the prophesied messenger of Malachi 3:1. Yet despite his status as a prophet of God, John and his message of repentance were rejected by the nation. Jesus and His message of repentance were likewise rejected by the nation. As a result, the Lord proclaimed divine judgment on all who witnessed His confirmatory miracles and still rejected Him, along with His disciples.

Yet even in the midst of His condemnation of the nation as a whole, Jesus made a gracious offer to relieve the afflictions of individuals who chose to follow Him. The religious leaders had placed an enormous burden on the nation, reducing the Mosaic Law to an extensive list of rules and regulations that needed to be rigidly followed. As a result, the Law had become a weighty yoke for individual Jews to bear. They were weary and heavy-laden. These leaders confused righteousness with religious practice. Jesus promised to replace the yoke of the Law with the yoke of discipleship. Although the yoke of discipleship may involve difficulty, and perhaps even death (cf. 10:17-23), the promised reward is great (v. 11).

When you are overwhelmed by the difficulties of life, come to Jesus. When you grow weary of trying to earn your way to heaven through self-righteousness, come to Jesus. His yoke is easy and His burden is light; and in Him you will find rest.

IL

Tuesday

BLOOD OR BELIEF
Read Matthew 12

For whoever does the will of My Father Who is in heaven, he is My brother and sister and mother. (12:50)

At first glance, it is difficult to see the connection between verses 46-50 and the rest of this chapter. However, this passage serves as a crucial pivot, emphasizing a major shift in Christ's ministry—from Jew to Gentile.

Chapter twelve marks the official rejection of Christ by the Jewish religious leaders. Although many Jews were on the brink of accepting Christ as the Messiah, the religious leaders were convinced that He was performing miracles by the power of Satan (vv. 23-24). After explaining the absurdity of their assertion, the Lord announced that the nation had reached a point of no return. They had rejected the Messiah and would therefore be condemned (vv. 31-32, 37, 41-42). The final sign they would be given was the sign of Jonah, a reference to the death and resurrection of the Messiah (vv. 39-40). From this point forward, the crucifixion was assured.

Verse fourteen describes the antagonism of the Pharisees, "But the Pharisees went out and conspired against Him, as to how they might destroy Him." But why were these religious leaders so hostile toward Christ? The answer lies in their belief that they were destined for the kingdom simply because they were related to Abraham by blood (3:9). However, John the Baptist announced that the Pharisees and Sadducees were in need of repentance in order to enter into the kingdom (3:7-8). Christ reiterated John's assertion at the beginning of the Sermon on the Mount (5:20). Naturally, the self-righteous Pharisees and Sadducees took offence at the suggestion that they were destined for wrath, responding with venomous rage.

Verses 46-50 reveal that repentant faith is more important than blood. A Jew's first birth was not sufficient to gain entrance into the kingdom—they needed to be born again (cf. Jn 3:3-6). Christ's true relatives are related to Him by faith, not blood.

Are you a relative of Christ? If so, do the will of the Father in heaven. Others will soon see your works and desire to join the family.

IL

Wednesday

WHEAT AND TARES
Read Matthew 13

But blessed are your eyes, because they see; and your ears, because they hear. (13:16)

Matthew thirteen contains eight parables designed to reveal mysteries concerning the kingdom of heaven to those whose hearts were prepared to receive these truths. Not everyone was prepared to hear Christ's teaching. "Therefore, I speak to them in parables; because while seeing they do not see, and while hearing they do not hear, nor do they understand" (v. 13). Christ was speaking here of those who had rejected His message of repentance and, by proxy, those miracles that proved the veracity of His message. Matthew 12:22-24 showed two responses to Christ's miracle of healing a demon-possessed man. The crowds were amazed, becoming convinced that Jesus was the Messiah. However, the religious leaders rejected this possibility, arguing that Jesus was doing miracles by the power of Satan.

Christ wanted to give additional revelation to those who had accepted His message. But He also wanted to keep this revelation from those who had rejected His message. Those who had repented were destined for the kingdom of heaven (cf. 5:3-10). Those who had rejected were condemned and would not see the kingdom of heaven (cf. 5:20; 12:31-32, 37, 41-42). Therefore, knowledge concerning the mysteries of the kingdom of heaven was restricted to those who would enter that kingdom.

These two groups are described in the parable of the wheat and the tares (vv. 24-30). The wheat represents those who are destined for the kingdom (v. 38), while the tares are those who will be kept from the kingdom and thrown into the furnace of fire (vv. 41-42). Ironically, those who had accused Christ of working by the power of the devil (12:24) were themselves the sons of the evil one (v. 38).

It can be difficult to distinguish between wheat and tares. Tares look just like wheat until the ear appears (the ear is the grain-bearing tip). Just as a tree is known by its fruit (12:33), so the stalk is known by its "fruit". Beware of tares! They may appear to be genuine Christians, but their lack of fruit (i.e., repentance) gives them away.

IL

Thursday

LITTLE FAITH
Read Matthew 14

Immediately Jesus stretched out His hand and took hold of him, and said to him, "You of little faith, why did you doubt?" (14:31)

Christ uses the phrase "little faith" four times in the Gospel of Matthew. In the Sermon on the Mount, The Lord uses it to criticize all those who worry about daily necessities (6:30). In 8:26, He uses it to admonish His disciples, who had grown fearful when a great storm arose on the Sea of Galilee. Here in chapter fourteen, Jesus scolds Peter, who became frightened while walking on water (v. 31). And in 16:8, he uses the phrase to correct His disciples' spiritual misunderstanding concerning the leaven of the Pharisees and Sadducees. In all four cases, the phrase is used as a sharp rebuke (see also 17:20).

The disciples possessed saving faith (i.e., justification)—what they needed was mature faith (i.e., sanctification). They showed their lack of spiritual maturity whenever they worried, or became afraid, or failed to trust Christ, or lacked understanding. This type of immature faith is described in James 1:6, "But he must ask in faith without any doubting, for the one who doubts is like the surf of the sea, driven and tossed by the wind." Peter initially showed great faith by getting out of the boat and walking on water. However, as soon as doubt crept in, he started to sink, and he became frightened.

By this time, the disciples had witnessed numerous miracles, including the feeding of the 5000 featured in verses 15-21. Amazingly, this miracle had taken place just hours before Jesus' appearance on the sea. Having witnessed so many of Christ's miracles, the disciples' faith should have grown to maturity. Yet, they still doubted. And they continued to doubt. It will take the Ascension to finally cure the disciples of their lack of faith (the disciples of the Book of Acts stand in sharp contrast to the disciples of the Gospel of Matthew).

How mature is your faith? Do you find yourself constantly worrying about the necessities of life (e.g., finances, health, relationships, etc.)? Or do you trust the Lord in all circumstances? Remember— "… the righteous (justification) will live by his faith (sanctification)" (Hab 2:4).

IL

Friday

GREAT FAITH
Read Matthew 15

Then Jesus said to her, "O woman, your faith is great; it shall be done for you as you wish." And her daughter was healed at once. (15:28)

Matthew fifteen begins with some religious leaders coming from Jerusalem to question Jesus as to why His disciples do not follow the tradition of the elders. As has been apparent for several chapters, these religious leaders were quite hostile to Jesus and His message of repentance (cf. e.g., 9:3; 12:14, 24). As a result, the Lord withdrew from Galilee to Phoenicia, a region dominated by its principal cities, Tyre and Sidon. This was the ancient birthplace of Baal-worship, a thoroughly Gentile region avoided by the Jewish religious leaders.

One day, a Canaanite woman approached Jesus and cried out, "Have mercy on me, Lord, Son of David; my daughter is cruelly demon-possessed" (v. 22). This Gentile woman recognized that Jesus was the Messiah—she used two titles commonly associated with the coming King (cf. 3:3; 12:23). Despite this acknowledgement, Jesus ignored the woman. She persisted until the disciples grew weary and begged the Lord to send her away. Jesus then turned to the woman and said, "I was sent only to the lost sheep of the house of Israel" (v. 24; cf. 10:6). Up to this point, Christ's ministry had been focused on the Jews, not Gentiles. Still the woman persisted, even bowing down to worship Him. So Jesus explained, "It is not good to take the children's bread and throw it to the dogs" (v. 26). Jesus' offer of the kingdom was for the Jews (children), not the Gentiles (dogs).

The woman's response is amazing, "Yes, Lord; but even the dogs feed on the crumbs which fall from their masters' table" (v. 27). In essence, she argues that dogs do get to eat the food that the children don't want. Acknowledging this fact, Jesus responds, "O woman, your faith is great" (v. 28). The only other time Jesus recognized someone for their great faith was the centurion in 8:10—another Gentile! This crucial passage demonstrates that the offer of the kingdom is for people of all nations (28:19), not just the Jews.

Is your faith great or little (cf. 14:31)? Trust in the Lord. He delights in those who do.

IL

Monday

WHEN FAITH IS NO LONGER EASY
Read Matthew 16

Simon Peter answered, "You are the Christ, the Son of the living God." (16:16)

The opening chapters of Matthew's Gospel carefully built the case proving Jesus was the promised Messiah. Despite the irrefutable evidence, the nation of Israel largely rejected His claims. The religious leaders claimed He was in league with the devil (12:24) and schemed to destroy Him (12:14).

Jesus then shifted the focus of His ministry from the crowds to the disciples. He took them through a curriculum designed to prepare them for a seismic shift. Instead of joining Jesus in establishing a glorious kingdom, they were following Him into a hotbed of hostility that would eventually lead to the cross.

The Master took the Twelve north to Caesarea Philippi, a region out of the conflict zone. There He asked, "Who do people say that I am?" His disciples parroted the answers they had heard from others. Christ followed up: "But who do *you* say that I am?" (16:15). Peter immediately replied, "You are the Christ, the Son of the living God."

People had identified Jesus with these titles before Peter. John the Baptist called Him the Son of God (Jn 1:34). Andrew exclaimed to his brother Peter that he had found the Messiah (Jn 1:41). When Jesus told the woman at the well that He was the Messiah (Jn 4:25-26), she spread the word to her town (Jn 4:29). The freshly-fed 5000 wanted to crown Him King (Jn 6:14-15). When He stilled the storm, His disciples called him the Son of God (Mt 14:33).

What was different about Peter's confession? It came at a time when the initial burst of enthusiasm had been battered by conflict and rejection. Clearly, Jesus was not the type of Messiah that the Jews had expected. In spite of this, Peter still believed that He was the promised Christ, the Anointed Son of God.

God's plan often looks different from what we expect. It is easy to trust Him when He grants our requests in the way we desire. But we still need to trust His character when His will for us is more difficult than anticipated.

JDB

Tuesday

THE KINGDOM BEYOND THE CROSS
Read Matthew 17

Behold, a voice out of the cloud said, "This is My beloved Son, with Whom I am well-pleased; listen to Him!" (17:5b)

Jesus had just revealed to His disciples that He was going to die (16:21). This was totally unexpected (cf. 16:22). Even though the religious leaders were hostile, Christ's followers surely did not expect the Messiah to end up on a cross.

The disciples were anticipating positions of honor in the King's court (cf. 20:20-21); and this announcement of rejection and death contradicted everything they believed about the Messiah. Did it mean that they had been tragically mistaken?

Jesus reassured them that "the Son of Man [a messianic title; cf. Dn 7:13] is going to come in the glory of His Father with His angels" (16:27). In fact, He promised that some would actually see the Son of Man coming in His kingdom (16:28).

Anyone who examined Jesus would see only a bearded, dusty rabbi. His royalty was hidden from view. Yet only a few days later, Jesus led Peter, James, and John up a high mountain. Suddenly, He began to glow—not a soft, soothing radiance, but an overpowering brightness like sculpted lightning. God momentarily pulled back the curtain to reveal the Son as He would appear in the kingdom. Decades later, John saw the unveiled Christ on the isle of Patmos, with His face shining like the sun in its strength (Rv 1:16).

Yes, He would be rejected. Yes, He would be crucified. Yet not even death could derail His Kingship. Jesus graciously gave the disciples a glimpse of His glory that would carry them through the trauma of rejection that lay ahead. Peter pointed to the transfiguration years later to prove that the gospel was no human invention, but a truth confirmed by the voice of God (2 Pt 1:16-18).

Many believers complain that following Jesus hasn't turned out the way they expected. Their problems haven't been erased; their irritations haven't been eased. In fact, life has actually gotten harder! God has not promised us an easy life in this age. The glory comes later. Don't doubt in the dark what God has shown you in the light!

JDB

Wednesday

THE PERILOUS SURGE FOR GREATNESS
Read Matthew 18

Whoever then humbles himself as this child, he is the greatest in the kingdom of heaven. **(18:4)**

Christ's disciples were poised to follow Him into a glorious kingdom where they would hold positions of power. When He announced that He would be rejected and killed, they were startled. But they still continued to push ahead in the race for the top posts in the King's new administration.

Jesus used much of His remaining time to start pulling the disciples toward the new attitudes required for a kingdom that would involve hardship, faith, and humility, not pomp and prestige. When the disciples asked, "Who then is greatest in the kingdom of heaven?" (v. 1), Jesus surprised them, as He often did, by calling over a child and pronouncing that greatness in His realm rested on childlike humility.

Humility can best be defined as regarding others as more important than oneself—looking out for their interests, not just your own (cf. Phil 2:3-4). How unlike the ambitious people who push aside those they feel are beneath them as they surge toward their goals. The great ones in Christ's kingdom don't shove people out of the way. Causing someone to fall has eternal consequences, both for the one who falls and the one who tripped them up (vv. 6-7).

God values those who are easily overlooked by the ambitious. His throne room contains a horde of angels who represent their interests (v. 10). He throws a party when one lost sheep is returned to the fold (vv. 12-14; cf. Lk 15). Jesus even outlined a procedure for helping to restore a wandering sinner (vv. 15-20).

We instinctively focus on achieving greatness. We surge toward goals and growth. But in the process we may accidentally trample those who don't contribute to our ambitions. God cares deeply about all people. And the greatest in His kingdom are those who are willing to hold a toddler's hand to make sure that no one falls on rough ground.

JDB

Thursday

MORE COMMITMENT THAN EXPECTED
Read Matthew 19

When the disciples heard this, they were very astonished and said, "Then who can be saved?" (19:25)

In Matthew nineteen, Jesus left Galilee to begin His final journey to Jerusalem (v. 1). Crowds still gathered to see His healings and hear His teachings, but Jesus increasingly devoted Himself to conversations with His closest disciples. As He neared the cross, He was preparing His followers for a future that would demand a much deeper level of commitment than they had expected.

As the chapter opens, a group of Pharisees approach Jesus with a question: "Is it lawful for a man to divorce his wife for any reason at all?" (v. 3). Divorce was one of the most controversial issues of the day. Some rabbis allowed divorce for almost any reason; others limited it to cases of infidelity.

Christ set the bar higher than either group. He declared that God had established marriage as a permanent relationship. Man has no right to sever what God has bound together (Gn 1:27; 2:24). Though the Law allowed for divorce, it was a divine concession—divorce was not God's original intent for marriage. Jesus demanded a deeper commitment to marriage than His hearers expected. A person should think twice before making such a commitment (v. 10).

God expects wholehearted commitment not only to marriage but to the kingdom. One day, a young man approached Jesus to ask what more he could do to obtain eternal life. He had scrupulously observed the Law of Moses and assumed he was well positioned to participate in the kingdom. Knowing his heart, Jesus zeroed in on his greatest weakness—his wealth. "Sell your possessions," He said, "and come, follow me" (v. 21). This was a much more drastic commitment than the young man had expected and he went away disappointed. The disciples were dumbfounded. Who can be saved if the standards are that high (v. 25)?

Discipleship often costs more than we anticipate. Make an open-ended commitment to do whatever the Lord may ask of you. You can trust the King to provide, no matter where He takes you.

JDB

Friday

REWARDS GO TO SERVANTS
Read Matthew 20

But whoever wishes to become great among you shall be your servant. (20:26b)

The final confrontation in Jerusalem loomed ahead, and Jesus was still preparing His disciples for the climactic events that would culminate in the crucifixion. Of course, the cross was not the end of the story. Jesus was still the King, and He would richly reward those who forsook all to follow Him (19:28-29).

The Lord's rewards are often surprising. Those who seem to be last in line may end up in first place (19:30). To illustrate the point, Jesus told a parable about a vineyard owner who had an unusual pay scale. Some men worked a full day in the vineyard, and he paid them the usual day's wage. Others spent only a fraction of the day, yet the owner rewarded them with pay for a full day! Like the vineyard owner, God distributes rewards just as He chooses. "So the last shall be first, and the first last" (v. 16).

But the promised rewards would come later. The immediate future held suffering, not rewards (vv. 17-19). His disciples, however, were still jockeying for prestige in the kingdom. The mother of James and John approached the Lord and asked him to appoint her boys to the places of highest honor. Jesus responded with a lesson on leadership. The world thinks of a ruler as one who exercises authority and wields power over others. But Christ's kingdom does not work that way. To be great in God's eyes, one must aim to serve others, not pursue self-glory. Christ Himself set the example (v. 28).

As the Lord walked along the road, two blind men shouted for help. The crowd sternly shushed them, assuming that the Messiah should not be bothered by a pair of nobodies. But Jesus heard them. He noticed them. He summoned them. And He healed them.

Do you want to be great in God's eyes? See the needs all around you and represent your King by serving as His hands and feet.

JDB

Monday

LOOK WHO IS COMING!
Read Matthew 21

Say to the daughter of Zion, "Behold your King is coming to you, gentle, and mounted on a donkey." (21:5a)

Jesus was a marked man. The religious leaders had determined to destroy Him (12:14) and He had spent the last several months preparing His disciples for the coming storm. Now the time had come. Jesus neared Jerusalem, knowing that this Passover week would end in His crucifixion.

Christ could have chosen to enter the city quietly, but instead He purposely arranged an entry so spectacular that no one could possibly miss it. Every action on that day of the week was a bold claim to be the Messiah, the King promised by God.

First, he borrowed a donkey and rode it down the road from the Mount of Olives through the eastern gate of the city. Anyone familiar with Old Testament prophecy would have recognized this as a demonstration of the prophesied arrival of Israel's King (cf. Zec 9:9). The crowds gathering for Passover picked up the theme, shouting phrases from the messianic Psalm 118. Even children joined the shouting, as predicted in Psalm 8:2.

Second, shortly after passing through the gate, Jesus found Himself in the courtyard of the temple. He saw it filled with money changers and merchants eager to rob the sojourners who came to worship God. To make an intentional statement, Christ cleared the courtyard, overturning the tables of the money changers and the seats of those who were selling doves. As the Son of God, He had the right to expel these transgressors from His Father's house.

Third, the blind and the lame came to Him, and He healed them, demonstrating that He wielded the power of a King.

Jesus drove the events of the week. He seized the initiative, asserting His Kingship so blatantly that the religious leaders could not miss it. His acts were like a slap in the face, a challenge to a duel. They could not ignore Him—they had to worship Him or kill Him.

Jesus offered the nation a choice, one that remains to this day. Will you reject Him or bow the knee to Him?

JDB

Tuesday

TRICK QUESTIONS
Read Matthew 22

No one was able to answer Him a word, nor did anyone dare from that day on to ask Him another question. (22:46)

It was the middle of the passion week, and Jesus had recently entered Jerusalem on a donkey to present Himself as the promised Messiah. As He rode, He was cheered by the crowds. He demonstrated His authority by clearing the merchants from the courtyard of the temple. No one could ignore Him. Now He was back, ready to spar with the religious leaders, who asked a series of questions designed to lure Him into an incriminating or embarrassing statement.

First, the Pharisees and Herodians asked whether the Jews should pay taxes to Caesar. An answer of "Yes" would drive away the crowds; but "No" would lead to arrest by the Romans. Jesus evaded their trap with a third answer: "Render to Caesar the things that are Caesar's; and to God the things that are God's" (v. 21).

Next, the Sadducees told the story of a woman who had seven husbands—all of whom died. Following her death, which one would be her husband in the resurrection? It was an attempt to ridicule the idea of resurrection, a doctrine rejected by the Sadducees. Jesus explained that life in the resurrection operates on an entirely new basis—there is no marriage in heaven. He then proved the doctrine of the resurrection with a quote from Exodus 3:6 to show that Yahweh is God of the living, not the dead.

Unwilling to give up, the Pharisees sent a lawyer to ask, "Which is the great commandment in the Law?" (v. 36). When Jesus replied, "You shall love the Lord your God with all your heart, and with all your soul, and with all your mind" (v. 37), no one could refute Him.

No matter what the question was, Jesus had the answer. He still does! Skeptics may try to trip us up by tossing questions at us that we can't answer. But we do not need to know all the answers. The Lord is omniscient; and He invites us to come to Him seeking the wisdom we need. When we humbly ask in faith, He has promised to give us the wisdom we need (cf. Jas 1:5-6).

JDB

Wednesday

TARGETING HYPOCRISY
Read Matthew 23

But woe to you, scribes and Pharisees, hypocrites! (23:13a)

Their answer was an emphatic "No!" Early in His passion week, Jesus had entered Jerusalem, presenting Himself as the promised King. But by the middle of the week, the Jewish leaders had made it clear that they rejected His messianic claims. While the crowds were still enthusiastic, events would soon show that few were truly committed to His cause. The nation had refused to acknowledge their Messiah. Now Jesus announced the consequences of that choice.

He began with the religious leaders—the scribes and Pharisees. These men were highly respected, known for their devotion to the Law and the traditions of Israel. They should have been the first to bow before the Messiah. Instead, they plotted to drive people away.

"Hypocrites!" That's what Jesus called them. The word *hypocrite* comes from the ancient Greek theater, where actors wore large masks that covered their faces. It literally means "one who is under a mask." These religious leaders wore masks of outer religiosity to hide the ugly reality of their true character.

Jesus presented a long list of charges against the scribes and Pharisees. For example, they failed to do themselves what they prescribed for others. Their good deeds sprang from wrong motives. They pushed people away from the kingdom. They followed trivial rules while ignoring the larger issues of justice and righteousness.

Why did Jesus issue such a harsh condemnation of the scribes and Pharisees in this chapter? Because these religious leaders were the teachers of the Law. They were supposed to lead others to the truth. Instead, Jesus called them "blind guides" (vv. 16, 24).

James said it well: "Let not many of you become teachers, my brethren, knowing that as such we will incur a stricter judgment" (Jas 3:1). This warning holds true today. Unless we are careful to make Christ the focus of our teaching, we are in danger of slipping into the same trap as the scribes and Pharisees. Make sure your reputation for godliness is backed by the reality of a heart that humbly follows God and lovingly serves others.

JDB

Thursday

THE ONLY SURE WAY TO BE READY
Read Matthew 24

For this reason you also must be ready; for the Son of Man is coming at an hour when you do not think He will. (24:44)

Jesus was nearing the end of a long day of confrontation with the scribes and Pharisees. He had just pronounced judgment on these religious leaders; now He foretold the fate of the city and nation.

The Lord revealed to His disciples that the temple would soon be destroyed. The disciples, eager to know the timing of the prophecy, started peppering Him with questions. His lengthy answers are recorded in the so-called Olivet Discourse (Mt 24-25). Though His original prophecy referred to the A.D. 70 destruction of the temple by the Romans, Jesus moved immediately to long-range predictions that will be fulfilled when He returns to set up His kingdom.

First, he listed the sequence of events leading to His return. Wars, famines, and earthquakes are going to be like birth pains, just the beginning of the end (v. 8). Prior to the Lord's return, the earth will suffer a time of horror beyond anything in history (v. 21). His actual coming will resemble a bolt of lightning, obvious to all (v. 27).

At this point in the message, Jesus stopped narrating a timeline and turned to a timely warning—the need to always be ready. The disciples had asked, "When will these things happen?" (v. 3). Christ replied, "Of that day and hour no one knows" (v. 36). We do not know the time of the rapture of the church, nor the time of Christ's arrival to set up the kingdom.

The people in Noah's day had no idea when the rain would fall. Unconcerned, they continued their daily routines until it was too late (vv. 37-39). The slave in Christ's parable assumed he had plenty of time to abuse the other slaves and carouse with his friends. But he paid the price when the master arrived unannounced (vv. 48-51).

If Christ returned today, would you be caught unprepared? Or would you be ready to welcome Him, having fulfilled your ministry here on earth? When you don't know the day of His coming, you can only be prepared by being ready every day!

JDB

Friday

SEEING THE KING IN HIS PEOPLE
Read Matthew 25

The King will answer and say to them, "Truly I say to you, to the extent that you did it to one of these brothers of Mine, even the least of them, you did it to Me." (25:40)

Matthew twenty-five contains the conclusion of the Olivet Discourse, Christ's detailed explanation of the events leading to His return to set up the promised kingdom. Having described the signs that foretell His appearing in glory, the Lord then told a series of parables emphasizing the need to always be ready for His return. Finally, beginning in verse thirty-one, He adds one more event to the prophetic timeline—the judgment of the nations.

When Jesus takes His place on the throne, His first act as King will be to gather all the nations before Him for judgment. Just as a shepherd divides a mixed flock into sheep and goats, the Lord separates the nations into two groups. The Greek word for "nations" is often translated "Gentiles" (e.g., 10:5), referring in this context to the non-Jewish peoples who have survived the Great Tribulation.

Christ announces the destiny of each group. He invites the "sheep" to enter His kingdom and enjoy its blessings. He sends the "goats" away to the lake of fire. Jesus carefully explains the criteria of judgment. Those who enter the kingdom are those who ministered to Him—feeding Him when He was hungry, providing hospitality when He was a stranger, and visiting Him when He was sick.

Surprised by the Lord's statement, the "sheep" asked, "When did we see You hungry, and feed You, or thirsty, and give You something to drink?" (v. 37). The Lord replied, "To the extent that you did it to one of these brothers of Mine, even the least of them, you did it to Me" (v. 40).

Jesus resides in heaven and we live on earth. Physically speaking, we cannot give him a cup of cold water. But any time we serve the ones He loves, He counts it as a gift to Him. Saul thought he was persecuting Christians. But Jesus asked, "Why are you persecuting Me?" (Acts 9:4). Would your behavior change if you knew that the needy person in front of you was really Jesus Himself?

JDB

Monday

A WILLING SACRIFICE
Read Matthew 26

How then will the Scriptures be fulfilled, which say that it must happen this way? (26:54)

Nothing about the cross was a surprise to Jesus. The first few days of the passion week consisted of a series of confrontations that made it clear that Israel had rejected their Messiah. Now Matthew records the climax of the conflict—Jesus' seizure and slaughter by self-righteous leaders who thought they were purging a dangerous charlatan.

Six times in this chapter, the Lord announced that His betrayal and death were imminent (vv. 2, 11-12, 21, 24, 31, 45). Yet He didn't run; He walked willingly to His death.

At the Passover meal, Christ identified Judas as the betrayer. He then sent him out to summon the arresting troops (cf. Jn 13:27). As the Lord shared the bread and cup, He explained that His death was part of a divine plan. His blood would be shed to provide for the forgiveness of sins.

When the troops arrived to arrest Jesus, Peter swung his sword, injuring a slave (v. 51; cf. Jn 18:10). The Lord immediately stopped him, explaining that He could say the word and have legions of angels come instantly to His rescue.

Jesus allowed them to bind His hands and lead Him away. He made no effort to plead His innocence when He was hauled before the Sanhedrin. When the kangaroo court was unable to find witnesses who could lie convincingly, Jesus said the words that sealed His fate. When the high priest questioned whether He was the Messiah, the Lord acknowledged that He was the Promised One, adding, "Hereafter you will see the Son of Man sitting at the right hand of power, and coming on the clouds of heaven" (v. 64). The priests did not even consider the possibility that He might be telling the truth. To them, His words were blasphemy, punishable by death.

Jesus willingly chose to undergo the whole process of humiliation, pain, and death. Why? To provide salvation for mankind. In light of Christ's sacrifice, how should we respond? By sharing the good news of this salvation with everyone we meet.

JDB

Tuesday

WHEN ALL SEEMS LOST
Read Matthew 27

And they went and made the grave secure, and along with the guard they set a seal on the stone. (27:66)

Matthew wrote to overcome Jewish objections to the idea that Jesus was the promised King. One of the main objections was His death. How could Jesus be the Messiah if He was slain by His own people?

The Gospel account shows that Israel's leaders decided early on that Jesus was a counterfeit; so they set out to silence Him. This opposition came to a head during His passion week, resulting in His arrest. Matthew twenty-seven records the events that took place on the morning and afternoon of Passover—from the hearing before the Jewish authorities to his trial before Pilate, continuing through His crucifixion leading to His death and burial.

All through that grueling day, Christ's followers must have hoped that somehow the fatal process could be reversed. Even His enemies shouted the sarcastic suggestion that He should come down from the cross. But in the end, Jesus died. When He "yielded up His spirit" (v. 50), many of His followers' dreams of a messianic kingdom died with Him. They believed that death is the door that never opens.

Of course, there were His strange words about rising again (v. 63; cf. v. 40; 12:40). His enemies were concerned that someone would steal His body, proclaim that He was still alive, and launch a movement in His name.

Matthew, however, records several details that made that sort of charade impossible. Jesus was buried in the personal tomb of a rich man named Joseph of Arimathea, so there could be no mistake in identifying the grave site. It was a new tomb, never used before, so there could be no confusion about a second corpse in the chamber. It was hewn out of solid rock and sealed with a huge stone, so theft was virtually impossible. On top of all this, the Jewish leaders arranged for a detachment of Roman soldiers to secure the tomb. Jesus was in the grave for good—unless …

When we face a hopeless situation, it is good to remember that God is in the business of opening doors that seem irrevocably shut!

JDB

Wednesday

THE KINGDOM IS STILL IN BUSINESS
Read Matthew 28

And Jesus came up and spoke to them, saying, "All authority has been given to Me in heaven and on earth." (28:18)

Were the religious leaders right? Was Jesus a fake; a pseudo-Messiah with big ideas and a magnetic personality? The supposed King was lying in a tomb. Now He was gone and life could return to normal.

However, there is one more chapter in Matthew's story. Amazingly, the biography continues even after the death of its subject. Jesus of Nazareth is indeed the King promised long ago—He proved it conclusively by rising from the dead.

Matthew begins his final chapter with the resurrection itself, as seen through the eyes of the women walking toward the tomb as the sky begins to lighten. Their arrival coincides with a series of incredible events: an earthquake, an angel who descended from heaven and rolled away the stone, a set of terrified guards, and the announcement that Jesus had risen. The angel then commanded the women to tell His disciples that Christ is alive and that He plans to meet them in Galilee.

A composite of the Gospels and 1 Corinthians fifteen reveals that the risen Christ would appear several times to various people, but Matthew moves quickly to the mountainside appointment in Galilee. There the Lord climaxes the account with a final statement worthy of a King. First, He emphasizes His authority over the entire universe. Second, He exercises His authority by giving His disciples instructions to follow in His absence. They are to make disciples everywhere they go, baptizing them and teaching them to obey the King. Finally, He promises His perpetual presence, enabling them to carry out His will.

The Book of Matthew is essentially a long answer to the question, "Is Jesus the Messiah?" Mankind has made every effort to say "No." But the carpenter from Nazareth is seated on the throne today. He can handle any problem that comes along. And even His worst enemies will one day bow before Him. Let us do the same!

JDB

Thursday

LIFE CHANGE
Read Mark 1

As He was going along by the Sea of Galilee, He saw Simon and Andrew, the brother of Simon, casting a net in the sea; for they were fishermen. And Jesus said to them, "Follow Me, and I will make you become fishers of men." Immediately they left their nets and followed Him. (1:16-18)

As Jesus began His public ministry, He selected twelve men to accompany Him in His ministry and travels. The Lord trained these disciples for several years, preparing them to pursue a new mission in life. These men had very different careers prior to meeting Jesus. Yet they willingly abandoned their professions to do something unlike anything they had ever done. They now had a greater calling—one with an eternal impact.

Four of these twelve were fishermen: Simon and Andrew, brothers, and James and John, also brothers. These four were called to a drastic life change—from fishing for personal profit to fishing for the souls of men and women for the kingdom of God.

These four men probably had their lives carefully planned out, no doubt looking forward to retirement by the Sea of Galilee in a quiet fishing village, eventually dying of old age. Then, one fateful day Jesus came along and told them to follow Him. They immediately dropped their nets and followed their new Master.

According to tradition, Simon's life would end on an inverted cross (cf. Jn 21:18-19); for James, death by a sword (Acts 12:2). Also, church tradition maintains that Andrew died on an X-shaped cross in northern Greece. John would be the only one to die of natural causes. Ask any of the apostles if their life change was worth devoting the rest of their lives to the Lord and assuredly they would each respond with a resounding "Yes!"

My life change was from a planned early retirement from the oil industry to an unpaid ministry of almost forty years (to date) in the pastorate. Has it all been worth it? Absolutely, without a doubt! If the Lord is currently calling you to a life change, immediately drop your nets and follow Him. His calling and retirement plan is eternal, and surely far greater than what you have planned for the rest of your life.

AL

Friday

LOAD SHARING
Read Mark 2

And they came, bringing to Him a paralytic, carried by four men. Being unable to get to Him because of the crowd, they removed the roof above Him; and when they had dug an opening, they let down the pallet on which the paralytic was lying. And Jesus seeing their faith said to the paralytic, "Son, your sins are forgiven." (2:3-5)

The news that Jesus was performing miraculous healings had spread rapidly. As a result, He was now overwhelmed with people coming to be healed (cf. 1:45). A paralytic man who desperately wanted to be healed was carried to Jesus by four men because he was unable to make the journey on his own. But when they arrived, they were unable to get to Jesus because the doorway was crowded and the interior of the house was full. So they carried the man to the roof of the house and made an opening so that they could lower him down to where Jesus was healing.

When Jesus saw their faith, He first chose to forgive the paralytic of his sins. The Lord then healed the man to prove that He had the authority to pronounce forgiveness. Finally, Jesus commanded the man, "Get up, pick up your pallet and go home" (v. 11).

The paralytic could never have reached Jesus if not for the four men that carried his pallet, lifted him to the roof, made an opening, and gently lowered him into Jesus' presence. Their efforts made it possible for the Lord to do a miraculous work in his life.

In Galatians 6:2, Paul commands us to bear one another's burdens. However, a few verses later he states, "Each one will bear his own load" (Gal 6:5). There is no contradiction—there are certain burdens in life that we need help with while other loads are designed for us to bear alone.

There will be times in your life where God calls you to assist others in getting the help they so desperately need. There will also be times when you are going to be the one in need. Always be willing to help share the load, because one day you may be the load.

AL

Monday

LOONEY TUNES
Read Mark 3

And He came home, and the crowd gathered again, to such an extent that they could not even eat a meal. When His own people heard of this, they went out to take custody of Him; for they were saying, "He has lost His senses." (3:20-21)

Jesus' ministry was now running at full force. Crowds of people were seeking Him wherever He went, be it on land or at sea (vv. 7-8). There was non-stop teaching and healing. When Jesus returned home, a great multitude appeared there as well, hoping to be ministered to by the Lord. The situation was so chaotic that Jesus and His disciples could not even eat a meal.

When His own relatives heard what was happening, they attempted to take custody of Jesus, thinking He had lost His senses. The religious leaders thought He was possessed by Beelzebul, the ruler of the demons. Today, some claim that those who sacrificially serve day in and day out, week in and week out, must be out of their minds. They'll declare, "Jesus or God or that Bible has made you crazy!" The Apostle Paul faced similar criticism (cf. Acts 26:24-25).

Looney Tunes was an animated series produced from 1930 to 1969. Two notable characters were the Road Runner and his archenemy Wiley E. Coyote. The Road Runner travelled the desert highways with boundless energy while the Coyote did everything he could to stop him. But no matter what he did, the Coyote could never stop the Road Runner. It was the same with Jesus. His own people tried to stop Him—but nothing they did was able to prevent Jesus from accomplishing His mission.

A person on fire for the Lord often goes day and night without stopping. Sometimes it's their own self-will pushing them; other times they are operating according to the will of God, relying on the power of the Holy Spirit to continue. Outside observers, maybe even family, might think you are crazy in your non-stop zeal. Ignore them. Be a "Road Runner" for the Lord. Don't let the "Wiley E. Coyotes" in your life prevent you from accomplishing everything the Lord wants you to do today.

AL

Tuesday

LISTENING, ACCEPTING, DOING
Read Mark 4

These are the ones who have heard the word, but the worries of the world, and the deceitfulness of riches, and the desires for other things enter in and choke the word, and it becomes unfruitful. And those are the ones on whom seed was sown on the good soil; and they hear the word and accept it and bear fruit, thirty, sixty, and a hundredfold. (4:18b-20)

Twin boys were playing a video game when their mother called them to immediately come downstairs to the kitchen. Both heard the call, both started down the stairs, but one decided to go back up and continue playing the game. The twin who heard the call and made his way to the kitchen was rewarded with all the cookies his mother had baked—his and his brother's. Both twins heard the same authoritative call, both accepted the command and started to obey, but one failed to complete the task while the other did just as he was commanded. One twin was a good "lad" to listen, accept, and do (l.a.d.); as a result, he received a blessing. The other missed out on his blessing because he had failed to complete the command, even though he had heard and accepted.

Jesus often used parables to teach spiritual truths. In this chapter, Jesus told the so-called "Parable of the Sower" (vv. 3-8). In this parable, the seed is identified as the Word of God (v. 14). The four soils represent four types of people who each heard the same Word yet experienced different results (vv. 15-20). The first three groups were unable to retain the Word for a variety of reasons. As a result, they were unproductive. However, a fourth group listened, accepted, and carried out the Word as they were commanded (l.a.d.). They put the teaching into practice so as to become productive to various degrees (v. 20).

If you want to be blessed and productive in your spiritual life, you must be a good "lad", that is, a Christian who "listens", "accepts", and "does" what God commands. You will then be of great use to your Master and bear fruit many times over.

AL

Wednesday

LEGION OF PROBLEMS
Read Mark 5

And He was asking him, "What is your name?" And he said to Him, "My name is Legion; for we are many." (5:9)

When Jesus arrived on the shores of the country of the Gerasenes, He was immediately confronted by a man who was possessed by a host of demons collectively named Legion. In the ancient world, a Roman legion was comprised of up to six thousand soldiers. The exact number of demons in the man is unknown, but there were enough to possess two thousand swine (v. 13).

This man lived alone among the tombs. He screamed night and day. He gnashed himself with stones. He was unable to be subdued, even with shackles and chains. He was possessed by a host of demons. Literally and figuratively, this man had a legion of problems in his life all at the same time.

As the man approached Jesus, he bowed down in submission to the "Son of the Most High God" (v. 7). At Jesus' command, the demons left the man and entered a herd of swine, which ran off a steep bank into the sea and drowned. The man was now free from his legion of demons, clothed, and in his right mind. He wanted to accompany Jesus as He prepared to get back into His boat, but Jesus commanded him to return home and share with his people what the Lord had done for him.

For some people, the problems of life are relatively few. For others, it may seem like a hundred, a thousand, or even six thousand problems all at the same time. Whether your problems are few or many, the "Son of the Most High God" can help you overcome them by His great authority, mercy, and love. And when the Lord has delivered you from your problems, be sure to give testimony of your deliverance to all you know. Praise the Lord, for He has demonstrated His providential care for you, someone who was once overwhelmed by "legions".

AL

Thursday

LEGACY
Read Mark 6

"Is not this the carpenter, the son of Mary, and brother of James and Joses and Judas and Simon? Are not His sisters here with us?" And they took offense at Him. (6:3)

When Jesus returned to His hometown Nazareth, he began to teach in the synagogue on the Sabbath. The crowd was amazed at His insights, His wisdom in the Scriptures, and His ability to perform miracles; however, they took offense at His claim that He was the fulfillment of Old Testament prophecy (Lk 4:16-30; cf. Is 62:1-2).

Because Jesus was raised in Nazareth, the local residents knew His family members by name. They also knew that He was a carpenter by trade, just like His father (cf. Mt 13:55). His family was poor—they offered the least expensive sacrifice when He was consecrated at the temple (Lk 2:24; cf. Lv 12:8). This small village, of which it was said, "Can any good thing come out of Nazareth?" (cf. Jn 1:46), was not expected to produce anyone of note, much less the promised Messiah.

So, they reasoned, how was a person with such a humble family legacy able to do such amazing things? What the hometown crowd did not realize was that Jesus' legacy came from His Father in heaven, not his family on earth. They only saw His human legacy from Mary and Joseph; they were not aware of His eternal legacy—"Son of the Most High God" (5:7). Jesus was God in the flesh dwelling among them (cf. Jn 1:14).

You may have a legacy that is not glamorous in the eyes of those who have known you from birth. Or you may come from a prominent family with a distinguished legacy. But once you have received Jesus Christ as Savior your legacy changes. You are now a member of the royal family, a child of the King. Give praise to God, because once you were saved your sins were forgiven, and you became a royal heir with an everlasting inheritance in heaven. You are now an ambassador of the kingdom. And those who knew you prior to your salvation will soon recognize your new legacy.

AL

Friday

LISTS OF MEN
Read Mark 7

The Pharisees and the scribes asked Him, "Why do Your disciples not walk according to the tradition of the elders, but eat their bread with impure hands?" (7:5)

The Pharisees, a sectarian group who believed in keeping the Law of Moses even beyond what it commanded, and the scribes, a group consisting of those who were the official copyists of the Law of Moses, and supposedly experts in it, confronted Jesus one day concerning the behavior of His disciples. The Pharisees and scribes had observed Jesus' disciples eating bread with unwashed hand, thus defiling themselves according to the "traditions of the elders", a man-made list of rules for determining a person's righteousness. The Pharisees and scribes were careful to keep these traditions in their entirety, including diligently washing their hands as well as their utensils. As a result, they believed that they were more righteous than those who did not follow their rules; in this case, Christ's disciples.

Jesus responded by pointing out the fact that they had exchanged God's Law for their self-made set of rules, i.e., "the traditions of the elders". These traditions allowed them to twist the Law to suit their own interests, including the right to get out of providing for one's own parents (vv. 9-13).

Jesus then turned to the crowd and explained that it is not what goes into a person's mouth that defiles him or her, but what proceeds from out of their heart (vv. 14-15). Evil thoughts and sinful desires defile a person—not dirty food going into the stomach.

Our culture is full of modern-day Pharisees and scribes, self-righteous individuals with their traditions or currently trending fads of what is right and wrong before God. Social media is full of people who are constantly critical of behavior that doesn't measure up to their own standards. Our standards for right and wrong should come from the Scriptures, not society. Man looks at the outward appearance, but the Lord looks at the heart (1 Sm 16:7). Let the Bible determine whether your behavior is godly, not the lists, tweets, posts, and critiques of men.

AL

Monday

LESSONS FROM THE LOAVES
Read Mark 8

And His disciples answered Him, "Where will anyone be able to find enough bread here in this desolate place to satisfy these people?" And He was asking them, "How many loaves do you have?" And they said, "Seven." (8:4-5)

Mark 6:34-44 records the account of the so-called "Feeding of the 5000". In this famous story, Jesus taught the crowds until late in the evening. When the disciples asked Jesus to send the crowds away to the surrounding towns to get something to eat, the Lord responded, "You give them something to eat" (6:37). The disciples, after calculating the cost, realized they would be unable to feed the crowd. Jesus then told them to collect all the food they could; and they found five loaves and two fish. After blessing the food, the Lord multiplied it to feed five thousand men with twelve baskets left over.

The narrative recorded in Mark 8:1-21 is very similar. After teaching for three days, Jesus realized that the large crowd had nothing to eat. Again His disciples wondered where they could find enough food to feed everyone. Jesus told them to gather the available food, and they found seven loaves and a few small fish. The Lord then repeated His earlier miracle. By this time, the disciples should have realized that Christ could perform wonders. However, instead of anticipating another miracle, the disciples again worried about the acquisition of food, "Where will anyone be able to find enough bread here in this desolate place to satisfy these people?" (v. 4).

Leaving the area in a boat with no more than one loaf of bread, Jesus told His disciples to beware of the leaven (sins and false teachings) of Herod and the Pharisees. The mention of leaven reminded the disciples that they did not have enough food. Yet again, they failed to learn from Jesus' lessons from the loaves.

If Jesus calls you to a task He will provide all you need, even in seemingly impossible situations. Take what you have, pray where you are, and ask God to bless. Don't follow the example of the disciples, who repeatedly lacked faith in God's ability to provide. Remember the lessons from the loaves and trust God for His provision.

AL

Tuesday

LAST IS FIRST
Read Mark 9

Sitting down, He called the twelve and said to them, "If anyone wants to be first, he shall be last of all and servant of all." (9:35)

The end of Jesus' earthly ministry was approaching. Christ informed His disciples that He was about to be delivered into the hands of men who would kill Him. Despite this, He promised that He would rise three days later (v. 31). The disciples did not understand what Jesus meant and were afraid to ask any questions about His statement.

Shortly after arriving in Capernaum, Jesus asked His disciples what they were talking about during their journey. The disciples kept silent, because they had discussed with one another which of them was the greatest. Assembling the Twelve, Jesus said to them, "If anyone wants to be first, he shall be last of all and servant of all" (v. 35). He then took a child in His arms and said, "Whoever receives one child like this in My name receives Me; and whoever receives Me does not receive Me, but Him Who sent Me" (v. 37).

Jesus was teaching His disciples that the greatest person in the eyes of God was not the person who was served by everybody else, but the person who was serving everybody else. This was contrary to the customary way of thinking. After all, who would humble themselves to welcome a child rather than hobnob with kings and other dignitaries? No one, they surely thought.

But when we humble ourselves to the point of recognizing children, we welcome the King of Kings; and in welcoming the King of Kings, we welcome the Father in heaven. When we serve the least among us we are serving God Himself. Jesus, the great King of Kings, was about to humble Himself to the point of death for us, thus providing an example of true servant leadership. Only then would He rise in glory to sit at the right hand of God (cf. 14:62).

In the kingdom of heaven, the greatest among us is the least among us. The servant of all is greater than those they are serving. If we desire to receive the highest reward, then we should live our lives as servants. For the last shall be first.

AL

Wednesday

LASTING ROI
Read Mark 10

Looking at him, Jesus felt a love for him and said to him, "One thing you lack: go and sell all you possess and give to the poor, and you will have treasure in heaven; and come, follow Me." (10:21)

As Jesus was setting out on a journey, a rich man approached Him and asked, "What shall I do to inherit eternal life?" (v. 17). Jesus first questioned the man about his moral life in relationship to the commandments, to which his response was, "I have kept all these things from my youth up" (v. 20). With that being determined, Jesus then said, "One thing you lack: go and sell all you possess and give to the poor, and you will have treasure in heaven; and come, follow Me" (v. 21). And with that statement, the rich man left deeply saddened because he owned a lot of property. He refused to part with his temporary treasures on earth, despite the fact that he would gain eternal treasures in heaven.

Jesus then turned to His disciples and explained just how difficult it will be for a wealthy person to attain salvation. While our salvation is not determined by our morals or our financial contributions or any human works, but by our faith in Christ alone (cf. Rom 3:21-28; Eph 2:8-9; Ti 3:5), the issue is that some in this world love their wealth so much that it hinders them from receiving Christ.

In stark contrast to the rich man, Peter and the other disciples had given up all their earthly treasures to follow Jesus. The Lord informed them that they would be rewarded a hundred times as much as they had given up, along with eternal life. The disciples had made a better investment.

Those who seek wealth want a high ROI (return on investment). Unfortunately, they will only see a high ROI in this life. The wealth they gain is temporary—they lose it all the moment they die. A spiritual investor makes a better investment, one with locked in rates and no losses ever. Their investment is in the kingdom. As a result, they are storing up lasting treasures in heaven.

Begin investing in the people, plans, and projects of the kingdom of God. The ROI will be well worth the time and money you invest.

AL

Thursday

LORD HAS NEED OF YOU
Read Mark 11

If anyone says to you, "Why are you doing this?" you say, "The Lord has need of it." (11:3a)

As Jesus the Messiah prepared to enter Jerusalem at the beginning of His passion week, He was careful to fulfill all of the Old Testament prophecies concerning Himself, right down to the smallest details. One of those prophecies is recorded in Zechariah 9:9, "Rejoice greatly, O daughter of Zion! Shout in triumph, O daughter of Jerusalem! Behold, your King is coming to you; He is just and endowed with salvation, humble, and mounted on a donkey, even on a colt, the foal of a donkey."

In order to fulfill this prophecy, Jesus instructed two of His disciples to go to a certain village where they would find a colt that had never been ridden, and to untie the colt and return with it. If anyone should question what they were doing, they were to simply say, "The Lord has need of it" (v. 3). Having acquired the colt, Jesus mounted it and entered Jerusalem. As the Messiah rode, many of the people spread their coats in His path while others spread leafy branches which they had cut from the fields. Then they all shouted, "Hosanna! Blessed is He Who comes in the name of the Lord" (v. 9; cf. Ps 118:26).

Jesus needed two of His disciples to go and retrieve the colt. Jesus also needed the owner of the colt to willingly loan the animal to Him. The two disciples, the owner, and the colt were like four seemingly nondescript pieces of a jigsaw puzzle. But if one single piece was missing, the picture would be incomplete.

Someday the Lord may ask you, His devoted disciple, to do something or to give something at a particular point in your life. Obey immediately. Even though it may seem small and insignificant to you, it may be just what the Lord needs to complete His master plan.

AL

Friday

LIVING NOT DEAD
Read Mark 12

But regarding the fact that the dead rise again, have you not read in the book of Moses, in the passage about the burning bush, how God spoke to him, saying, "I am the God of Abraham, and the God of Isaac, and the God of Jacob"? He is not the God of the dead, but of the living; you are greatly mistaken. (12:26-27)

The Sadducees, who did not believe in the resurrection, tried to trick Jesus with a hypothetical situation. In the Law of Moses, when a man died without an heir, his wife was to marry his brother to produce offspring and raise an heir in his name. In the Sadducees' example, a series of seven brothers were married to the same woman as each one died without producing an heir. They then questioned Jesus as to which of these brothers would be the woman's husband in the resurrection (vv. 18-23).

First, in response to the marriage issue, Jesus revealed that in the resurrection the woman would not be married to any of them because they would all be like the angels in heaven, which do not marry (vv. 24-25).

Second, in response to the resurrection issue, Jesus used Exodus 3:6 to prove the fact of the resurrection. In this verse, God spoke to Moses at the burning bush in the present tense, "I *am* the God of" Abraham, Isaac, and Jacob, rather than the past tense, i.e., "I *was* the God of" these three, as though they no longer existed (vv. 26-27). At the time of the burning bush Abraham, Isaac, and Jacob had all been dead for 400 years, yet they were still alive!

Upon the physical death of our body, our spirit moves into the presence of God (cf. 2 Cor 5:8), awaiting the rejoining of body and spirit (cf. 1 Thes 4:14-16). So, for Christians, God is the God of the living, not the dead. It doesn't matter whether they have a body or not—those who believe in Christ are always alive. At the time of this writing, I am about to bury my sister. At her upcoming funeral I will say, "Brenda *is*", not "Brenda *was*". Praise God for the certainty of eternal life and the hope of our future resurrection!

AL

Monday

LEARNING THE SEASONS
Read Mark 13

Now learn the parable from the fig tree: when its branch has already become tender and puts forth its leaves, you know that summer is near. Even so, you too, when you see these things happening, recognize that He is near, right at the door. (13:28-29)

As the disciples of Jesus marveled at the magnificent temple complex built by Herod, the Lord surprised them by revealing that the temple would soon be completely destroyed (vv. 1-2). Naturally, this statement inspired questions from His disciples concerning the timing of this destruction and the signs associated with it (vv. 3-4).

While Jesus chose not to elaborate on the question of the timing of this climactic event, which is now known to have occurred in A.D. 70 at the hands of the Romans, He does describe the signs associated with the future period of Tribulation. These signs, including the "abomination of desolation" (v. 14), will culminate in the return of the Son of Man accompanied by angels (vv. 26-27).

To illustrate the need to be attentive to the signs preceding the Second Coming, Jesus told a parable about the fig tree. The fig tree exhibits changes that announce a change in season. When someone observes these changes, they know that summer is approaching.

The blossoming of the fig tree is just one of many events in nature that signal a change of season. We respond appropriately by unpacking our winter coats, or by planting trees, or by wearing sunscreen, or by harvesting crops. As believers, we should likewise be aware of the prophecies in the Bible that announce the end times. We can then more accurately analyze current events, especially those concerning the Middle East and the nation of Israel, knowing that our prophetic summer is close.

Carefully pay attention to the prophetic seasons and respond appropriately. As you see world events unfold, realize that the Lord's coming is near—it is almost summer. Urgently share the gospel with your loved ones, so that when the Master returns no one in your house will be found asleep (vv. 35-37).

AL

Tuesday

LIMITATIONS OF THE FLESH
Read Mark 14

But Peter said to Him, "Even though all may fall away, yet I will not." And Jesus said to him, "Truly I say to you, that this very night, before a rooster crows twice, you yourself will deny Me three times." (14:29-30)

As He celebrated His final Passover with His disciples, Jesus revealed that He was about to be betrayed by one of them (v. 18). Jesus later informed the rest of them that they would all fall away and be scattered—a fulfillment of Zechariah 13:7 (v. 27).

Upon hearing this statement, Peter boldly proclaimed his unfailing loyalty. Jesus responded by informing Peter that he would surely deny Him. In fact, he would deny Him three different times that very night. Peter persisted, asserting that even if he had to die with Jesus, he would never deny Him.

Yet this same Peter could not even stay awake with Jesus while He was praying in Gethsemane. Although his spirit was willing, his flesh was weak (v. 38). When the hour of betrayal finally came, Peter initially rose to Christ's defense and cut off the ear of the slave of the high priest. However, almost immediately after this Peter fled, just as prophesied. Later, as he loitered in the courtyard, Peter three times denied being associated with Jesus, once again fulfilling prophecy.

Growing up in my neighborhood, we had a saying, "Don't let your mouth write a check that your body can't cash". Our prideful human nature often boasts about our intentions to make a meaningful contribution to God's kingdom. Yet those intentions are limited, because they rely on the ability of our flesh to fulfill them, not on God's power.

Elijah, in his human flesh but operating by the power of God, outran Ahab's chariot (1 Kgs 18:46). Likewise, Samson used his physical body and killed a thousand men with a donkey's jawbone (Jgs 15:15). Peter, having learned the limitations of his flesh, would get another chance to fulfill his pledge. Years later, Peter died a martyr's death because he refused to deny the Lord (cf. Jn 21:18-19). Your flesh has limitations, but God working through your flesh has no limitations. Learn to trust the power of God instead of relying on your own abilities. AL

Wednesday

LAID IN A TOMB
Read Mark 15

Joseph bought a linen cloth, took Him down, wrapped Him in the linen cloth and laid Him in a tomb which had been hewn out in the rock; and he rolled a stone against the entrance of the tomb. (15:46)

Shortly after Christ's crucifixion, Joseph of Arimathea approached Pilate and asked for the body of Jesus. Joseph, a prominent member of the Sanhedrin, was a good and righteous man (Lk 23:50) who was eagerly awaiting the kingdom of God (v. 44). When Pilate granted his request, Joseph, accompanied by Nicodemas (cf. Jn 19:38-40), took the body of Jesus, prepared it for burial, and laid Him in a tomb. A stone was then rolled in front of the entrance to the tomb (v. 46). Finally, the chief priests and Pharisees convinced Pilate to set a guard and put a seal on the tomb (cf. Mt. 27:62-66). This was the end of the story, right?

Two devout followers of Jesus personally handled and prepared Jesus' body, laid Him in a tomb, and put a stone in front of the entrance. Meanwhile, two groups who were adversaries of Jesus procured a Roman guard and put an official seal on the tomb. For the first group, their hope and dreams had seemingly been laid to rest. For the second group, their nightmare of dealing with a troublemaker was apparently over.

Sometimes, when we think something is over and laid to rest, God reminds us it is not over until He says so. At the end of my favorite movie Gladiator, Maximus dies and is laid to rest. There will be no part two with my hero. However, with God stories end differently. Jacob thought his son Joseph was dead and laid to rest, yet Jacob lived to see Joseph again. Daniel was thought to have died in the lion's den; instead, he came out alive. Because of their old age, both Sarah and Elizabeth laid to rest their hope of having a child, but God blessed their wombs and they each had a son.

Joseph and Nicodemas thought they had laid to rest their hopes in Jesus and the kingdom of God when they buried the Lord. However, their hopes were resurrected after three days. Have you laid to rest your hopes? Remember Luke 1:37, "For nothing will be impossible with God." May your dreams rise again. AL

Thursday

LOOKING FOR JESUS THE NAZARENE
Read Mark 16

And he said to them, "Do not be amazed; you are looking for Jesus the Nazarene, Who has been crucified. He has risen; He is not here; behold, here is the place where they laid Him." (16:6)

Early in the morning on the first day of the week, three women came to the tomb of Jesus to anoint His body with spices. However, when they arrived they discovered that the stone sealing the tomb had been rolled away—there was no body to anoint! Instead, they saw a young man in a white robe sitting in the tomb. The man, clearly an angel, informed the women that Jesus the Nazarene had risen from the dead. He then told the women to tell the disciples that Jesus would meet them in Galilee.

The women who had come looking for the dead Jesus were informed that He was now risen. To ensure that the women realized that this was the one and the same Jesus, the angel added the descriptors "the Nazarene", "Who has been crucified", and "here is the place where they laid Him" (v. 6). Why was it so important to identify the dead Jesus with the risen Jesus? Because some deceptive followers could have stolen the body of Jesus and falsely claimed that He had risen from the dead.

Many today are trusting in their own personal saviors. While these saviors may share some similarities with the actual Jesus, there are many differences. Pay attention to their descriptors! Like counterfeit money that looks real but is not, so too are the counterfeit messiahs and saviors of today. They might use spiritual language and look righteous, but do they have lives that correspond with Scripture? They may even be able to perform miracles, but Satan can do such things in order to lead God's people astray (cf. 13:21-22; 2 Thes 2:9).

We know we believe in the legitimate Savior, because He was Jesus of Nazareth, born of a virgin, perfectly righteous, crucified until death, buried in a tomb, raised from the dead after three days, seen of men, and He currently sits at the right hand of the Father.

AL

Friday

PERSIST IN PRAYER
Read Luke 1

But the angel said to him, "Do not be afraid, Zacharias, for your petition has been heard, and your wife Elizabeth will bear you a son, and you will give him the name John." (1:13)

Prayer is an act of faith trusting that God both hears and is able to respond with assistance. But unanswered prayer often causes disappointment. In such cases, it might appear as if God is indifferent and insensitive. Natural questions follow, such as, "Why doesn't God hear?" or "Why doesn't God help?" It is tempting to simply give up. But doing so may deprive you of seeing and savoring the answer to your prayer that might be just around the corner.

In the days preceding the birth of Jesus Christ, there was a priest named Zacharias. He was married to a woman named Elizabeth. They were elderly and without child, which would have been a source of great anguish in that culture. Zacharias was graciously given the privilege to enter the temple of the Lord and burn incense—a once in a lifetime opportunity for a Levitical priest! While performing his duties in the temple, the angel Gabriel appeared, causing Zacharias fear and shock. The angel immediately reassured him and informed him that God had heard his prayer. The answer fulfills what was lacking in Zacharias' life, a child, and what was lacking in Israel, a savior! As Darrell Bock notes: "God's answers sometimes come at a surprising time, in a surprising place, and in a surprising way" (*Luke 1:1-9:50*, p. 83, Baker, 1994).

Zacharias was told that he would be given a child who was to be named John, a shortened form of the Hebrew name Jonathan, meaning "Gift of Yahweh." Indeed, God had graciously answered the greatest prayer of an elderly husband as well as the greatest need of a nation and the world—John the Baptist was the precursor to Jesus Christ.

If your prayers are not immediately answered, don't give up. Continue to seek the Lord and to trust in His timing. And remember to rejoice in the grace of the Lord when He responds.

AH

Monday

GOOD NEWS!
Read Luke 2

But the angel said to them, "Do not be afraid; for behold, I bring you good news of great joy which will be for all the people." (2:10)

With so much pain and suffering in the world, good news is always refreshing. Perhaps you have received news of a promotion at your job. Maybe a colleague and his spouse are expecting their first child. Or perhaps a family member has been given a cancer-free diagnosis. Good news certainly has a way of lifting our spirits and putting a pep in our step.

Shortly after the birth of Jesus Christ, an angel appeared to a group of shepherds who were keeping watch over their sheep in the fields near Bethlehem. Just like Mary and Zacharias before them, the shepherds were initially terrified; however, they were soon reassured by the angel, "Do not be afraid" (vv. 9-10; cf. 1:12-13, 29-30). The announcement of the birth of Jesus was good news that was intended to elicit great joy, not fear—the Savior had come (v. 11)! In Luke's Gospel, "joy" is often associated with salvation, as it is in these verses (cf. 6:23; 15:7, 10).

The good news of great joy was for "all the people" (v. 10). In the immediate context, this phrase referred to God's covenant people, the Israelites, who were eagerly awaiting the coming of their promised Messiah. However, the good news of Jesus' arrival would soon extend to people of every land across the globe. Luke 2:32 provides a hint of the worldwide significance of the good news of the birth of Jesus. In this verse, He is identified as "a light of revelation to the Gentiles."

Christ the Savior has come. That is surely good news. Such news is too good to keep to oneself. It should be proclaimed to all people everywhere. Share the good news of Jesus Christ with an unbelieving family member, colleague, friend, classmate, or neighbor. Jesus offers his love and forgiveness, and a rich and satisfying life. That is good news indeed!

AH

Tuesday

REPENT AND REFORM
Read Luke 3

Therefore bear fruits in keeping with repentance, and do not begin to say to yourselves, "We have Abraham for our father," for I say to you that from these stones God is able to raise up children to Abraham. (3:8)

About-face! The military command means to turn around so as to face in the opposite direction. When used in a spiritual sense, it essentially serves as a synonym for repentance, which means to change one's mind. Repentance is what happens when someone comes to faith in the Lord. Jesus Christ is no longer rejected as a mere man, but rather acknowledged as the Son of God—the sole and sufficient Savior. This change of mind should encourage a change in lifestyle as well.

Crowds streamed out from the nearby towns and villages to receive John's baptism at the Jordan River. Some came to seek John's baptism because they believed that his baptism guaranteed salvation. John, however, exhorted his Jewish audience to bear fruits in keeping with repentance—they must denounce sin and express devotion to God through a lifestyle of obedience. The Jews were commanded not to trust in their religious heritage as descendants of Abraham. In hyperbolic fashion, John declared that God is able to create children for Abraham from lifeless stones. In sum, the performance of a rite (baptism) or one's physical ancestry is of no value apart from repentance.

There is no ordinance or ritual that can produce a right relationship with God. Similarly, the Lord is no respecter of persons (cf. Rom 2:11)—He doesn't care who your ancestors were. God wants genuine repentance followed by outward deeds that give testimony to that repentance. These deeds also give testimony to the outside world of the transformation that has taken place inwardly. So make sure your lifestyle is consistent with your profession. In modern language, "don't just talk the talk, walk the walk," "practice what you preach," or simply "live out your Christian faith."

AH

Wednesday

ARE YOU MALNOURISHED?
Read Luke 4

And Jesus answered him, "It is written, 'Man shall not live on bread alone.'" (4:4)

Most people eat every day. Some are even fortunate enough to eat three or more meals per day. For those who don't eat every day, they are in danger of becoming malnourished. It is alarming to learn that only 32% of churchgoers say they read the Word of God every day. About a quarter (27%) say they read the Scriptures a few times a week. Tragically, more than 40% say they read the Bible once a week or less. This is a clear indication that many Christians are spiritually malnourished.

Shortly after being baptized by John the Baptist, Jesus was led by the Holy Spirit into the wilderness, where he was tempted by the devil for forty days. His experience was similar to that of the nation Israel, who had been tempted in the wilderness for forty years. Jesus faced a long and arduous trial—forty days without family, friends, fellowship, and food. Satan's first temptation was an effort to get Jesus to turn stones into bread, knowing that He was in need of physical sustenance. By performing this miracle, Jesus could prove to the devil that He was the Son of God (v. 3). Rather than fall prey to the devil's scheme, Jesus countered Satan's attack by quoting from the Scriptures. Just as Israel needed to depend on the Lord for sustenance in the wilderness, so did Jesus Christ (cf. Dt 8:1-3). Jesus understood that one's ultimate survival is not dependent upon the satisfaction of physical hunger—a person needs something more substantial than mere bread—a person needs to feed on the Word of God.

Avoid spiritual malnourishment. Become dependent on the Word of God for sustenance. Set aside a specific time to read and meditate on the Scriptures every day. Get to the place where you long for the nourishment that the Word of God provides, so much so that it seems impossible to live without it. This way, you will feed your soul and grow in intimacy with your God and Savior.

AH

Thursday

SLIP AWAY TO PRAY
Read Luke 5

But Jesus Himself would often slip away to the wilderness and pray. (5:16)

People slip away from all sorts of things. Some slip away from work early. Others slip away from parties. Many slip away from their homes. The slipping away is usually for some type of relief—maybe to get something to eat, or to get some needed rest, or for mental rejuvenation.

In the midst of grueling days filled with serving the needs of the crowds, Jesus would often slip away to pray. Prayer is a prominent theme in the Gospel of Luke, which records several instances when Jesus prayed. The Lord routinely communicated with His Father at the most significant times in His life, including at His baptism (3:21), before choosing the Twelve (6:12), at the Transfiguration (9:29), in the Garden of Gethsemane (22:41-42; cf. Mt 26:36-39), and while on the cross (23:46). Jesus taught the disciples to pray the so-called Lord's Prayer (11:1-4). The disciples were also commanded to pray throughout the passion week (21:36; 22:40, 46). All believers are encouraged to persist in prayer (11:5-8), to express total trust in God through prayer (11:9-13), and to pray at all times (18:1).

For Jesus, nothing was more satisfying, restful, and refreshing as spending time with His Father in prayer. Christians should follow the example of Christ, especially in the midst of a busy season, during times of trouble, or while facing conflict.

What's going on in your life today? What has you completely exhausted or overwhelmed? Is it your finances, your marriage, or your studies? Whatever is taxing you today, slip away to pray. Stop holding on to your concerns and hand them over to the Lord. He is more than able to grant the nourishment, refreshment, peace, comfort, and rest your soul needs.

AH

Friday

LOVE OTHERS WELL
Read Luke 6

Treat others the same way you want them to treat you. (6:31)

Love, respect, and kindness are all universal longings. While many will, at best, reciprocate love, respect, and kindness, few will actually initiate those qualities toward others. What better way for Christians to make a difference in a world full of so much hate, disrespect, and hostility!

While teaching His followers concerning how to live out true righteousness, Jesus mentioned seven aspects of unconditional love: 1) love your enemies (v. 27a); 2) do good to those who hate you (v. 27b); 3) bless those who curse you (v. 28a); 4) pray for those who mistreat you (v. 28b); 5) do not retaliate when wronged (v. 29); 6) give freely (v. 30); and 7) treat others the same way you want to be treated (v. 31). The final aspect is perhaps the most summative charge. Commonly known as the Golden Rule, it is a compelling challenge. It is no wonder that other religions have similar statements. Confucius taught, "What you do not want for yourself, do not do to others." The acclaimed Rabbi Hillel summed up the entirety of the Law when he taught, "Whatever angers you when you suffer at the hands of others, do not do it to others, this is the whole Law." However, notice that the aforementioned teachings are reactive while the Lord's instruction is proactive. As a result, Jesus' teaching is much more difficult to accomplish. In fact, it often requires supernatural enabling (cf. Gal 5:22-23). Nevertheless, by doing so, Christians will make a distinctive mark in a world where self-centeredness is the norm.

Love well today by respecting and showing kindness toward others. Take the initiative. Your love will not always be appreciated nor reciprocated, but God's heart will be well-pleased and others will be well-served.

AH

Monday

SPIRITUAL MATHEMATICS
~Corresponding Ratios~
Read Luke 7

Then He said to her, "Your sins have been forgiven." (7:31)

Sin is a universal problem. It is a disease all humans are born with and will struggle with until their last breath. It infects the poor as well as the prosperous. It contaminates the young and the old. It defiles both men and women. It affects every race. Because of sin, we live in a world filled with murder, adultery, theft, sexual exploitation, abortion, terrorism, lying, child abuse, racism, drugs, and countless other evils.

On one occasion, while Jesus was dining in the home of a Pharisee named Simon, a sinful woman (probably a prostitute) approached the Lord and began to kiss His feet while anointing them with perfume. The self-righteous Simon was appalled. He muttered to himself that Jesus couldn't be a prophet because if He was then He would know that the woman touching Him was full of sin. Jesus responded by telling Simon a parable. In the parable, one man was forgiven a debt ten times greater than another—one was forgiven 500 denarii while the other was forgiven 50 denarii. In the time of the New Testament, a denarius was worth a day's wages, so these were both very significant debts. Jesus then asked Simon which of the two men would be more grateful. Simon correctly answered the person who was forgiven the larger debt. Jesus then rebuked Simon, criticizing him for his lack of reverence when He had entered his home. The sinful woman had shown Christ far more honor and respect than the proud Pharisee. As a result, Jesus informed her that her sins had been forgiven. The point of the parable was clear—the woman was forgiven an enormous debt because of the magnitude of her sins; she would therefore be immensely grateful for what Jesus had done.

Have you been forgiven by Jesus? If so, has it prompted a love response? Do you long to spend time with the Lord through Bible reading, prayer, and meditation? Are you eager to gather with other Christians regularly for mutual encouragement? Are you involved in making disciples? These are just a few of the ways we can demonstrate our gratitude to Jesus, Who has forgiven us a great debt.   AH

Tuesday

CULTIVATING GOOD SOIL
Read Luke 8

But the seed in the good soil, these are the ones who have heard the word in an honest and good heart, and hold it fast, and bear fruit with perseverance. (8:15)

Cultivation is an agricultural term that means to prepare and use land for crops and gardening. Cultivating soil has a twofold purpose. First, it breaks up the crusty surface, allowing for easier penetration of air, water, and nutrients deep in the soil where plant roots can gain access to them. Second, it enables newly germinated seeds to sprout effortlessly through the surface of the soil to reach the sunlight they need to grow to maturity.

The teachings of Jesus drew various responses from the crowds that followed Him. The Lord illustrated these reactions with a well-known parable—the so-called Parable of the Sower. Jesus highlighted four types of people represented by four kinds of soils. All four soils received the same seed (i.e., the Word of God). The first group (beside the road) represents those who hear but do not respond in faith due to the devil's work. The second group (rocky soil) denotes those who listen and rejoice but lack deep roots, with the result that times of testing cause them to fall away. The third group (among the thorns) symbolizes those who listen but the cares of this world (i.e., materialism, riches, pleasures of life) prevent them from reaching maturity. The fourth group (good soil) illustrates those who hear the Word of God, hold fast to it, and persevere until they yield a good harvest.

Is the Word of God producing fruit in your life? If not, consider how well you are cultivating the soil in your heart to allow the Word of God to easily penetrate and provide the nourishment you need. Spiritual growth begins from the inside out. Read the Word of God. Meditate on it and memorize key verses. Pray for insight and guidance. These are all wonderful ways to begin cultivating good soil in your life.

AH

Wednesday

NO MORE EXCUSES
Read Luke 9

And He said to another, "Follow Me." But he said, "Lord, permit me first to go and bury my father." (9:59)

It has been said that excuses are like armpits—everybody has them and they all stink! When it comes to failing to honor commitments, excuses abound. Oftentimes, excuses are used to save face and prevent embarrassment. Other times, they serve as a way to avoid responsibility. But in the Christian walk, a committed lifestyle is an essential part of being a devoted follower of Jesus. The Lord is looking for serious, selfless, and sacrificial Christians.

Luke 9:51-19:27 is a composite record of several of Jesus' journeys to Jerusalem. Discipleship is the major theme of the narrative. As Jesus and His disciples were going along the road, a man approached them and expressed a desire to follow Jesus; that is, until he realized what that kind of commitment entailed (vv. 57-58). Jesus then offered an invitation to a second man with the same words He had previously used to call His disciple Levi (i.e., Matthew), "Follow Me" (v. 59; 5:27; cf. Mt 9:9). The man, however, explained that he first needed to go and bury his father. The text does not indicate whether the father was terminally ill or had recently passed away, although both options are unlikely since the man was not currently with his father. What's more likely is that the man was asking for permission for an indefinite delay until his father died.

Too many Christians are waiting for a better time to fully commit to the Lord. Some want to wait until they have finished with their studies. Others want to wait until they are married. Still others want to wait until retirement. But when that retirement finally comes, the excuse is that there is no more energy. The young are often too busy and the old are just too tired. However, the Lord doesn't want excuses. Put aside the fear of failure, embarrassment, uncertainty, or change, or your perceived lack of confidence or resources. Discern what the Lord is asking you to do today and trust that He will accompany you as you step out in faith. The Lord's invitation is clear: Follow Me. Now. No matter what.

AH

Thursday

PRAYING WHILE GOING
Read Luke 10

And He was saying to them, "The harvest is plentiful, but the laborers are few; therefore beseech the Lord of the harvest to send out laborers into His harvest." (10:2)

In Luke ten, Jesus sent out seventy disciples in pairs on a mission to prepare cities for His arrival. Equipped with clear instructions but few provisions, the disciples were commanded to peacefully enter appointed locations, heal their sick, and proclaim, "The kingdom of God has come near to you" (v. 9). Jesus knew that these two-man teams, as His representatives, would encounter both reception and rejection as they carried out their mission. Yet, despite resistance from some of the cities, the size of the harvest would soon exceed the number of workers. As a result, Jesus exhorted His disciples to "beseech the Lord of the harvest to send out laborers into His harvest" (v. 2).

This call to prayer has both theological and practical significance. Theologically, it reinforces the Father's sovereign control of the harvest. It is "His harvest" and He is "the Lord of the harvest." Therefore, no one can enter the harvest fields on his own volition—one can only be called by the sovereign Lord of the harvest and assigned a place of labor. The Lord will then produce the harvest He desires.

Practically, the call to prayer is directed not to those who are seated on the sidelines—and therefore unengaged in the mission—but to those who have been called. Jesus gave this command to "them", i.e., the seventy who were sent. This means that as they were going, they were to be praying. As they fulfilled their calling, thus increasing the size of the harvest, they were to be asking God to call more workers into the fields.

Until the Great Commission is fulfilled, the need for laborers will remain. The Lord commands us to pray for laborers so that the fields can be fully harvested. But we are to pray *while* going. Where has the Lord of the harvest called you?

PN

Friday

SHAMELESS PERSISTENCE
Read Luke 11

So I say to you, ask, and it will be given to you; seek, and you will find; knock, and it will be opened to you. (11:9)

In Luke 11:1-13, Jesus gave His disciples some valuable instruction on prayer. The first section of this teaching provides a model prayer for His disciples, commonly referred to as the Lord's Prayer (vv. 2-4). This prayer is followed by a parable (vv. 5-8) and a series of commands (vv. 9-13).

Jesus' parable was a story about a bothersome neighbor who must find a suitable solution to a dilemma. A friend from afar had unexpectedly come to the neighbor's house at midnight and he had no bread to set before him. Facing embarrassment, the man decided to boldly awaken his neighbor and ask him for bread to serve his friend. Although the neighbor is initially reluctant to answer the door, he finally relents and provides what is needed because of the man's "persistence" (v. 8).

The biblical word translated "persistence" conveys two equally important ideas. First, it carries the idea of shamelessness, in that we should never be embarrassed to ask God for anything we need through prayer. Second, it carries the idea of boldness, in that we should have the courage to approach His throne without fear. It is this kind of bold, shameless persistence in asking that Jesus commends in this parable.

To reinforce this truth, Jesus concluded His discourse with a series of present tense commands. He said, "Ask (and keep on asking), and it will be given to you"; "Seek (and keep on seeking), and you will find"; "Knock (and keep on knocking), and it will be opened to you" (v. 9). In light of the preceding parable, these commands exhort us to never become weary, but to remain shamelessly persistent in our prayers, knowing that our God is a compassionate Father Who delights in meeting the needs of His children.

Have you given up praying about a need in your life? Stay shamelessly persistent like the bothersome neighbor and boldly continue to ask the Lord to meet your need.

PN

Monday

WHEN PERSECUTION COMES
Read Luke 12

When they bring you before the synagogues and the rulers and the authorities, do not worry about how or what you are to speak in your defense, or what you are to say; for the Holy Spirit will teach you in that very hour what you ought to say. (12:11-12)

As Jesus neared the time of His crucifixion, He wanted to warn His disciples of the persecution they will inevitably face as His representatives. A commitment to Him will not result in joyful acceptance from others, but hostile rejection (cf. v. 53). Loyalties will be disrupted, families will be divided, and persecution will be inevitable.

To prepare His disciples for this reality, Jesus gave them a pair of practical instructions here in Luke twelve. First, He commanded His disciples not to be afraid of the civil authorities who would one day oppose them, perhaps even to the point of locking them up and executing them. Jesus explained that these authorities might be capable of killing the body, thus bringing an end to this earthly life; but they were unable to touch the soul, for that was exclusively God's domain. Rather, their fear should have been directed towards the Lord, Who "has authority to cast into hell" (v. 5).

Second, Jesus commanded His disciples not to be anxious about how they should respond when dragged before the civil authorities in court. They were not to worry about their defense nor rehearse a speech, for they would be given the right words to say at that moment. The Holy Spirit, Who lives within them, would provide the appropriate words to speak. The disciples were to merely trust Him for His timely grace.

As our modern society continues to grow ever more hostile to Jesus Christ and His Word, believers will increasingly find themselves living in this first-century context. Persecution will soon become the norm, not the exception. If persecution knocks on your door, how will you respond? Will you be fearful of those who are able to harm your body? Or will you place your trust in the One Who owns your soul?

PN

Tuesday

OF MUSTARD SEED AND LEAVEN
Read Luke 13

So He was saying, "What is the kingdom of God like, and to what shall I compare it?" (13:18)

The rabbis of Jesus' day thought that God's kingdom would quickly and powerfully overtake sinful human structures. They believed victory would be swift and complete.

The Lord corrects this erroneous opinion through the telling of two short parables, the first focusing on a mustard seed and the latter on leaven. Together, these parables answer the question raised by Jesus: "What is the kingdom of God like, and to what shall I compare it?" (v. 18).

In the first parable, Jesus likens the kingdom of God to a mustard seed, which starts very small—the smallest of all seeds in that region—but grows into such a sizeable tree that birds are able build nests in its branches. In the second parable, Jesus compares the kingdom of God to leaven which a woman kneads into a lump of dough. Inevitably, the leaven is able to permeate and penetrate the entire lump.

These two parables inform us concerning the nature of God's kingdom. Contrary to the common thinking of the religious leaders, the kingdom is not destined to arrive with sizzle and size. Instead, the kingdom will launch as an entity so small that it will appear to be insignificant. But like the mustard seed, the kingdom will continue to grow until its stature is unmistakable. Along with its increasing reach is the promise, like leaven, of its inevitable, almost invisible, permeation and penetration into all of human society.

The church started in Jerusalem with a tiny group of 120 persons huddled in an upper room (cf. Acts 1:15). Since its humble beginnings, the church has grown to such an extent that there are now believers in every country of the world, perhaps numbering in total more than a billion. Despite opposition from Satan, the church will continue to grow until Christ returns to establish His kingdom. When we encounter hardship and setbacks, let us persevere with optimism and confidence. For one day soon, Jesus will indeed rule!

PN

Wednesday

JESUS' FAMILY VALUES
Read Luke 14

If anyone comes to Me, and does not hate his own father and mother and wife and children and brothers and sisters, yes, and even his own life, he cannot be My disciple. (14:26)

As a result of his compassionate love for people coupled with His incredible displays of power, Jesus' popularity had swelled considerably. Now large crowds were going along with Him wherever He went (v. 25). It is at this point that Jesus delivered one of the most difficult teachings that His followers could have ever heard (vv. 26-35). In His sermon, Jesus outlined the priority of the kingdom of God, admonishing those who wanted to follow Him to "calculate the cost" (v. 28) of being His disciple.

But was Jesus really saying that only the one who gave up all his own possessions (v. 33) or only the one who hated his own family (v. 26) was worthy of following Him? Moreover, was the Lord declaring that only those who die for Him (v. 27) are to be considered disciples? Of course not. However, Jesus was emphasizing the depth of commitment needed by those who sought to follow Him. His message is clear—those who prioritize the cares of this world over the needs of the kingdom are not worthy of being His disciples.

Christ's disciples have priorities that are starkly different from those of this world. While the Christian life should be marked by love and grace, it can also be characterized by division, because many do not understand the priorities of those who are truly sold out for Christ. While we should always seek to "be at peace with all men" (Rom 12:18), we should never allow human relationships to take priority over our commitment to the Lord. Are you a true disciple of Christ? Have you fully committed to Him? Or are you refusing to give up those things in your life (e.g., relationships, possessions, selfish desires, physical comforts) that are hindering your ability to wholeheartedly follow the Lord?

BH

Thursday

THREE PARABLES, TWO AUDIENCES, ONE THEME
Read Luke 15

And he said to him, "Son, you have always been with me, and all that is mine is yours. But we had to celebrate and rejoice, for this brother of yours was dead and has begun to live, and was lost and has been found." (15:31-32)

As Jesus continued on His journey to Jerusalem, He told a series of interconnected parables about the nature of God's kingdom. Many Christians know these parables by their common titles—the Lost Sheep, the Lost Coin, and the Prodigal Son. Luke presents these three stories as concentric tales circling one incredible theme.

This set of parables addresses two distinct audiences: a) the Pharisees and the scribes (v. 2); and b) the tax collectors and the sinners (v. 1). Jesus frequently surrounded himself with those individuals the self-righteous religious leaders (Pharisees and scribes) considered unclean (tax collectors and sinners). Therefore, it is not surprising that Jesus directed the first two parables solely at those who would have been regarded as the most lost. Consistent with His nature, God leaves everything to seek out the lost sheep and stops at nothing to find the lost coin.

But the second audience in this chapter is often overlooked. Evaluate closely the father's response to the "righteous" son: "all that is mine is yours" (v. 31). His words are truly filled with gentle compassion and understanding. In Luke 13:33-35, Jesus expressed the same kind of pursuing love in the painful relationship that He had with Jerusalem, saying, "How often I wanted to gather your children together, just as a hen gathers her brood under her wings" (v. 34). The Lord patiently handled His self-righteous children with tenderness while also disciplining them perfectly for their correction.

The one theme that these three parables have in common is the description of the nature of the heavenly Father. He diligently seeks after the lost and rejoices whenever one is found. The Father's love is steadfast and deeply compassionate (v. 20). If you are feeling lost today, take comfort in the fact that God is seeking after you, eager to demonstrate His steadfast love when you return.   BH

Friday

WISDOM WITH TRUE RICHES
Read Luke 16

For the sons of this age are more shrewd in relation to their own kind than the sons of light. (16:8b)

As Jesus continued to instruct His disciples as to how they should operate in light of both current and future realities, He told them a parable about an unrighteous manager. Jesus had previously spoken of the contrast between the wise and foolish slaves in 12:42-48 as it related to the timing of the master's return, praising the wise slave and criticizing the foolish one. And similarly, he had chastised the crowds in 12:54-59 for not applying the same level of shrewdness in regard to the current spiritual realities as they did in regard to physical realities. The parable about the unrighteous manager was quite different, however, because in this story Jesus revealed that the master "praised the unrighteous manager because he had acted shrewdly" (v. 8). Was Jesus really saying that the heavenly Master is going to be pleased with servants who act dishonestly in order to make friends for themselves "by means of the wealth of unrighteousness" (v. 9)? Of course not!

If Jesus was not condoning dishonesty, then what was the point of the parable? Jesus was not focused on the dishonesty of the manager, but rather the shrewdness of the manager's solution to his dilemma. Since he was about to get fired for mismanagement, the manager had to act quickly to build favor with his master's debtors. By collecting only a portion of the outstanding debts, he not only gained the favor of the debtors, but, incredibly, he gained back some of the favor that he had lost with his master.

The main point of the parable is that believers should be uncommonly shrewd as it relates to how they take care of the Master's business. We should approach our spiritual responsibilities with the same intensity and practicality as the world pursues wealth and pleasure? After all, the spiritual realm is where we find our "true riches" (v. 11). Consider a variety of ways that you can implement a more strategic approach to expanding the spiritual territory for which God has given you responsibility.

BH

Monday

INCREASE YOUR FAITH
Read Luke 17

Increase our faith! (17:5b)

As Jesus continued to teach lessons to His disciples, they finally acknowledged their spiritual inadequacy, crying out to Jesus, "increase our faith!" (v. 5b). From the calling of the Twelve Apostles (6:13-16) to the current passage, Luke provides accounts of a number of miracles (cf. e.g., 7:1-10, 11-15; 8:27-33, 41-56; etc.). And due to the nature of Gospel writing, it can be safely assumed that there were many more miracles during this same time period that Luke chose not to mention. In light of all these miracles, why are the Apostles crying out to the Lord, asking Him to increase their faith? Why hadn't their faith already grown strong?

The answer lies in Christ's response. After describing how even a little faith can have a tremendous effect (v. 6), Jesus used an illustration to describe the proper attitude that God's servants should possess (vv. 7-10). Servanthood is thankless; and the true servant doesn't expect praise from his Master. The Master expects—and is justified in expecting—His servants to do just as He commands, without hesitation or complaint. The Apostles had previously demonstrated a misunderstanding of God's kingdom values, seeking to be the greatest (9:46-48). This parable emphasizes the need for faithful dedication without the expectation of reward or honor.

How do we increase our faith? Our faith grows as we consistently live a life of humble obedience to our heavenly Master. As we faithfully follow the Lord, our lives are changed, and we become more like Christ. We learn to become dependent upon the Master to give us direction and to meet our needs. Our faith grows day by day; and we slowly become the type of servant that can be of use to the Master. The Exodus generation witnessed a number of miracles, yet their faith never grew. It was not until the following generation obediently walked with God for forty years that the faith of the Israelites was sufficient to conquer the Promised Land. Live a life of faithful and humble obedience as you wait patiently for the call of the Master. Ask Him what He wants you to do. Then be a faithful servant.

BH

Tuesday

SPIRITUAL AND PHYSICAL BLINDNESS
Read Luke 18

Those who led the way were sternly telling him to be quiet; but he kept crying out all the more, "Son of David, have mercy on me!" (18:39)

Luke frequently connects the parables and stories of Jesus with object lessons from the experiences of the disciples. However, these connections are not always made plain in the passages themselves. As a result, it is up to the reader to make these connections by analyzing both passages.

One excellent example of this is found at the end of this chapter, where Jesus outlines for the disciples His impending mistreatment, death, and resurrection (vv. 31-33). Despite having spent the last several years with Jesus, the disciples had grasped little concerning these things. Luke punctuates this point by repeating the same idea three different ways: 1) they "understood none of these things," 2) "the meaning of this statement was hidden from them," and 3) they "did not comprehend the things that were said" (v. 34). In effect, the disciples were spiritually blind as to the ultimate meaning of the words of Jesus.

To highlight the disciples' blindness, Luke followed up this passage with a story about a blind beggar outside of Jericho (vv. 35-43). The beggar, upon hearing that Jesus of Nazareth was passing by, called out, "Jesus, Son of David, have mercy on me!" (v. 38). Members of the crowd shouted at him to be quiet. Yet, he repeated his cry, this time even louder. Eventually, his persistent plea caught the attention of Jesus, Who healed the man, saying, "Receive your sight; your faith has made you well" (v. 42).

The connection between the spiritual blindness of the disciples and the physical blindness of the beggar should not be missed. At that moment, without the illumination of the Holy Spirit, the disciples remained blind to the meaning of their Master's words. Fortunately, we have the Holy Spirit to help us make the connection between the spiritual and the physical in our daily lives. Take advantage of this amazing opportunity. Through persistent prayer and petition, ask the Lord to reveal and illuminate your areas of blindness.

BH

Wednesday

THE THINGS WHICH MAKE FOR PEACE
Read Luke 19

If you had known in this day, even you, the things which make for peace! But now they have been hidden from your eyes. (19:42)

The long central section of the Gospel of Luke (9:51-19:27) ends with a chilling parable about the Master's plan for faithful and unfaithful stewards (vv. 11-27). Beginning in verse twenty-eight, Luke's account shifts to Jesus' final act, which takes place in Jerusalem. On Monday of Passion Week, Jesus rode into Jerusalem amid shouts of joy from His followers, who quoted a psalm of praise in honor of their Messiah, "Blessed is the King Who comes in the name of the Lord; peace in heaven and glory in the highest!" (v. 38; cf. Ps 118:26). It seemed that all of Jerusalem, even the religious leaders, had gathered to behold the spectacle of Jesus' arrival (cf. v. 39).

The Messiah's arrival is reminiscent of Jesus' birth, where Luke records the praises of the angels as heralding a future time of peace on earth, a promise that will be fulfilled at Christ's second advent (2:13-14; cf. Hg 2:9). Both sets of cheers contain similar themes: "glory in the highest" and "peace" (v. 38; cf. 2:14). When Jesus was ordered to rebuke His disciples by the religious leaders, who were skeptical that Jesus was the promised Messiah, He announced that nothing would be able to silence praises to the Most High God (cf. v. 40). In the following verses, the "man of sorrows" wept (Is 53:3; cf. v. 41) as He brought with Him an understanding of the coming destruction of Jerusalem (vv. 42-44). The phrase "peace in heaven" (v. 38) chanted by the crowd is different from the "on earth peace" (2:14) sung by the angels at Jesus's birth. In His first advent, the Lord did not come to bring "peace" on the earth, but a "sword" (Mt 10:34; cf. 12:51).

Jerusalem did not recognize the time of her "visitation" (v. 44). Therefore, she never repented. What about you? Has the Lord visited you with judgment for some sin in your life? If so, repent, and practice "the things which make for peace" (v. 42).

BH

Thursday

RENDER UNTO CAESAR
Read Luke 20

Then render to Caesar the things that are Caesar's, and to God the things that are God's. (20:25b)

Shortly after Jesus drove out those who were selling goods in the temple area (19:45-46), the "chief priests and the scribes with the elders" confronted Him (v. 1). These groups, who were often at odds with one another, had found common ground in their opposition to the Messiah. Therefore, they collectively began to test Jesus, attempting to catch Him speaking blasphemy (vv. 2-8), promoting anti-government rhetoric (vv. 20-26), or siding with one group over another (vv. 27-38).

In perhaps the most well-known of these attempted entrapments, spies sent by the religious leaders asked Jesus whether it was lawful to pay taxes to Caesar (v. 22). The Lord responded by asking to see a denarius (a Roman coin). He then posed a simple question, "Whose likeness and inscription does it have?" (v. 24). The crux of his question lies in his use of the word "likeness" (Greek *eikon*, from which we get the word "icon"). This term is often translated "image". The word is used in reference to the way sinful humanity exchanged the glory of the incorruptible God for an "image" in the form of corruptible man and other creatures (Rom 1:23). The denarius contained the "image" of a corruptible man—Caesar. Elsewhere, the word is used to identify Jesus as the "image" of the invisible God (Col 1:15). Believers are each commanded to put on the new self, corresponding to the "image" of God, Who created them (Col 3:10). And believers are destined to become conformed to the "image" of the Son (Rom 8:29). Each of these uses are in reference to deity. As the Lord said, "Render to Caesar the things that are Caesar's, and to God the things that are God's" (v. 25).

Whose image is engraved on your heart? Does your life reflect the image of the incorruptible God? Or are you reflecting the image of corruptible man?

BH

Monday

PREPARING FOR A DIFFICULT FUTURE
Read Luke 21

And He said, "See to it that you are not misled; for many will come in My name, saying, 'I am He,' and, 'The time is near.' Do not go after them." (21:8)

Luke recorded a historical account which was informed by eyewitness testimony of the life and teaching of Jesus Christ. His purpose was to confirm to his predominately Gentile audience that Jesus was the prophesied Son of God who became the Son of Man to provide forgiveness of sins for everyone.

In Luke 19:43-44, Jesus had prophesied about the impending attack on the city of Jerusalem. Here in this chapter, He foretells the destruction of the temple and His eventual return (vv. 5-6; 27). The first part of this chapter presents an interesting contrast between what impresses Jesus and what impresses others (vv. 1-5). "While some were talking about the temple, that it was adorned with beautiful stones and votive gifts" (v. 5), Jesus focused His attention on a widow who gave "all that she had to live on" (v. 4) to honor God.

Concerning the temple, Jesus told His disciples, "the days will come in which there will not be left one stone upon another which will not be torn down" (v. 6). His disciples asked when this would happen and what would be the preceding sign. In response, Jesus revealed few clues about the precise timing of these events; instead, He gave them instructions on how to best prepare themselves. He warned them about the coming of false Christs who say, "The time is near" (v. 8), and counseled them not to be concerned about news of wars (v. 9). He then gave instructions on how to respond in the midst of persecution (vv. 12-19) and warned them to flee Jerusalem when they see approaching armies so that they would not be led away captive (vv. 20-24). He also promised that the Son of Man coming in a cloud would be the sign of the Jewish redemption (vv. 27-28). Jesus concluded His speech by encouraging His disciples to have hearts that are not worried, but alert and prayerful (vv. 34-36).

In a world that is more concerned about when the end will come than being spiritually prepared for the end, are we alert and prayerful?

JP

Tuesday

BUT I HAVE PRAYED FOR YOU
Read Luke 22

The Lord turned and looked at Peter. And Peter remembered the word of the Lord. (22:61a)

As Luke's gospel races toward its climax, the death of Jesus, the author punctuates the rising tension with his narrative of the Last Supper. This Passover meal (cf. v. 1) commemorated the Exodus of the children of Israel from Egypt, their redemption from slavery, and resultant freedom to live in communion with God. Every year, the parents of Jesus had brought Him to Jerusalem for this feast (2:41-43). The sense of foreboding is apparent in the words of Jesus as He reveals to His disciples that He had "earnestly desired to eat this Passover" with them (v. 15). Jesus knew this day would come; and He knew what it would mean for those who followed Him. During this meal, and in the days leading up to it, Jesus leveraged the symbolic acts associated with the Passover ritual (cf. Ex 12) to illustrate the importance of His final hours (cf. e.g., vv. 7-20).

Near the end of the meal, Jesus informed Peter that he was going to deny Him three times before the rooster crowed (v. 34). As the Lord began to speak, He twice addressed Peter as Simon (v. 31), knowing that Peter would fail to be the "rock" (cf. Mt 16:18) that Jesus needed during the most difficult time of His earthly ministry. Yet Jesus still encouraged him, saying, "But I have prayed for you" (v. 32).

Whether it was out of fear of persecution, having just seen his Rabbi taken into custody, or out of embarrassment of being associated with an accused criminal, Peter fulfilled the words of Jesus by denying Him three times (vv. 54-62). Sadly, in the drama of the moment, "The Lord turned and looked at Peter" (v. 61). Imagine the shame Peter felt as his Master's gaze pierced him. How could he ever be forgiven for such a betrayal? Had Satan really won (cf. v. 31)?

Surely not! Jesus knew all along exactly what would happen. We all falter; and Satan desires to paralyze us with shame. But have confidence—Jesus intercedes on our behalf (cf. Rom 8:34), just as He prayed for Peter. God wants you, just as He wanted Peter, to maintain your faith and to "strengthen" those around you (v. 32).

BH

Wednesday

CURIOSITY'S GOT YOUR TONGUE?
Read Luke 23

And he questioned Him at some length; but He answered him nothing. (23:9)

In the first three chapters of the Gospel, Jesus speaks in just one verse (2:49). In the first twenty-seven verses of this chapter, He speaks in just one verse (v. 3). In fact, once Jesus' ministry launches in earnest in chapter four, there is no greater gap in Jesus's words than that of verses 4-27. There was no longer any need for lengthy discourses—Jesus had spoken sufficiently to demonstrate that He was the promised Messiah.

When Pilate discovered that Jesus was from Galilee, and therefore under the jurisdiction of Herod Antipas, he sent him to the tetrarch, who was himself in Jerusalem at that time, probably to celebrate the Passover (v. 7). Herod Antipas found Jesus to be a curiosity, and he "was very glad when he saw Jesus; for he had wanted to see Him for a long time, because he had been hearing about Him and was hoping to see some sign performed by Him" (v. 8).

At this point, Herod viewed Jesus as little more than a court jester for his own personal entertainment. It is no wonder, then, that Jesus chose to remain completely silent in front of Herod, who was joined by the chief priests and scribes, who were serving as Christ's accusers (vv. 9-10). Just as Jesus had prophesied before entering Jerusalem, this Gentile was mocking and mistreating Him (v. 11; cf. 18:32). Herod's perception of the identity of Christ could not have been farther from the truth. As a result, the Lord would not speak or act in the presence of such unbelief. Consequently, every question was returned with silence. Herod was enamored with his own glory, not the glory of the Most High God, and Jesus saw right through his royal façade.

This episode should serve as a harsh warning to those who approach God without faith in Who He is, but rather with a sense of curiosity about the things He might be able to do for them. Let us not make an idol out of the things we see God doing and thus miss the glory of His identity. Praise God simply for Who He is; and stop treating Him like a divine Genie Who is able to grant wishes.   BH

Thursday

ONE ENDING MARKS A NEW BEGINNING
Read Luke 24

Then He opened their minds to understand the Scriptures. (24:45)

For a period of forty days following His resurrection (cf. Acts 1:3), the followers of Christ—not just the Eleven, but also "those who were with them" (v. 33; cf. Acts 1:15; 1 Cor 15:6)—once again had the opportunity to sit at their Master's feet. During this period, the Lord taught His followers (vv. 27, 44-48), ate with them (vv. 30, 41-43), showed them His scars (vv. 39-40), reminded them of the coming of the Holy Spirit (v. 49), and blessed them (v. 50). The Lord then ascended into heaven (v. 51).

In the midst of these events, the Lord gave His followers an explicit order, "But you are to stay in the city [Jerusalem] until you are clothed with power from on high" (v. 49; cf. Acts 1:8). Luke's story did not end with the Ascension. In fact, his narrative was only half finished. The Gospel of Luke was just the "first account" that Luke wrote to Theophilus (Acts 1:1; cf. 1:3)—the Book of Acts was the second account. And in Acts, many of the promises Jesus gave to His followers were fulfilled, including the promise of the Holy Spirit.

It is the coming of the Holy Spirit that will allow the followers of Christ to more fully understand the power and meaning of the cross, just as the story of the two travelers on the road to Emmaus exemplifies (vv. 13-32). In his Gospel, Luke records several occasions where the followers of Christ were unable to comprehend the words of the Lord (cf. 2:50, 9:45, 18:34). However, the coming of the Holy Spirit marked the beginning of a new age for the followers of Christ. Thanks to the teaching ministry of the Holy Spirit, they were now able to understand all the things Jesus had told them (cf. Jn 16:13).

This shift in the experience of the followers of Jesus was critically important. Their new knowledge was not the result of their own intelligence or personal gifts—it came from the presence of the Holy Spirit. It is the same with believers today. We are indwelt by the same Holy Spirit. Let us strive today to allow Him to open our "minds to understand the Scriptures" (v. 45) so that we may proclaim the gospel to "all the nations" (v. 47).

BH

Friday

WAS JESUS HUMAN OR DIVINE? YES!
Read John 1

And the Word became flesh, and dwelt among us, and we saw His glory, glory as of the only begotten from the Father, full of grace and truth. (1:14)

The Book of John paints a vivid picture of both the humanity and the deity of Jesus Christ. From the outset, John proclaims the deity of Christ—the Word Who was with God and is God (v. 1). Verse fourteen then weds Jesus' deity with His humanity through the advent.

Throughout this Gospel, Jesus Himself demonstrates both His humanity and His deity as the "God-man." He is tired (4:6). He thirsts (19:28). Yet, He declares that He and the Father are One (10:30).

The rest of the New Testament supports this concept as well. In Philippians 2:5-8, Paul explains how Jesus voluntarily chose not to utilize some of his divine attributes in donning human flesh. John and Paul both confirm Jesus' deity via His work in creation (vv. 3, 10; Col 1:15-17; cf. Heb 1:2).

Nevertheless, for centuries many have denied the union of Christ's divine and human natures. Some believed that Jesus only appeared to be human (Docetism). Others believed Jesus to be fully human but not divine (Ebionism). Another group held to the teaching that Jesus was a created being with divine attributes (Arianism). There were even those who went as far as stating that Jesus' human spirit was replaced by a divine spirit (Apollinarianism).

However, John staunchly verifies that Jesus became a human being and that His divine glory was undeniable (v. 14). Jesus was God's one and only unique son in human flesh—Immanuel (cf. Mat 1:23).

Regardless of what others said, John the Baptist believed Jesus to be the God-man (v. 29). Andrew and Peter believed and followed (vv. 35-41). Even Nathaniel, though a bit skeptical at the outset, believed and declared Jesus to be both the Son of God and the King of Israel (v. 49). Who do *you* believe Jesus is?

KB

Monday

FAN OR FOLLOWER?
Read John 2

Now when He was in Jerusalem at the Passover, during the feast, many believed in His name, observing His signs which He was doing. (2:23)

John two describes the commencement of Jesus' ministry, where the Lord uses a variety of signs to demonstrate His deity. The specific miracle mentioned in this chapter is one that most people know about—turning water into wine at Cana (vv. 1-10). However, it appears from this verse that there are many other signs that Jesus performed that John does not record.

Notice, though, John's emphasis on how the people responded to seeing those signs: "…*many* believed in His name, observing His signs which He was doing." Undoubtedly, the air was electric from the miracles that Jesus had performed. The audience was excited to see what else He would do. The crowd was growing, anticipating more from this newcomer in town.

Yet, something was wrong and Jesus knew it. In verse twenty-four, John indicates that Jesus was not ready to commit to a deep relationship with the people "for He knew all men". The omniscient God-man knew their *hearts*. He knew many of the eyewitnesses were just along for the ride to see how they could personally benefit from His miracles. The Bible describes man's heart as deceitful and desperately sick (Jer 17:9); and left to itself, will naturally focus on its own wants and desires. For these spectators it was, "We want more miracles, Jesus!"

Many in the crowd that followed were just fans of Jesus. They would eventually show that they were not *true* followers. Unfortunately, it is no different today. Being a fan is about comfort and pleasures. Being a follower, though, is about giving up all you have to follow Him (cf. Lk 9:23). So the question remains: Are you a fan or a follower?

KB

Tuesday

THE WITNESS
Read John 3

He who believes in the Son has eternal life; but he who does not obey the Son will not see life, but the wrath of God abides on him. (3:36)

For most people, John 3:16 is the most familiar verse in the Bible—"For God so loved the world, that He gave His only begotten Son, that whoever believes in Him shall not perish, but have eternal life." This is the "witness" verse; the primary passage used to evangelize the lost and the crux of the Christian faith. Jesus is the Savior of the world. Believe in Him and you will be saved.

Unfortunately, times are changing. In our pluralistic culture, Jesus is no longer viewed as *the* Savior, the **only** way to heaven. Instead, He is considered one of many religious teachers, one way among numerous ways to eternal life.

In John 3, we see a similar perspective. Nicodemus, a Pharisee, believed Jesus was a teacher "come from God" (v. 2). He had observed the works Jesus had performed and knew He was different. Yet, he was about to find out Jesus was far more than he imagined.

Interestingly enough, Jesus does not patronize Nicodemus. Instead, he goes right to the heart of the matter, informing Nicodemus that he must be "born again" if he wants to see the kingdom of God (v. 3). To be born again one must believe in the Son, the One Whom the Father sent (v. 17). In verse thirty-six, John the Baptist proclaims the same truth, "He who believes the Son has eternal life; but he who does not obey the Son will not see life, but the wrath of God abides on him."

Two thousand years later, the question remains: "Is Jesus, the Son of God, really the **only** way to heaven? Yes! Believe and you will receive eternal life!

KB

Wednesday

LIVING WATER
Read John 4

Jesus answered and said to her, "Everyone who drinks of this water will thirst again; but whoever drinks of the water that I will give him shall never thirst; but the water that I will give him will become in him a well of water springing up to eternal life." (4:13-14)

First century Samaria—arid, hot, scorched. A place where, if someone went without water for very long, they would surely die. It was here, at the well of Jacob, that a noteworthy encounter took place. Here Jesus and a Samaritan woman had a conversation that would change not only her own life, but the lives of many others in her community.

This encounter was amazing for two reasons: 1) Samaritans and Jews despised each other and routinely refused to have anything to do with each other; and, 2) Men and women who didn't know each other in that culture usually didn't converse. Despite these facts, in this situation a male Jew initiated a conversation with a female Samaritan. It was a simple request, yet one that would dramatically alter her life—"Give Me a drink" (v. 7).

Over the course of a relatively short conversation, Jesus transformed His need for a physical drink of water into her need for spiritual living water. A simple object lesson became the vessel through which Jesus was able to present Himself as the source of living water through which the woman would never thirst again. In fact, she was about to discover that this water would become "a well of water springing up into everlasting life" (v. 14).

The world is filled with items that can be used as conversation starters leading to spiritual encounters. Unfortunately, for many of us, sharing the Gospel seems to be tantamount to scaling Mount Everest. In reality, it can be as simple as asking for a drink of water.

Look around you. What objects do you see that would allow an entry point into a conversation that could lead to someone discovering eternal life? Always be prepared to use whatever you can to facilitate a "living water" encounter.

KB

Thursday

DISPLAYING HIS DIVINITY
Read John 5

For this reason therefore the Jews were seeking all the more to kill Him, because He not only was breaking the Sabbath, but also was calling God His own Father, making Himself equal with God. (5:18)

"Get up, pick up your pallet and walk" (v. 8). And with those three simple commands, a man who had been lame for thirty-eight years of his life was able to stand and walk. However, at the same time, this act of love and kindness was a catalyst for the religious leaders' attacks on Jesus.

In John five, Jesus began to encounter greater opposition than He had faced up to this point. The religious leaders were indignant that Jesus had healed this man on the Sabbath. They ignored the fact that a lame man had been healed. Instead, they focused on condemning Jesus for breaking *their* sacred law.

Jesus, though, did not back down. On the contrary, He escalated the altercation. Jesus had previously displayed His divinity through the healing of the lame man, now He made the direct claim that God was His Father (vv. 17-18), a relationship that provided Him with the authority and ability to perform miracles. This blasphemous (at least in the minds of the religious leaders) assertion drove the religious leaders crazy—so much so that they began looking for a way to kill Jesus (v. 18).

In His interaction with the religious leaders, Jesus made a bold claim—that He is God. But the Lord didn't just show and tell. He proceeded to back up His claim by listing multiple witnesses that testified to His deity—John the Baptist (vv. 32-35), His ability to perform miracles (v. 36), the Father (vv. 37-38), and the Scriptures themselves (v. 39). In spite of this, the Jews were so blinded that they could not perceive Jesus' divinity because they were not willing to come to Jesus so that they could have life (v. 40).

Jesus continues to display His divinity today through the testimony of His words and actions. Do you believe that He is Who He claims to be? Come to Jesus; in Him is life!

KB

Friday

PASS THE BREAD
Read John 6

Jesus said to them, "I am the bread of life; he who comes to Me will not hunger ..." (6:35)

When people think about bread, they usually think about the types of bread vital for physical life (e.g., white, wheat, rye, cornbread, etc.). But in John six, Jesus introduced a type of bread that was vital for spiritual life.

At the beginning of the chapter, John recounted an event where Jesus was on a mountain when large crowds approached Him. Jesus questioned His disciples as to where they could get enough bread to feed thousands of people. Eventually, they located five loaves and two fish. After Jesus distributed the bread and fish to the people, His disciples gathered the remaining fragments—twelve baskets full (vv. 1-14)!

Following a rough night on the water, Jesus and His disciples arrived on the other side of the Sea of Galilee. The crowds followed Him, seeking to be filled with more bread. Jesus admonished them, explaining that they needed "the food which endures to eternal life" (v. 27).

Despite the fact that they had recently witnessed an amazing miracle, the multitudes had the audacity to ask Jesus for yet another sign. They proudly proclaimed that their fathers had eaten the manna that had come down from heaven.

Jesus then revealed that He is the bread of life, "He who comes to Me will not hunger" (v. 35). Jesus Himself is the bread that comes down from heaven (cf. vv. 33, 38). And there will be no need for any other bread for those who "consume" Jesus; for those who believe in Him whom God has sent (v. 29). Those who believe are not to *add* "Jesus Bread" to their diet; rather, they are to clean out their bread box of all other breads, thus making Jesus their only bread for life. They are to be committed to the heavenly diet of Jesus alone.

So, what's in your bread box? Whether it's a famous name brand, or from the local bakery—nothing can compare to the wonder of all breads—Jesus. Please pass the Bread of Life!

KB

Monday

GOD'S TIMING
Read John 7
So Jesus said to them, "My time is not yet here ..." (7:6)

As Jesus' popularity among the masses continued to grow, so too grew the religious leaders' animosity toward the One who claimed to be the Son of God (cf. 5:18). Here in chapter seven, Jesus' brothers, who at this point did not believe in Him (v. 5), were preparing to travel to Jerusalem to celebrate the Feast of Booths (also known as Tabernacles). However, Jesus had determined that it would be best if He no longer travelled through Judea because the Jews were attempting to kill Him (v. 1). So Jesus encouraged His brothers to go to the feast on their own. Soon after they left, Jesus decided to attend the feast secretly.

At first glance, it seems quite odd that the Son of God—the One who has all power and authority over life and death—would go to the feast secretly. Did Jesus fear for His life? Was He worried about what might happen to Him? Of course not. On the contrary, Jesus was simply following the will of His Father.

The key to the Lord's departure and subsequent arrival at the feast is found in His statement, "My time is not yet here" (v. 6). This statement demonstrated the Son's submission to His Father as well as His total commitment to the Father's timetable of events. Jesus' human will was completely dependent on the will of the Father. Simply put, His time to die had not yet arrived.

How often do we, as believers, trust God's timetable? Do we really have complete confidence that the Father is in control when events do not go the way we planned? Do we truly believe that God is sovereign over all of life, especially when we encounter pain and suffering?

Jesus' focus was not on Himself—He was focused on the will of His Father (6:38). This should also be the focus of every believer—"not my will, but Yours be done" (Lk 22:42). If you are not focused on the will of the Father, confess your unfaithfulness. Don't doubt His sovereign plan. Trust your omniscient, omnipotent, and omnipresent God in everything.

KB

Tuesday

DIVINE LIGHT
Read John 8

Then Jesus again spoke to them, saying, "I am the Light of the world; he who follows Me will not walk in the darkness, but will have the Light of life." (8:12)

At the end of chapter seven, the Pharisees made a bold assertion, "Search, and see that no prophet arises out of Galilee" (7:52). Jesus, of course, was claiming to be a prophet from Galilee. Jesus contradicted the Pharisees' statement when He declared, "I am the Light of the world" (v. 12). His declaration is an obvious allusion to Isaiah 9:1-2, "But there will be no more gloom for her who was in anguish; in earlier times He treated the land of Zebulun and the land of Naphtali with contempt, but later on He shall make it glorious, by the way of the sea, on the other side of Jordan, Galilee of the Gentiles. The people who walk in darkness will see a great light; those who live in a dark land, the light will shine on them."

The Pharisees challenged Jesus' assertion, claiming that His testimony could not be proven to be true because He was testifying about Himself. Jesus responded with the claim that the Father Himself testifies on His behalf (cf. Mt 3:17).

The Pharisees could not understand Jesus' claim to be the prophet from Galilee Who had brought light to the world because they were themselves in spiritual darkness (cf. v. 19). They were from below, whereas Christ was from above; they were of this world, Christ was not of this world; they were destined to die in their sins, Christ was destined to die for their sins; they were children of the devil, Christ was the Son of God (cf. vv. 19, 23-24, 28, 44).

Jesus tried to shine the light of truth on the Pharisees' inability to see that the religion they were practicing had nothing to do with a relationship with God. Their claim that they were the children of Abraham should have manifested itself in their performing the deeds of Abraham; but since they were trying to kill Christ, they were showing that they were no relation to Abraham (vv. 39-40).

Do you walk in darkness? Jesus is the Light of the world. Make the decision today to believe in the Son and receive the divine Light!

KB

Wednesday

SPIRITUAL OPTOMETRY
Read John 9

And Jesus said, "For judgment I came into this world, so that those who do not see may see, and that those who see may become blind." (9:39)

While Jesus was in Jerusalem, He happened to pass by a beggar who had been born blind. His disciples inquired of Him as to why the man had been born blind, naturally assuming that it was because of his own sin or perhaps because of the sin of his parents. The Lord replied that he had not been born blind because of sin, but "so that the works of God might be displayed in him" (v. 3). After repeating his earlier proclamation, "I am the Light of the world" (v. 5; cf. 8:12), Jesus spat on the ground, made clay, placed it on the beggar's eyes, and told him to go wash in the pool of Siloam. When the blind man did as he was commanded, he received his sight and became living proof that Jesus was indeed the source of Light.

Once healed, the beggar was brought before the Pharisees, who inquired as to how he had been cured. The man testified that Jesus was the cause of his newfound vision. After interviewing the beggar's parents and engaging in a heated exchange with him, the exasperated Pharisees decided to excommunicate him (v. 34).

Thankfully, that is not the end of the account. When Jesus heard that the formerly blind man had been excommunicated, He found him and endowed him with spiritual vision. Jesus introduced Himself as the Son of Man, a notable messianic title (1:49, 51; cf. Dn 7:13). The beggar immediately believed in Jesus and worshiped Him.

The key to this chapter is the phrase, "though I was blind, now I see" (v. 25). Jesus is the source of Light to all who believe in Him. Those who were once blind are now able to see because they have been to the Spiritual Optometrist. Paradoxically, those who believe they can see are actually still blind and remain in darkness—they have not seen the Light, they remain in their sin (v. 41). How's your spiritual vision? Do you remain in darkness? Or have you seen the Light?

KB

Thursday

THE DOOR & THE SHEPHERD
Read John 10

My sheep hear My voice, and I know them, and they follow Me; and I give eternal life to them, and they will never perish. (10:27-28a)

John ten records a series of stories told by Jesus centered around the relationship between sheep and their shepherd. The first story emphasizes the fact that sheep obediently follow their shepherd but are unwilling to follow a stranger (vv. 1-5). The second story contrasts the shepherd who guards the sheep with thieves and robbers who seek to steal and destroy (vv. 7-10). The third story contrasts the shepherd who owns the sheep with a person who is simply hired to guard the sheep (vv. 11-16).

In the midst of these stories, Jesus boldly makes two "I am" statements. He first declares, "I am the door of the sheep" (v. 7). Then, just a few verses later, He proclaims, "I am the good shepherd" (v. 11). Jesus is the door in the sense that He guards the sheep and determines who is allowed to enter and exit the pasture. Jesus is the good shepherd because He is willing to lay down His life for His sheep.

In His role as the divine Shepherd, Jesus has His own sheep. These sheep willingly follow Him because they know His voice. He protects them and gives them abundant life. Other sheep are able to join this flock and become one with them, likewise receiving abundant life.

In these stories, Jesus serves as a sharp contrast to the Jewish religious leaders, who are characterized as strangers, thieves, robbers, and hired hands. These unfaithful leaders don't really care about the sheep—that's why they flee when danger approaches instead of being willing to lay down their lives for their flock.

Whose voice are you listening to? Are you listening to the divine Shepherd and following Him as He leads you? Or are you listening to false teachers, the "hired hands" who selfishly seek their own interests?

KB

Friday

RESURRECTION AND LIFE
Read John 11

Jesus said to her, "I am the resurrection and the life; he who believes in Me will live even if he dies, and everyone who lives and believes in Me will never die. Do you believe this?" (11:25-26)

This chapter of John includes one of the most familiar events in the life of Jesus—the raising of Lazarus from the dead. Mary and Martha, close friends of Jesus, sent word to Him that their brother Lazarus was sick. Instead of rushing immediately to the village of Bethany, Jesus remained where He was for two days. In the meantime, Lazarus died. It should be noted that the Lord's delayed departure was intentional, for it was designed to bring the greatest glory to both God and the Son of God (v. 4).

By the time of Jesus' arrival, Lazarus had already been in the tomb four days. As Jesus approached Bethany, Martha rushed out to meet Him, immediately confronting Him as to why He had delayed His coming. She was certain that if Jesus had been there, Lazarus would not have died. Mary later echoes this same response when she meets Jesus (v. 32). The Lord comforted Martha by assuring her that Lazarus would rise from the dead.

Martha misunderstood Jesus' statement, mistakenly believing that He was talking about the future resurrection on the last day. However, Jesus was about to reveal His true power as the Son of God. After boldly declaring that He was the resurrection and the life, Jesus proved the veracity of His claim by raising Lazarus from the dead.

Many of those who had witnessed the raising of Lazarus believed in Jesus (v. 45). However, for the chief priests and Pharisees the miracle reinforced their desire to kill Him. The religious leaders were afraid of losing their power and authority over the people—they were sure that the Romans would come and destroy the nation if the people continued to believe in Jesus (v. 48).

What is your response to the raising of Lazarus? Do you truly believe that Jesus is the resurrection and the life? If so, you will gain everything. If not, you will lose everything.

KB

Monday

PREPARATIONS FOR DEATH
Read John 12

And I, if I am lifted up from the earth, will draw all men to Myself. (12:32)

Less than a week before His death, Jesus traveled to Bethany to visit Mary, Martha, and the recently-resurrected Lazarus. The Lord, realizing that the time of His sacrifice was near, had decided to spend His final days with His closest friends. The grateful family welcomed Him with a specially prepared dinner.

During the meal, a variety of actions and attitudes stand out with regard to Christ's imminent death. First, Mary opened a bottle of expensive perfume, anointed the feet of Jesus, and carefully wiped His feet with her hair.

Second, in the midst of this beautiful act of worship, Judas questioned why the perfume had not been sold so that the money could have been given to the poor. The future betrayer of Jesus was not really concerned about the impoverished—he selfishly wanted the proceeds put into the money box, which he routinely pilfered.

Third, the Lord rebuked Judas, explaining that Mary was to keep the perfume so that she could use it for His burial. While there would always be poor people in need of aid, the Messiah would not be around much longer.

The responses of Mary and Judas stand in stark contrast—one was an act of selfless dedication while the other was an act of selfish avarice. Mary displayed a humble heart, willingly sacrificing the perfume to express her devotion. On the other hand, Judas demonstrated a self-centered heart, greedily seeking his own prosperity. It is doubtful that either knew the pain and agony that Jesus was about to go through—their actions simply revealed the state of their hearts.

Those whose hearts are devoted to the Lord attract people to Him, with the result that many experience eternal life. Those whose hearts are devoted to themselves repel individuals, with the result that many remain in darkness. Is your heart reflecting your Savior, or yourself?

KB

Tuesday

LESSONS OF HUMILITY
Read John 13

Then He poured water into the basin, and began to wash the disciples' feet and to wipe them with the towel with which He was girded. (13:5)

It was just before the Passover and Jesus knew that his time had come to leave this world. The disciples had recently had an argument over which one of them would be regarded as the greatest (cf. Lk 22:24), and at this point there was no way they would wash each other's feet. Therefore, like any good teacher, Jesus used this as a teachable moment to demonstrate lessons of humility.

The first lesson shows us how to love others, even when they don't deserve it. In spite of the recent dispute between the disciples, as well as His knowledge of Judas' imminent betrayal (vv. 18-30) and Peter's future denial (vv. 37-38), Jesus still loved them (v. 1). Loving others does not come without challenges. However, our Master commands us to love one another as an outward demonstration of our relationship with Him (v. 34).

The second lesson is that we must to be willing to take on the role of a servant (vv. 4-11). Jesus came not to be served, but to serve, and to give his life as a ransom for many (cf. Mt 20:28). Accordingly, He got up and performed a task which at that time was typically done only by servants and slaves. Just as Jesus provided an outward demonstration of humility, we also should be willing to take on the role of a servant who humbly takes care of the needs of others.

The final lesson that Jesus provides for us is cleansing. Cleansing is important because of where we walk—in a dirty, sinful world. Therefore, Jesus wanted to make it very clear to Peter that washing his feet was not about hygiene, but holiness. Beware of demanding holiness in others prior to caring for their needs.

Praise God today for His undeserved love towards us, serving us unconditionally, and cleansing us from our sins. And look for opportunities to lovingly serve others in humility.

HF

Wednesday

COMFORT FOR TROUBLED HEARTS
Read John 14

"Do not let your heart be troubled; believe in God, believe also in Me." (14:1)

A great deal of anxiety is created whenever young adults are heading to college. This is especially true for their parents, because there are a number of uncertainties. Similar uncertainties were apparent when Jesus made the announcement that He was soon leaving His disciples during the so-called Upper Room Discourse (cf. 13:33, 36). Immediately following His announcement, the Lord perceived that His disciples were deeply troubled. As a result, He sought to calm their anxious spirits with comforting words. Jesus was essentially telling His disciples, "Don't be anxious, set your heart at ease, and trust Me." Christ's actions should also comfort us. Whenever we are worried or fearful, God will speak comforting words to our troubled hearts.

During times of trouble, we should not only trust God's words, we should also trust in His promises. Notice that Jesus promised to prepare a place for His disciples and then return (v. 3). The Lord's departure was not the end of the story. Christ's departure meant that His disciples would eventually have a secure dwelling place (v. 2). Although His imminent departure greatly troubled His disciples, the Lord comforted them with news of His eventual return.

The only way that we can be assured of receiving the place He has promised is if we trust in the Lord as Savior. In "truth", Jesus is the only "way" to have "life" with the Father (v. 6). We cannot be saved by any other way. We must believe in the death and resurrection of the Lord Jesus Christ.

Jesus never promised a life without trouble or anxiety. However, when we do experience hardship, even when things seem out of control and uncertainty has overwhelmed us, we can trust in the One Who has provided comforting words for troubled hearts. We know what tomorrow holds—the Lord is coming back one day. We will meet Him in the sky (cf. 1 Thes 4:16-17), and live with Him forever in the place He is preparing for us.

HF

Thursday

IS THERE A CONNECTION?
Read John 15

"Abide in Me, and I in you. As the branch cannot bear fruit of itself unless it abides in the vine, so neither can you unless you abide in Me." (15:4)

An elderly man was having problems getting his new computer to work. Since his daughter was an expert in computers, he called her for assistance. When she answered the phone, the exasperated man cried out, "My computer will not turn on; what should I do?" His daughter responded with a simple question that solved the problem, "Is the computer plugged in?" This is the same question that believers should ask themselves daily—"Am I plugged in to my source of power, Jesus Christ?"

In John 15:1-2, Jesus taught His disciples using an extended metaphor, describing Himself as a vine, His Father as the vinedresser, and believers as branches. In viticulture, unproductive branches are cut off and taken away while productive branches are carefully pruned so that they will produce more fruit. In the same way, unproductive believers may suffer chastisement; not the loss of salvation, but the occurrence of discipline with the goal of spiritual growth (cf. Heb 12:5-11). For productive believers, pruning must take place so that they can produce even more spiritual fruit (Jas 1:2-4; cf. Gal 5:22-23). However, in order to produce fruit, a branch must remain attached to the vine. In His speech, Jesus emphasized the need for the branches to abide in the vine more than ten times. To abide means to stay connected. For believers, it means being in constant fellowship with the Lord.

When we abide in Jesus, the source of nourishment, He enables us to produce fruit (vv. 4-5). We are incapable of producing fruit on our own. It is only when we are connected with our power source that we can be productive. We can take advantage of this connection by consistently reading God's Word and interacting with Him through prayer. Furthermore, our prayers will be answered (v. 7). Abiding disciples receive what they ask for and bring glory to God (v. 8). Stay connected to your power source! You will be amazed at how productive you can be!

HF

Friday

PEACE IN TROUBLESOME TIMES
Read John 16

"These things I have spoken to you, so that in Me you may have peace." (16:33a)

Soon after reminding His disciples that He was about to leave this world (v. 28), Jesus announced the coming of a time of intense persecution (vv. 32-33; cf. v. 2). Ultimately, this was the primary purpose of His extended lecture (chs. 13-16). Jesus was preparing His disciples to carry on the ministry of the kingdom of God in His absence.

At the end of His speech, Jesus revealed a startling contrast, "In me you may have peace; in the world you have tribulation" (v. 33). There is a crucial distinction between being in the world and being in Christ. It is the difference between finding peace and finding tribulation.

Tribulation can be defined as "intense oppression and persecution." Tribulation is an integral part of God's process for redeeming the world. Since the world has rejected Him, God will judge the world (9:39; 12:31; cf. vv. 8-11). Yet in the midst of this tribulation, Christ's disciples have the opportunity to experience peace. Here, peace refers to the inner tranquility experienced by those who "abide" in Christ (14:2).

At this time, you may be experiencing oppression and persecution. It may be taking place in your home, or at school; on the job, or in your ministry. It might appear as if the world is winning. In fact, the world may even be celebrating and rejoicing (cf. v. 20). In the midst of this trial, you might feel like you are all alone. But take comfort. The Lord has given you a Comforter Who will allow you to experience peace (14:26-27; cf. vv. 13-14), even in the midst of the worst of storms.

Christ has overcome the world (v. 33); therefore, we have no reason to be anxious. Ultimately, our citizenship is in heaven (Phil 3:20). One day, Christ will return and take us home (14:2-3). Once there, we will never again experience pain, or distress, or tribulation (cf. Rev 21:4).

HF

Monday

TRUE INTERCESSORY PRAYER
Read John 17

I ask on their behalf ... (17:9)

John seventeen contains the longest prayer of Jesus recorded in the Gospels. This prayer is commonly known as Christ's High Priestly Prayer. Jesus probably spoke the words of this prayer in the Upper Room shortly after He had finished giving a series of instructions to His disciples (chs. 13-16). What was the purpose of this prayer? To pray for Himself (vv. 1-5), to pray for His disciples (vv. 6-19), and to pray for those who would believe in Christ through the testimony of the disciples (vv. 20-26).

Just before He spoke, Jesus lifted His eyes to heaven. In the modern age, we commonly pray with our eyes closed. Yet the Bible never mentions praying with eyes closed. Nor does the Bible demand a certain posture. Hannah prayed while standing (1 Sm 1:26). King Solomon prayed while kneeling on his knees with his hands spread toward heaven (1 Kgs 8:54). Ezra prayed while prostrate (Ezr 10:1). Additionally, lengthy prayers are not necessary. Christ's High Priestly Prayer takes approximately 3 minutes to recite. Short, orderly prayers can be far more effective than long, rambling prayers.

At the time of this prayer, Jesus was preparing to give His life as a ransom on the cross. He acknowledged His impending death with His opening words, "Father, the hour has come" (v. 1). Jesus began by praying for Himself. Praying for yourself is not selfish when God gets the glory in your petitions (vv. 1, 5). Next, Jesus interceded for others—first for his disciples and then for those who would believe through their testimony. This latter group includes modern believers. In a few hours, Jesus would even make intercession for those who are crucifying Him (cf. Lk 23:34).

Christ continues to make intercession today (cf. Heb 7:25). Following His example, we should make intercession for all people (cf. 1 Tm 2:1). True intercessory prayer is not about posture, or prolonged soliloquies—it is about petitions. We should always seek to glorify God, both through our own requests and through our pleas on behalf of others.

HF

Tuesday

MAKING THE RIGHT CHOICE
Read John 18

So Jesus, knowing all the things that were coming upon Him, went forth and said to them, "Whom do you seek?" (18:4)

Shortly after He finished His High Priestly Prayer, Jesus led His disciples to the Garden of Gethsemane, where they often met. Leaving His disciples, Jesus went off by Himself to pray (cf. Mt 26:36). When He returned, three significant events took place as recorded in this chapter: Jesus was betrayed (vv. 2-12); Jesus was denied (vv. 15-18, 25-27); and Jesus was tried (vv. 13-14, 19-24, 28-40).

Soon after Jesus finished praying, Judas approached the Garden with a group of Roman soldiers and Jewish religious leaders in order to arrest Him. Shortly thereafter, Peter three times denied that he was one of Christ's disciples. Over the course of the next few hours, Jesus participated in several trials designed to find a charge worthy of a death sentence. In each case, Jesus was able to predict what would happen. He had identified Judas as the betrayer at the Last Supper (13:21-27). At the same meal, He informed Peter that he would deny Him three times before the rooster crowed (13:37-38). And John 13:1 reveals that Jesus knew "that His hour had come that He would depart out of this world to the Father."

Since Jesus knew these events were going to take place, why would He allow them to happen? Because the Lord knew that He had a mission to fulfill that had been given to Him by God (17:4). He was obediently carrying out His Father's will (cf. Mt 26:39, 42; Lk 22:42). Seen in this manner, Jesus made the right choice. As God incarnate, the Lord could have easily called on more than twelve legions of angels to rescue Him from His dilemma (cf. Mt 26:53). Yet He didn't. Jesus could have hidden Himself from those seeking to kill Him (cf. 8:59). But He didn't.

As believers, we have two choices every day—to either humbly obey God or selfishly do what we want to do. Following the example of our Savior, we should seek to complete our mission, willingly taking up our cross daily, and living in total obedience to God.

HF

Wednesday

IS BLOOD REALLY THICKER THAN WATER?
Read John 19

When Jesus then saw His mother, and the disciple whom He loved standing nearby, He said to His mother, "Woman, behold, your son!" Then He said to the disciple, "Behold, your mother!" From that hour the disciple took her into his own household. (19:26-27)

There is an ancient proverb, blood is thicker than water. This statement is used to convey the idea that loyalty to family takes precedence over any other form of relationship. However, is this really true when it comes to the kingdom of God?

Over the previous several hours, Jesus had been betrayed (18:2-11), arrested (18:12), put on trial (18:12-14, 19-24, 28-40), denied (18:15-18, 25-27), scourged (v. 1), and mocked (vv. 2-3). Now, He was being crucified at a place called Golgotha between two thieves. Yet, after enduring hours of unjust suffering, just minutes before He bowed His head and gave up His spirit, the Savior demonstrated love and compassion by arranging for the care of His mother.

Standing near the cross were several women, including Mary, the mother of Jesus, and the mother of John, the son of Zebedee (cf. Mt 27:56). John, the author of this Gospel, was the "disciple whom He [Jesus] loved" (v. 26). While on the cross, Jesus turned to His mother and said, "Woman, behold, your son" (v. 26). The Lord addressed His mother as "woman" to distance Himself from her. It was the same term He used in 2:4 to indicate that she was no longer in a position of authority over Him. Jesus' words transferred the care of His mother from Himself to John, the referent of the term "son". As the oldest son, Jesus would have been responsible for the care of His mother.

At first glance, it seems unusual that Jesus did not entrust this responsibility to one of His younger brothers, who were of His own blood (cf. Mt 12:46). The most likely explanation is that His brothers had not yet believed in Him (cf. 7:5). Therefore, Jesus bypassed His unbelieving relatives and chose a believing disciple for this important task, which was a great honor. In the kingdom, water (whoever does the will of the Father) is thicker than blood (cf. Mt 12:46-50).

HF

Thursday

THE POWER OF THE RESURRECTION
Read John 20

Blessed are they who did not see, and yet believed. (20:29b)

A few days after He had been laid in a tomb, Mary Magdalene, along with Mary, the mother of James, and Salome, came early in the morning to anoint the body of Jesus with spices (v. 1; cf. Mk 16:1). They had come to the tomb expecting to find a dead body. After all, as a wise man once quipped, "You don't go to a cemetery to look for the living." However, when the women arrived, they saw that the stone sealing the tomb had been rolled away—there was no body to anoint!

In a panic, Mary Magdalene rushed to Peter and John, exclaiming, "They have taken away the Lord out of the tomb, and we don't know where they have laid Him" (v. 2). Peter and John then sprinted to the tomb to see for themselves. In truth, these individuals should not have been surprised—the Lord had announced His resurrection after three days early in His ministry (cf. 2:18-22). That is why the angel posed the question, "Why do you seek the living One among the dead?" (cf. Lk 24:5).

Rather than rejoice after recognizing that the empty tomb meant that Jesus had been resurrected, Mary Magdalene wept, believing that some group had taken His body. It was at this point that Jesus revealed Himself to Mary. And it was not until the Lord revealed Himself that Mary finally believed that He had resurrected.

We see the same pattern throughout the rest of the chapter. The disciples were hiding behind closed doors because of their fear of the Jews when Christ appeared before them and showed them the wounds in His hands and His side (vv. 19-20). Then they experienced peace (v. 21). Thomas doubted the resurrection until he was able to place his hands on Jesus' wounds; then his doubt turned to belief (vv. 27-28).

Such is the power of the resurrection. It is able to turn sorrow to joy, fear to peace, and doubt to belief. The disciples were blessed because they were able to see the risen Lord. Yet we are further blessed because we believe without seeing.

HF

Friday

BOUNCING BACK FROM FAILURE
Read John 21

He said to him the third time, "Simon, son of John, do you love Me?" (21:17a)

Peter's life can be described as consistently inconsistent. He had the audacity to rebuke the Lord when He revealed that He would be going to Jerusalem to die (Mt 16:21-23). In the Upper Room, Peter refused to let Jesus wash his feet until the Lord informed him that he could no longer participate in His ministry unless he allowed Him to wash his feet (13:8). Shortly thereafter, Peter vowed to never deny the Lord (Mt 26:33-35), only to deny Him three times over the next few hours (18:17, 25-27). In each case, Jesus immediately confronted Peter, rebuking him for questioning His behavior.

A similar confrontation takes place in the final chapter of John's Gospel. Seven of Christ's disciples had gathered on the shore of the Sea of Galilee. When Peter decided to go fishing, the others quickly joined him. After spending the night in a futile attempt to catch fish, the Lord appeared to them from the shore at daybreak and told them to cast their net on the right-hand side of the boat. They then gathered in an enormous amount of fish. Peter, in a rush to greet the Lord, jumped overboard and swam to shore.

As they were celebrating their catch, Jesus questioned Peter regarding his inconsistent devotion. Three times the Lord asked, "Simon, son of John, do you love me?" (vv. 15, 16, 17). Three times Peter responded, "You know that I love you" (vv. 15, 16, 17). These questions revealed to Peter the great difference between his brotherly love towards Jesus and the sacrificial love Jesus had for him. Jesus then proved to Peter that he did indeed have sacrificial love for Him by announcing that he would one day die on His behalf (cf. 15:13).

The events of Peter's life show that God loves unconditionally. Accordingly, He permits us to recover from past failures as long as we are repentant. Our failures allow us to develop spiritually so that we can be of greater use in the future (cf. Lk 22:31-32). Don't let failure discourage you to the point where you give up in your spiritual life. Repent and recover; for we serve a God of second chances.

HF

Monday

MARCHING ORDERS
Read Acts 1

But you will receive power when the Holy Spirit has come upon you; and you shall be My witnesses. (1:8a)

Acts one is a chapter of great change. The disciples hear the final instructions of the Lord, Jesus ascends to heaven, the disciples gather to wait for the Holy Spirit to fall upon them, and they replace Judas with Matthias.

The things that had been foretold by the Lord had come true. He had been crucified, He had remained in a tomb for three days, and He had risen from the dead. From a mountain in Galilee, the resurrected Lord gave marching orders to His disciples, "Go therefore and make disciples of all the nations!" (Mt 28:19). The Book of Acts records the initial stages of the fulfillment of this mission.

The apprehension that existed in each of the disciples evaporated with the resurrection of the Lord. The fearful followers have now become powerful proclaimers. Filled with the presence of the Holy Spirit, these disciples, along with several other apostles, are destined to take the Gospel from Jerusalem to "the remotest part of the earth" (v. 8).

Today, the church has the awesome responsibility to continue the work of the apostles and present the hope of Christ to everyone we meet. The Lord's promises and commands are as true in the present age as they were for those who heard them. When people are introduced to the saving knowledge of Jesus, their lives are changed. Spiritually speaking, the blind see, the lame walk, the sick are healed, and the deaf hear (cf. Mt 11:5).

The Lord has given you marching orders. You have the power of the Holy Spirit. What are you doing to help fulfill the divine mission? In what ways are you contributing to the spread of the Gospel to the remotest part of the earth?

JTB

Tuesday

PENTECOST
Read Acts 2

And the Lord was adding to their number day by day those who were being saved. (2:47b)

The Holy Spirit arrived on the Day of Pentecost, roughly fifty days after the Lord had spoken of His coming in the Upper Room (cf. Jn 14:16, 26; 15:26). This was also about one week after the promise of 1:4-5. As the Holy Spirit filled the disciples, He gave them the ability to speak in foreign languages. This was necessary because many in the audience were visiting from other countries. These devoted worshipers were about to hear the gospel in their own language.

To explain what was happening, Peter preached a sermon beginning with a quote from Joel 2:28-32. Peter's sermon was accusatory, placing the blame for Jesus' crucifixion squarely on the Jews. Many in the audience were pierced to the heart with conviction and inquired of Peter what they should do. Peter responded, "Repent, and each of you be baptized in the name of Jesus Christ for the forgiveness of your sins; and you will receive the gift of the Holy Spirit" (v. 38). About three thousand souls did as they were instructed; and so the church began.

The church grew quickly as many witnessed the unity of the new converts. They met together to hear the apostles' teaching, to have fellowship, to break bread, and to pray. The needs of individual believers were met as everyone had everything in common. As a result, the Lord blessed them, and their number grew daily.

Acts two reminds us of the need to share the gospel. We should expect God to open the hearts of unbelievers wherever we are—in our workplaces, in our families, in our neighborhoods, in our schools. The same Spirit that filled the apostles is working through us today. Preach the good news to those around you. Expect a great outpouring of salvation among those who hear.

JTB

Wednesday

THE MAKING OF THE BEAUTIFUL
Read Acts 3

And on the basis of faith in His name, it is the name of Jesus which has strengthened this man whom you see and know; and the faith which comes through Him has given him this perfect health in the presence of you all. (3:16)

One day, Peter and John were on their way to the temple when they met a lame beggar who sat near the temple at a gate called Beautiful. Peter approached the beggar and said, "I do not possess silver and gold, but what I do have I give to you: In the name of Jesus Christ the Nazarene—walk!" (v. 6). The man immediately stood upright and walked into the temple with Peter and John, praising God. When those in the temple saw the man, they were filled with amazement—many recognized the beggar because he had begged at the Beautiful Gate for quite some time. Peter spoke to the crowd, explaining that God had healed the man in the name of Jesus. He then encouraged the crowd to repent, so that their sins could be wiped away.

Over the course of perhaps several years, this man had sat a few feet from the temple, unable to enter because the sick and broken were unwelcome inside. This man watched for years as the healthy walked inside to worship and pray. The name of the gate was ironic, for surely those who passed the lame beggar would not have pictured him as beautiful.

As you read the story, perhaps you were able to identify with the beggar—physically, emotionally, or spiritually broken. Perhaps you are experiencing a sense of hopelessness, or the feeling of a lack of worth. Perhaps your afflictions have persisted for so many years that they now seem normal. You need restoration. You need healing. Hope is found in the name of Jesus. Through Him, the broken can be made whole. The sick can become healthy. The disfigured can be made beautiful.

JTB

Thursday

UNTRAINED MEN
Read Acts 4

Now as they observed the confidence of Peter and John and understood that they were uneducated and untrained men, they were amazed, and began to recognize them as having been with Jesus. (4:13)

Shortly after the healing of the lame beggar (3:2-8), Peter began to preach at the temple, showing how Jesus fulfilled Old Testament prophecy (3:12-22). Almost immediately, the priests and Sadducees approached Peter and John, being accompanied by the captain of the temple guard. They arrested the two disciples and put them in jail overnight. In the morning, the religious leaders held a trial, where they inquired, "By what power, or in what name, have you done this?" (v. 7). Peter responded, boldly declaring that they had healed the man in the name of Jesus Christ the Nazarene.

Just a few months prior, a frightened Peter had denied any association with Jesus on three different occasions (cf. Jn 13:38; 18:17, 25-27). Following the death of Christ, the disciples had hid themselves behind closed doors because of their fear (cf. Jn 20:19). Yet now, Peter spoke with a new sense of confidence. He bravely proclaimed, "There is salvation in no one else; for there is no other name under heaven that has been given among men by which we must be saved" (v. 12). When the religious leaders commanded them to stop speaking in the name of Jesus, Peter and John gave a fearless response, "Whether it is right in the sight of God to give heed to you rather than to God, you be the judge; for we cannot stop speaking about what we have seen and heard" (vv. 19-20).

These uneducated and untrained men spoke with great confidence (v. 13). They were able to challenge the intellectual religious leaders, who were amazed at their response. The reason for this dramatic change—they were now filled with the Holy Spirit (v. 8).

The same Holy Spirit resides in us. Don't be afraid. Don't focus on your own deficiencies or lack of talent—the Holy Spirit will speak through you. Boldly proclaim the name of Jesus Christ. Take advantage of every opportunity to tell others about the salvation that comes through His name.

JTB

Friday

OBEY GOD RATHER THAN MEN
Read Acts 5

And we are witnesses of these things; and so is the Holy Spirit, Whom God has given to those who obey Him. (5:32)

What degree of obedience does God expect from believers? In this chapter, God punished Ananias and Sapphira for lying about a piece of property that they had sold. He put them to death because they were not fully committed to Him. Their death led to great fear over the whole church (v. 11).

The story of Ananias and Sapphira is followed by an account of the persecution of the apostles. The apostles were having great success as they preached and healed in the name of Jesus. New believers were being added to the church each day. The Sadducees, filled with jealousy, arrested the apostles and put them in jail. Later that evening, an angel freed them from their cell and commanded them to preach to the people in the temple.

The apostles were quickly apprehended and brought before the Sanhedrin. The high priest questioned the apostles, reminding them that they had been ordered not to preach in the name of Jesus. Peter responded with the immortal words, "We must obey God rather than men!" (v. 29). The Sanhedrin initially decided to kill the apostles. However, after hearing the wise counsel of Gamaliel, they decided to release the apostles, but only after flogging them and once again ordering them to refrain from preaching in the name of Jesus, a command that was quickly ignored.

Believers should devote themselves entirely to God. The Lord demands full commitment, not partial. Ananias and Sapphira exhibited partial commitment—they lied about their offering, which reveals that their hearts were divided. The apostles were fully committed to the Lord, even if their devotion resulted in their death. These two stories serve as a direct challenge for those who want to serve Christ, but are unwilling to count the cost. Preach the gospel with boldness. Although you may experience opposition, always remember the words of the apostles, "We must obey God rather than men!"

JTB

Monday

ARE YOU WILLING TO BE USED?
Read Acts 6

The word of God kept on spreading; and the number of the disciples continued to increase greatly in Jerusalem, and a great many of the priests were becoming obedient to the faith. (6:7)

As the church continued to grow, the Twelve soon found it impossible to fully minister to all the people. So they laid their hands on seven men, choosing them to perform serving roles while the Twelve devoted themselves to prayer and preaching. Those chosen were no ordinary individuals. They were "men of good reputation, full of the Spirit and of wisdom" (v. 3).

One of these seven was particularly noteworthy. Stephen is further described as "full of faith" (v. 5), "full of grace and power" (v. 8), capable of performing great wonders and signs (v. 8), and able to speak with wisdom (v. 10).

As Stephen used his spiritual gifts to proclaim the gospel, he was opposed by some men from the Synagogue of the Freedmen, a religious group that included former slaves from North Africa and Asia Minor. These men were unable to silence Stephen because of his great wisdom, so they secretly induced men to accuse Stephen of blasphemy. The accusations soon found their way to the Sanhedrin, and Stephen was arrested.

There are some valuable lessons to be learned from this chapter. First, churches should be flexible as they grow. The leadership structure may need to be changed so that no group is neglected. Second, supporting roles need to be filled by spiritually qualified individuals (cf. 1 Tm 3:8-13). Servants in the church are still performing the work of the ministry. Third, spiritual gifts are absolutely vital, both for ministering to the needs of people and also for the advancement of the gospel. Each believer should look for ways to use their spiritual gift for the benefit of the body of Christ. Finally, those who minister for the Lord will inevitably encounter opposition. In the midst of persecution, they should exhibit "the face of an angel" (v. 15), for they reflect the glory of God (cf. 7:55).

JTB

Tuesday

THE SACRIFICE OF LIFE
Read Acts 7

But being full of the Holy Spirit, he gazed intently into heaven and saw the glory of God, and Jesus standing at the right hand of God. (7:55)

In this chapter, Stephen defends himself against the accusation of speaking "blasphemous words against Moses and against God" (6:11). Stephen's speech surveys the time period of the Old Testament, highlighting the pattern of rebellion against God exhibited by His chosen people. Stephen began his sermon with the calling of Abraham and his immediate descendants, Isaac, Jacob, and Joseph (vv. 2-16). He then reviewed the deliverance of the children of Israel from slavery in Egypt that God provided through His servant Moses (vv. 17-34). Finally, Stephen emphasized the nation's history of rebellion against God, beginning with the time of Moses and continuing through the period of the prophets (vv. 35-53).

From Moses to Malachi, God had used leaders to announce the coming of the Messiah and to encourage His people to repent of their sins. Now, Stephen was standing as God's representative, boldly comparing the current generation to those that had previously rebelled against God. Together, they are characterized as "stiff-necked", "uncircumcised in heart and ears", "always resisting the Holy Spirit", "betrayers", "murderers", and those who did not keep the Law (vv. 51-53).

When the officials heard Stephen's words, their anger burned out of control. They rushed at him and dragged him out of the city to stone him. The mob was led by a young man named Saul (also known as Paul), who would later would convert to Christ on the road to Damascus.

Stephen's commitment to the Lord ranged from serving tables to preaching to dying as a martyr. Stephen performed faithfully behind the scenes, doing menial tasks among the widows. He performed just as faithfully on a more public platform, preaching God's word. Stephen was willing to give everything he had to fulfill his calling. His story is a reminder that we need to display boldness and be faithful in every situation, even if it results in the sacrifice of life.

JTB

Wednesday

PERSECUTION TO SALVATION
Read Acts 8

Therefore, those who had been scattered went about preaching the word. (8:4)

Luke's summary passage (vv. 1-4) reassures the reader that Saul's campaign of religious persecution had failed to stop the preaching of the word. It has been noted that Saul was to Christians what Adolf Eichmann would become to the Jews of 1930s Germany—the architect of a holocaust. Driven by religious zeal, Saul determined to exterminate the followers of Jesus. However, instead of wiping out the church, Saul's efforts actually helped facilitate God's plan.

Stage one of God's plan saw the arrival of the Holy Spirit and the evangelization of Jerusalem (2:1-7:60). Now, Saul's persecution became the catalyst for *stage two* in "Judea and Samaria" (cf. 1:8). As believers were scattered throughout the surrounding regions, they continued to proclaim the name of Jesus.

Philip, one of the seven original deacons (cf. 6:5), fled Jerusalem and witnessed in Samaria (vv. 5-24). Philip's ministry exhibited three qualities of a genuine ministry flowing from the power of the Holy Spirit. *First*, Jesus Christ was the central focus of his message (v. 5). As noted in verse thirty-five, "Philip opened his mouth, and beginning from this Scripture [Is 53:7-8] he preached Jesus" to the Ethiopian eunuch, who then confessed, "I believe that Jesus Christ is the Son of God" (v. 37).

Second, there was a dynamic of liberating power present (vv. 6-7). Philip healed and cast out demons with the power of God. As those who believed gained freedom from their physical afflictions, they also gained freedom from their spiritual afflictions through Jesus Christ.

Finally, Philip's ministry resulted in contagious joy (v. 8). The people rejoiced in their freedom; they experienced a happiness and contentment like never before.

Even in the face of opposition, always remember, "to live is Christ and to die is gain" (Phil 1:21). God is still sovereign!

MS

Thursday

NURTURING NEW BELIEVERS
Read Acts 9

So Ananias departed and entered the house, and after laying his hands on him said, "Brother Saul, the Lord Jesus, who appeared to you on the road by which you were coming, has sent me so that you may regain your sight and be filled with the Holy Spirit." (9:17)

Saul's conversion was like no other. Most people don't receive a supernatural, personal encounter with the risen Christ! Yet in Saul's experience there are two significant concepts that apply to the nurturing of all new Christians. Take note of the events following Saul's conversion.

A Relationship. Immediately after Saul's encounter with Christ, the Lord sent Ananias, a mature believer, to minister to him (vv. 10, 17). Ananias became his friend, advocate, and guide. Saul had questions and Ananias offered answers. It's a jolting, sometime overwhelming experience when the Holy Spirit first takes up residence in a new convert. The believer needs someone to help with those first halting steps as life begins from a completely new perspective.

A Community. Ananias did not shoulder this burden alone. He quickly introduced Saul to the community of believers in Damascus, and Saul stayed with them for several days (v. 19). Those believers then helped Saul escape from an attempt on his life (v. 25). When Saul arrived in Jerusalem, Barnabas interceded on his behalf with the apostles, thus allowing him to continue freely preaching in Jerusalem, "But Barnabas took hold of him and brought him to the apostles and described to them how he had seen the Lord on the road, and that He had talked to him, and how at Damascus he had spoken out boldly in the name of Jesus" (v. 27). When another life-threatening situation arose, the brethren helped Saul escape to Tarsus (v. 30).

Think about those believers who were of assistance when you first trusted in the Lord. Eagerly pursue and take advantage of opportunities to get involved in the life of a new Christian who needs nurturing.

MS

Friday

ALL ARE CLEAN
Read Acts 10

All the circumcised believers who came with Peter were amazed, because the gift of the Holy Spirit had been poured out on the Gentiles also. (10:45)

The importance of Cornelius to the history of the church is reflected by the space devoted to the events surrounding his conversion in the Book of Acts. The various issues posed in this account were crucial for future progress (e.g., laws concerning cleanliness, dietary regulations, conversion of Gentiles, Jewish-Gentile relations).

By this time, the gospel had been firmly established in Jerusalem. It was now being extended throughout the rest of Judea and Samaria. It was only a matter of time until the outer borders of the Jewish community would be reached, and the problem of Gentile eligibility would be raised. It may well be that the question had already been faced to a limited degree—the Ethiopian eunuch may have been a Gentile; it's also possible that some of the preaching among Greeks at Antioch had already begun (cf. 11:19-20). The ancient divide between Jew and Gentile must certainly have caused many to view these contacts with grave suspicion. A test case was needed to deal squarely with the issue, and to know exactly what God's will was in the matter. The episode with Cornelius provided the occasion for the young church to confront the matter that it could no longer sidestep. And the implications of what took place in this passage have affected the character of the church from that time forward.

When Peter was given the vision of the sheet, he was initially resistant to change, protesting, "By no means, Lord, for I have never eaten anything unholy and unclean" (v. 14). The Lord responded, "What God has cleansed, no longer consider unholy" (v. 15). Peter later said to Cornelius and his friends, "You yourselves know how unlawful it is for a man who is a Jew to associate with a foreigner or to visit him; and yet God has shown me that I should not call any man unholy or unclean" (v. 28). People of all races and colors are fellow heirs and members of the body of Christ (Eph 3:6). Preach the gospel to all, without prejudice or discrimination!

MS

Monday

JEWS + GENTILES = THE CHURCH
Read Acts 11

Therefore if God gave to them the same gift as He gave to us also after believing in the Lord Jesus Christ, who was I that I could stand in God's way? (11:17)

Shortly after the conversion of Cornelius and those close to him, Peter returned to Jerusalem. He was soon accosted by a group of Jews who accused him of eating with "uncircumcised men" (i.e., Gentiles; v. 3). This accusation revealed the great prejudice that existed on the part of Jews toward Gentiles—Jews typically avoided any contact with Gentiles because they regarded them as unclean; and dining together was especially forbidden. These Jews were resistant to Gentiles becoming part of the church because that meant that they would then be regarded as equal to Jews.

Peter responded by explaining what had happened, beginning with his vision of a sheet in Joppa and culminating with the Holy Spirit falling upon those Gentiles who believed. He emphasized the fact that a voice from heaven had declared, "What God has cleansed, no longer consider unholy" (v. 9). Gentiles were now to be regarded as clean! When the Jews heard this, they quieted down and glorified God, acknowledging, "Well then, God has granted to the Gentiles also the repentance that leads to life'" (v. 18). As always, God has the last word!

A similar conversion took place 300 miles north of Jerusalem. Some men from Cyprus and Cyrene traveled to Antioch, where they preached the Lord Jesus to the Greeks who were living there. "And the hand of the Lord was with them, and a large number who believed turned to the Lord" (v. 21). When the news reached the church at Jerusalem, they sent Barnabas to investigate. "When he arrived and witnessed the grace of God, he rejoiced and began to encourage them all with resolute heart to remain true to the Lord" (v. 23). Gentiles were now accepted as part of the church. To signify their union in the body of Christ, the collective group of Jews and Gentiles were now called "Christians" (v. 26). Praise the Lord! Jesus Christ was and is building His church, uniting people of all races.

MS

Tuesday

EXPECTANT PRAYER
Read Acts 12

When Peter came to himself, he said, "Now I know for sure that the Lord has sent forth His angel and rescued me from the hand of Herod and from all that the Jewish people were expecting." (12:11)

Creatively, Luke contrasts the sincere love of the church at Antioch (11:19-30) with the coldhearted animosity of Herod and the Jews toward the church (vv. 1-23). The chapter begins with the death of John's brother James, who Herod had put to death with a sword. When Herod saw that this pleased the Jews, he had Peter arrested and put in prison. These incidents clearly demonstrate that the church had become hated and despised by the Jews. One of the major subthemes of Acts is the spread of the gospel despite opposition.

Herod made certain Peter's imprisonment was secure, handing him over to be guarded by four squads of soldiers. But God was faithful, and for the second time He sent an angel to help Peter escape (cf. 5:18-19). Supernaturally, the chains fell off Peter's wrists, the guards remained asleep, and the iron gate was opened; and the angel led Peter along the streets of the city. When Peter realized that he had escaped, he said, "Now I know for sure that the Lord has sent forth His angel and rescued me from the hand of Herod and from all that the Jewish people were expecting" (v. 11).

Amazingly enough, even though the saints were fervently praying for Peter's release (v. 5), they did not expect an answer so soon. When Rhoda informed them that Peter was at the door, they said, "You are out of your mind!" (v. 15). When she persisted, they replied, "It is his angel" (v. 15). Finally, they opened the door and were amazed to see Peter standing there.

God continues to do amazing things today. When we pray, let us be ever mindful of His power, and let us expect that He will answer our prayers, no matter how difficult the circumstances.

MS

Wednesday

THE POWER OF THE WORD
Read Acts 13

The next Sabbath nearly the whole city assembled to hear the word of the Lord. (13:44)

A number of prophets and teachers gathered at Antioch to minister to the Lord. Yet, even among these spiritual leaders, two individuals stood out. The Holy Spirit identified them, "Set apart for me Barnabas and Saul for the work to which I have called them" (v. 2). This divine mission was a missionary journey to the island of Cyprus and several cities in Asia Minor.

As the missionaries journeyed from city to city, they preached a number of sermons highlighting the person and work of Jesus Christ. When they arrived in Pisidian Antioch, the synagogue officials invited them to speak one Sabbath. Paul's preaching was so effective that the crowds begged them to return the following Sabbath. The next week, nearly the whole city assembled to hear "the word of the Lord" (v. 44). This key phrase, or its equivalent, occurs four times in six verses.

In verse forty-four, it was "the word of the Lord" that stimulated the interest of the people and caused them to flock to the synagogue. In verse forty-six, it was "the word of God" that rebuked the jealous Jews who accused Paul of blasphemy. In verse forty-eight, those who believed "the word of the Lord" were appointed to eternal life. And in verse forty-nine, "the word of the Lord" was being spread throughout the whole region.

It was not the words of Paul that were effective. It was not the words of Barnabas that were effective. It was the word of the Lord that stimulated the interest of the people as the Holy Spirit blessed it. Our commission is to take the word of the Lord to "the remotest part of the earth" (1:8). It is the word of the Lord that is "the power of God for salvation to everyone who believes" (Rom 1:16), because "faith comes from hearing, and hearing by the word of Christ" (Rom 10:17). Preach the word of the Lord!

MS

Thursday

PREACHING DESPITE PERSECUTION
Read Acts 14

Through many tribulations we must enter the kingdom of God. (14:22b)

Acts 14:1-6 repeats a pattern that can be observed in Acts 13:14-52: the apostles arrive in a city; preach the word of the Lord in the local synagogue; and, following the sermon, there is division, persecution, and growth. When Paul and Barnabas arrived in Iconium, they entered the synagogue and spoke "in such a manner that a large number of people believed, both of Jews and of Greeks" (v. 1). But the Jews who did not believe "stirred up the minds of the Gentiles and embittered them against the brethren" (v. 2). Despite this opposition, Paul and Barnabas "spent a long time there speaking boldly with reliance upon the Lord" (v. 3). Soon, a division formed among the people, with some siding with the Jews, and some with the apostles. Persecution quickly followed, and the apostles fled the city when the situation became life-threatening.

The apostles then traveled to the cities near Lycaonia. Wherever they went, they continued to preach the gospel (v. 7). As the apostles were ministering in Lystra, some Jews came from Pisidian Antioch and Iconium and incited the crowds to stone Paul. They then dragged him out of the city, believing him to be dead. The following day, a revived Paul accompanied Barnabas to Derbe. There, they preached the gospel and made many disciples. Amazingly enough, Paul and Barnabas then returned to the very cities that had persecuted them—Lystra, Iconium, and Pisidian Antioch. When they arrived in each city, they strengthened and encouraged the new converts to continue in the faith. They also warned them concerning persecution, "Through many tribulations we must enter the kingdom of God" (v. 22).

Jesus never promised an easy life for those who minister in His name. In fact, the opposite is true. Jesus said, "If anyone wishes to come after Me, he must deny himself, and take up his cross daily and follow Me" (Lk 9:23). When you encounter opposition and persecution in your ministry, remain faithful, and continue to preach the word of the Lord.

MS

Friday

GRACE ON TRIAL
Read Acts 15

Some men came down from Judea and began teaching the brethren, "Unless you are circumcised according to the custom of Moses, you cannot be saved." (15:1)

When they returned to Antioch, Paul and Barnabas gathered the church together and reported on what God had accomplished on their first missionary journey. Of special note was the fact that God "had opened a door of faith to the Gentiles" (14:27). Unfortunately, some Judaizers arrived from Judea and began teaching that circumcision was necessary for salvation. Paul and Barnabas immediately confronted these Judaizers, debating them until there was great dissension in the church. Finally, the brethren determined that Paul and Barnabas should go to Jerusalem and question the elders concerning this issue.

Soon after they arrived at Jerusalem, some of the sect of the Pharisees who had believed maintained, "It is necessary to circumcise them [Gentiles] and to direct them to observe the Law of Moses" (v. 5). After much debate, Peter stood up and addressed the congregation. He explained that God had used him to preach the gospel to Gentiles during the early days of the church. And when those Gentiles believed, they were given the gift of the Holy Spirit. God had made no distinction between Jew and Gentile, cleansing the hearts of both groups solely by faith.

Peter then confronted the Judaizers with a piercing question, "Now therefore why do you put God to the test by placing upon the neck of the disciples a yoke which neither our fathers nor we have been able to bear?" (v. 10). Peter silenced the Judaizers with his final words, "But we believe that we are saved through the grace of the Lord Jesus, in the same way as they also are" (v. 11).

Beware of modern Judaizers who demand that people need to do something before they can be saved (e.g., be baptized, change one's lifestyle, quit sinning, etc.). It is impossible to obtain salvation through human activity. We are all saved by grace alone through faith alone (vv. 9, 11; cf. Eph 2:8).

MS

Monday

FINDING DISCIPLES
Read Acts 16

Paul came also to Derbe and to Lystra. And a disciple was there, named Timothy, ... and he was well spoken of by the brethren. (16:1-2a)

Acts 15:40-18:22 is a record of Paul's second missionary journey. Paul, having recruited Silas to join him, began his journey by visiting nearby churches in Syria and Cilicia, where he strengthened the believers (15:40-41). At Lystra, they were joined by a young man named Timothy, whose mother was Jewish while his father was Greek. Timothy, highly praised by the local churches, would soon become Paul's student in ministry. Paul expressed glowing praise for his protégé in Philippians 2:20-22. In this passage, Timothy is described as: 1) a kindred spirit (sharing a similar perspective as Paul); 2) genuinely concerned for the welfare of others; 3) one who seeks out the interests of Christ Jesus; and 4) one with a proven track record of faithful service. As you faithfully serve the Lord, search out faithful individuals to disciple who will eventually be able to teach their own disciples (cf. 2 Tm 2:2).

As Paul, Silas, and Timothy continued their journey, the text records three instances where they were given divine guidance. First, the Holy Spirit prevented them from preaching the gospel in the province of Asia (v. 6). Second, the Spirit of Jesus did not permit them to go to Bithynia (v. 7). Third, at Troas God gave Paul a vision of a Macedonian man appealing for the missionaries to come to Macedonia (v. 9). Troas was also the place where Luke joined the journey (note the "we" in v. 10). As you faithfully serve the Lord, seek divine guidance each step of the way.

When the missionaries arrived in Macedonia, they immediately visited Philippi, a leading city of the district. Several noteworthy events took place in Philippi: Lydia and her household believed and were baptized; Paul cast a demon out of a fortune-telling slave-girl; Paul and Silas were thrown in prison; and the jailer and his household believed and were baptized. As you faithfully serve the Lord, expect persecution; but also expect a bountiful harvest.

MS

Tuesday

THE UNKNOWN GOD
Read Acts 17

For while I was passing through and examining the objects of your worship, I also found an altar with this inscription, "To An Unknown God". (17:23a)

Paul's sermon in Acts 17:22-31 is a masterful example of preaching to a lost, yet religious, audience. Approaching his subject from the audience's perspective, Paul began with a compliment, "Men of Athens, I observe that you are very religious in all respects" (v. 22). Having recently toured the extensive altar complex located near the Areopagus, Paul had quickly realized that the Athenians were comprehensive in their pursuit of spiritual knowledge. He used this dedication to his advantage. Paul called attention to the fact that the Athenians had an altar with the inscription, "To An Unknown God" (v. 23). The presence of this altar indicated that the Athenians had an all-inclusive culture, accepting any and all gods. He then used this altar to build a bridge to the main subject of his sermon, "Therefore what you worship in ignorance, this I proclaim to you" (v. 23).

Paul revealed that the Athenians' "Unknown God" was actually the God of the Bible. His sermon included four main points. First, as the Creator, God does not dwell in temples made by human hands (v. 24). Second, as the Sustainer, He has no need to be served by humans (v. 25). Third, as the accessible Sovereign, the Lord has predetermined the lives of all humans (vv. 26-27). Fourth, as the Father of all, God cannot be represented with images made of gold, silver, or stone; formed by the art and thought of humans (vv. 28-29).

Paul closed his sermon with a call for repentance. He explained that even though God has been patient, a certain day of judgment has been fixed. The only way to obtain righteousness was through the Man God has appointed, confirming the identity of the Savior by raising Him from the dead.

As we seek to evangelize the lost, we should look for ways to bridge the gap between their knowledge and ours. We know the God that is unknown to them. Proclaim His name to the remotest part of the earth so that all may come to know Him (cf. 1:8)!

MS

Wednesday

THE LORD IS WITH US
Read Acts 18

For I am with you, and no man will attack you in order to harm you, for I have many people in this city. (18:10)

When Paul left Athens, he traveled to the nearby city of Corinth. There, he met a Jew named Aquila and his wife Priscilla, who had recently come to the city from Rome, because Claudius had expelled Jews from the imperial city. In Corinth, Paul stayed with Aquila and Priscilla because they were of the same trade, tent-makers. Every Sabbath, Paul would speak in the synagogue, trying to persuade Jews and Greeks concerning the gospel. When Silas and Timothy came down from Macedonia, he began devoting himself completely to the word, testifying to the Jews that Jesus was the Christ.

When the Jews resisted and blasphemed, Paul shook out his garments and said, "Your blood be on your own heads! I am clean" (v. 6). Paul then decided to focus his ministry on the Gentiles. Amazingly, Crispus, the leader of the synagogue, believed in the Lord with all his household. He was joined by many of the Corinthians, who responded to Paul's preaching with belief and were subsequently baptized.

The Apostle Paul had experienced persecution and intimidation in Macedonia, including in the cities of Philippi, Thessalonica, and Berea. Now he was experiencing the same in southern Greece. To comfort His faithful messenger, the Lord spoke to Paul in a vision, saying, "Do not be afraid any longer, but go on speaking and do not be silent; for I am with you" (vv. 9-10). Paul would eventually remain in Corinth for a year and a half, teaching the word of God throughout the city.

The Lord's promise to Paul ("I am with you") is reminiscent of similar promises given to Jacob (Gn 28:15), Moses (Ex 3:12), Joshua (Jo 1:5), Jeremiah (Jer 1:8), and many others. Jesus made a similar promise to His disciples as part of the Great Commission, "I am with you always, even to the end of the age" (Mt 28:20). As you seek to fulfill your calling, remember that the Lord is with you wherever you go.

MS

Thursday

EFFECTIVE MINISTRY
Read Acts 19

This took place for two years, so that all who lived in Asia heard the word of the Lord, both Jews and Greeks. (19:10)

On Paul's third missionary journey (cf. 18:23-21:17), he finally got to spend a considerable amount of time in Ephesus, the principal city of the Roman province of Asia and one of the most populous cities in the Empire. It is likely that Paul had intended to visit Ephesus near the beginning of his second missionary journey but had been prevented from doing so by the Holy Spirit (cf. 16:6). Paul would eventually remain in Ephesus for three years (cf. 20:31), longer than in any other city.

Paul began his ministry in Ephesus by anointing some of John the Baptist's disciples with the Holy Spirit. He then preached in the synagogue for three months, persuading the Jews about the kingdom of God. When the Jews became belligerent, he withdrew from them and reasoned daily in the school of Tyrannus. This school served as the center of Paul's teaching ministry for two years. The Apostle's ministry was so effective that eventually everyone who lived in Asia heard the word of the Lord, both Jews and Greeks.

Paul was also able to perform a number of extraordinary miracles throughout the city. The sick were healed of diseases and the demon-possessed were delivered from oppression. As a result, great fear fell upon the entire city and the name of Jesus was magnified. Even those who practiced magic brought their books and began burning them in the sight of everyone. Paul's ministry was so effective that it eventually began to negatively affect the business of the craftsmen who made idols and shrines for Artemis (also known as Diana), the chief goddess of the Ephesians.

Effective ministry accomplishes two things—it builds the kingdom of God and damages the kingdom of Satan. This is why persecution is so prevalent in Acts—the devil was fighting back. As you serve the Lord, don't be surprised to see evil forces attempt to hinder your ministry. Trust in the power of the Holy Spirit. "Greater is He Who is in you than he who is in the world" (1 Jn 4:4).

MS

Friday

A CHARGE FOR SHEPHERDS
Read Acts 20

Be on guard for yourselves and for all the flock, among which the Holy Spirit has made you overseers, to shepherd the church of God which He purchased with His own blood. (20:28)

Near the end of his third missionary journey, Paul summoned the elders of the church at Ephesus to meet with him at Miletus. Knowing that he would probably never see them again, Paul gave a final charge to these elders (vv. 18-35).

Paul began his speech by reminding the elders of his faithful service to the church at Ephesus in the midst of persecution. He then informed them of his intention to travel to Jerusalem despite the fact that the Holy Spirit had testified to him that bonds and afflictions await, even though he was innocent of all wrongdoing.

Next, Paul turned to the future responsibilities of the Ephesian elders. Using pastoral language, the Apostle encouraged the elders to shepherd the flock that had been given to them by the Holy Spirit. Paul here identified the elders as "overseers" because this title emphasized their responsibility to watch over and protect their congregation. Accordingly, He warned them to be on guard against "savage wolves" (i.e., false teachers) who would soon infiltrate the flock (v. 29). This phrase is reminiscent of the words of Christ in Matthew 7:15, "Beware of the false prophets, who come to you in sheep's clothing, but inwardly are ravenous wolves" (cf. Mt 10:16; Lk 10:3). This was a timely warning, proven by later events at Ephesus (1Tm 1:3-7, 19-20; 6:20-21; Rv 2:2).

Paul concluded his speech by urging the elders to follow the example he had set. The Apostle had not sought after gold, silver, or clothes. He had diligently fulfilled his ministry without thought of personal gain. When Paul finished, he prayed for the elders as they wept and embraced him. They then accompanied him to his ship.

As spiritual shepherds, we need to faithfully care for those God has entrusted to our care. We need to protect them from false teaching by carefully discerning truth from error. And we need to fulfill our ministries with no thought for personal gain.

MS

Monday

TO GO OR NOT TO GO
Read Acts 21

After looking up the disciples, we stayed there seven days; and they kept telling Paul through the Spirit not to set foot in Jerusalem. (21:4)

Did Paul disobey the Holy Spirit by going to Jerusalem? It should be remembered that Paul's ministry was characterized by a sensitivity to divine guidance (cf. e.g., 16:6-10). This practice increases the probability for right action here. Furthermore, the Apostle was making this trip by the Spirit's leading, "Paul purposed in the Spirit to go to Jerusalem after he had passed through Macedonia and Achaia" (19:21). The Spirit had already revealed to Paul that "bonds and afflictions" awaited him "in every city" (20:23). Surely, the Spirit's declaration included the city of Jerusalem, where numerous apostles had already experienced persecution and imprisonment (cf. e.g., 4:3; 5:18, 40; 12:1-4). Additionally, this warning was in keeping with the Apostle's original commission, "For I will show him how much he must suffer for My name's sake" (9:16).

The situation here in verse four was probably similar to a subsequent event in Caesarea (vv. 8-14). While staying at the house of Philip the evangelist, a prophet named Agabus approached Paul and announced that the Holy Spirit had informed him that Paul would be bound by the Jews in Jerusalem and delivered into the hands of the Gentiles. The Apostle certainly did not regard Agabus' prophecy as a prohibition, but rather as a divine forewarning so that he could be spiritually prepared for what would take place. In fact, even those who had urged Paul not to go to Jerusalem eventually came to the realization that ultimately it was the Lord's will that would be done in the matter (v. 14). Paul's response to Agabus' prophecy is especially noteworthy. He passionately declared, "For I am ready not only to be bound, but even to die at Jerusalem for the name of the Lord Jesus" (v. 13).

Let us faithfully follow the leading of the Holy Spirit as we serve the Lord. And may we have the same attitude as the Apostle Paul, being willing to suffer affliction, and even death, for the name of the Lord Jesus.

MS

Tuesday

SPIRITUAL TRANSFORMATION
Read Acts 22

Go! For I will send you far away to the Gentiles. (22:21b)

At the end of the previous chapter, an angry mob of Jews attempted to kill Paul as he was worshipping in the temple in Jerusalem. However, the commander of a Roman cohort delivered Paul from the mob and arrested him so that he could determine who he was and what he had done. Just before he was brought into the barracks, the Apostle was given permission to speak to the people.

Paul's Life before Christ (vv. 1-5). Paul began his speech with a description of his previous life. He was a Jew, born in Tarsus of Cilicia but brought up in Jerusalem. He was educated under Gamaliel, one of the most respected teachers in Judea (cf. 5:34). He was exceedingly zealous for God, having persecuted the early church, imprisoning both men and women, and putting some to death.

Paul's Encounter with Christ (vv. 6-16). While on his way to Damascus to arrest believers and bring them to Jerusalem, Paul encountered Jesus the Nazarene, Who questioned him concerning his actions. When Paul realized that it was the Lord Who was speaking to him, He asked, "What shall I do?" (v. 10). The Lord told him to go to Damascus and await further instructions. Finally, a man named Ananias came to Paul and informed him that he would testify to all men of what he had seen and heard. Paul's narrative made it clear that he was following divine direction—he had been specifically "appointed" to "be a witness" for God (vv. 14-15).

Paul's Ministry in Christ (vv. 17-21). Soon after Paul returned to Jerusalem, the Lord appeared to him in a vision and told him to leave the city "because they will not accept your testimony" (v. 18). The Lord then informed Paul that he would minister to the Gentiles.

The trajectory of Paul's life completely changed when he met Jesus. The same is true of everyone who encounters the Lord. Think about your life before you were saved. How did you live and act? What were your goals and aspirations? Now compare your previous life to your life today. What changes have you experienced as a result of your own divine encounter?

MS

Wednesday

DIVINE ENCOURAGEMENT
Read Acts 23

Take courage; for as you have solemnly witnessed to My cause at Jerusalem, so you must witness at Rome also. (23:11b)

When the Roman commander who had arrested Paul found out that he was a Roman citizen, he brought him before the Sanhedrin to determine exactly why the Jews wanted him put to death (22:25-30). The fact that Paul was a Roman citizen gave him considerable rights, including the right to a trial (cf. 22:25). Eventually, Paul's citizenship would allow him to appeal to Caesar himself (cf. 25:11-12).

Paul began his address before the Sanhedrin with a statement of innocence, "Brethren, I have lived my life with a perfectly good conscience before God up to this day" (v. 1). Immediately, the high priest Ananias, who presided over the Sanhedrin, ordered that he be struck on the mouth. This was in violation of Jewish law, which considered a person innocent until proven guilty (v. 3; cf. Dt 19:15). Ananias, who came to power in A.D. 47, was one of Israel's cruelest and most corrupt high priests. Many Jews hated him because of his notorious greed. Less than a decade after the events recorded here, Ananias was assassinated by a mob of anti-Roman Jewish zealots.

Paul responded by calling Ananias a "whitewashed wall". This phrase is probably an allusion to Ezekiel 13:8-16, where the Lord used similar terms to describe the false prophets who were misleading the people. The Apostle then initiated a disagreement between the Pharisees and Sadducees by referring to the resurrection of the dead. The debate became so heated that the commander rescued Paul and returned him to the barracks. The following night, the Lord appeared to Paul, commanding him to "Take courage!" and informing him that he would serve as His witness in Rome. Almost immediately, the Lord began to fulfill His promise as he provided Paul with safe transport to Caesarea, despite the fact that the Jews had formed a conspiracy to put him to death (cf. v. 12).

Just as the Lord stood at Paul's side (v. 11), He stands at our sides. Take courage! God will rescue us and protect us from the threats of "evil men" and the schemes of the "evil one" (cf. 2 Thes 3:1-3).

MS

Thursday

A GOOD CONSCIENCE
Read Acts 24

Knowing that for many years you have been a judge to this nation, I cheerfully make my defense. (24:10b)

Paul was facing a plot against his life. There were more than forty Jewish conspirators who declared, "We have bound ourselves under a solemn oath to taste nothing until we have killed Paul" (cf. 23:13-14). Despite this threat, he was safely transported from Jerusalem to Caesarea in order to stand trial before Felix, the governor.

Five days after Paul's arrival in Caesarea, Ananias, the high priest, came down from Jerusalem with some elders and an attorney named Tertullus to bring charges against the Apostle (v. 1). The Jews claimed that Paul had stirred up dissension among the Jews and that he was a ringleader of the sect of the Nazarenes. They even accused him of trying to desecrate the temple.

Paul defended himself by informing the governor that the Jews were not able to prove any of the charges of which they had accused him. The Apostle did admit, however, that he believed there would be a resurrection of the dead, both the righteous and the wicked. And that it was on account of this belief that the Jews had brought him before the governor. Felix, unwilling to decide the case, left Paul imprisoned. Nevertheless, he routinely sent for the Apostle so that he could converse with him.

Paul was innocent. He had a blameless conscience, both before God and before men (v. 16). Yet he was still suffering for the cause of Christ. In spite of his tribulations, the Apostle was given the amazing opportunity to speak about his faith in Christ Jesus to the governor and his wife (v. 24). The Lord was accomplishing His plan to bring the gospel to the world (cf. 1:8).

As you serve the Lord, you may experience mocking and ridicule. When you do, "keep a good conscience so that in the thing in which you are slandered, those who revile your good behavior in Christ will be put to shame" (1 Pt 3:16). "If you are reviled for the name of Christ, you are blessed, because the Spirit of glory and of God rests on you" (1 Pt 4:14).

SE

Friday

WHY DID PAUL APPEAL TO CAESAR?
Read Acts 25

You have appealed to Caesar, to Caesar you shall go. (25:12b)

Paul remained imprisoned in Caesarea for two years until Felix was succeeded by Porcius Festus. Shortly after Festus arrived in the province, the chief priests and elders of the Jews again brought charges against Paul. The Jews wanted Paul to be brought to Jerusalem, hoping to kill him as they set up an ambush along the way. However, Festus invited the Jews to come to Caesarea if they wanted to prosecute Paul. During the trial, the Jews were unable to prove the charges against Paul. The Apostle provided his own defense, "I have committed no offense either against the Law of the Jews or against the temple or against Caesar" (v. 8). When Paul was asked whether he was willing to go to Jerusalem to stand trial before Festus, he appealed to Caesar.

Why did Paul appeal to Caesar? The simple answer is that the Apostle was being obedient to the will of God. The Lord had appeared to him in a vision and commanded, "Take courage; for as you have solemnly witnessed to My cause at Jerusalem, so you must witness at Rome also" (23:11). Paul, knowing that he was destined to preach the gospel in Rome, took advantage of the opportunity his Roman citizenship granted—the ability to appeal to Caesar himself. This plan of action would also fulfill the original commission that God had given concerning Paul, "to bear My name before the Gentiles and kings and the sons of Israel" (9:15).

David Livingstone, a missionary in Africa, once said, "I'd rather be in the heart of Africa in the will of God, than on the throne of England, out of the will of God." Are you following the will of God in your own life? If not, then you will experience nothing but anxiety and spiritual unrest. Jonah tried to flee from the will of God and ended up in the belly of a great fish. But if you are obedient to the Lord's calling, you will experience the comfort of peace (cf. Heb 13:20-21). Allow the Holy Spirit to direct your paths, and you will achieve great success.

SE

Monday

WORDS OF SOBER TRUTH
Read Acts 26

Agrippa replied to Paul, "In a short time you will persuade me to become a Christian." (26:28)

Paul had previously appeared before the governors Felix and Festus. Now he was summoned to present his defense before King Agrippa (cf. 9:15). Herod Agrippa II was the great-grandson of Herod the Great. The final ruler of the Herodian dynasty, he was overthrown by his Jewish subjects in A.D. 66.

Paul began his defense by explaining that he had spent his youth in Tarsus and in Jerusalem, and that he had lived as a Pharisee, the strictest sect of Judaism. The Apostle then addressed the reason that he was on trial—the fact that he believed in the resurrection of the dead. To offer proof of the resurrection of the dead, Paul recounted his experience on the road to Damascus, where he had encountered the risen Lord, Jesus, Who had been crucified by the Jews. He then revealed the mission that had been divinely give to him, "to open their [Jews and Gentiles] eyes so that they may turn from darkness to light and from the dominion of Satan to God, that they may receive forgiveness of sins and an inheritance among those who have been sanctified by faith in Me" (v. 18).

When Paul finished speaking, Festus said in a loud voice, "Paul, you are out of your mind! Your great learning is driving you mad" (v. 24). Paul answered, "I am not out of my mind, most excellent Festus, but I utter words of sober truth" (v. 25). He then turned to the king and said, "King Agrippa, do you believe the Prophets? I know that you do" (v. 27). Paul was implying that if the king truly believed the Prophets, then he would recognize the fact that they testified the truth about the Lord Jesus Christ (cf. vv. 22-23). Agrippa offered a light-hearted response, realizing that Paul was trying to persuade him to become a Christian.

As you share the gospel, you will encounter many who think you are out of your mind. Many will deny your spiritual experience. Many will deny the resurrection of Jesus Christ. Your responsibility is simply to preach the Word of God—to utter words of sober truth.

SE

Tuesday

PROVIDENTIAL CARE
Read Acts 27

Do not be afraid, Paul; you must stand before Caesar; and behold, God has granted you all those who are sailing with you. (27:24b)

When Paul's defense before Agrippa was concluded, the king confessed to Festus, "This man might have been set free if he had not appealed to Caesar" (26:32). Nevertheless, Paul had appealed to Caesar, and it was to Caesar that he would go (cf. 25:12).

When the preparations for the voyage to Rome were complete, Paul and some other prisoners were delivered to a centurion named Julius. Julius treated Paul with kindness, even allowing him to go ashore at Sidon to receive care from his friends. After a stop at Myra in Lycia, the party changed ships and sailed to Crete. There, Paul warned the centurion of the danger in attempting to continue the voyage since it was growing late in the year. The centurion, however, decided to follow the advice of the sailors and thus ordered the journey to carry on. Almost immediately, a violent storm caught the ship and carried it far out to sea. The storm raged for several days, and the crew had to throw the cargo and tackle overboard. Just as they were abandoning hope, Paul informed the sailors that an angel had appeared to him and told him that they would all be saved, yet the ship would be lost. Sure enough, all 276 (cf. v. 37) persons on board made it safely to land on the island of Malta, though the vessel ran aground and was broken up by the waves.

In this chapter, the Lord demonstrated His providential care to Paul in several ways. First, Julius treated Paul with consideration. Second, an angel was sent to comfort the Apostle with a promise of deliverance. Third, the centurion allowed Paul to swim to shore rather than be killed according to the plan of the soldiers. Fourth, everyone who was on the boat, including Paul, made it safely ashore.

God's sovereign plan will never lead you where His grace cannot protect you. Trust God always, especially in the midst of difficult times. His providential care will see you through (cf. 1 Pt 5:7).

SE

Wednesday

THE GOSPEL REACHES ROME
Read Acts 28

When we entered Rome, Paul was allowed to stay by himself, with the soldier who was guarding him. And he stayed two full years in his own rented quarters and was welcoming all who came to him. (28:16, 30)

When Paul and his companions arrived on the island of Malta, the natives showed them great kindness. They kindled a fire so that the castaways could warm themselves. As Paul laid sticks on the fire, a viper bit him on his hand. The natives, expecting Paul to suffer hardship, were amazed when nothing happened. Next, Paul healed the father of Publius, the leading man of the island who owned a considerable amount of land. Soon, the rest of the inhabitants were coming to the Apostle for healing. The islanders supplied the castaways with everything they needed and they departed for Rome after three months.

When Paul arrived at Rome, the Christian brethren greeted him warmly. These believers were probably saved as a result of Peter's sermon on the day of Pentecost (cf. 2:10). Three days later, Paul was given an opportunity to speak to the leading men of the Jews. After proclaiming his innocence, he informed them that he was "wearing this chain for the sake of the hope of Israel" (v. 20).

From morning to evening, the Apostle testified about the kingdom of God. He tried to persuade the Jews concerning Jesus, using passages from both the Law of Moses and from the Prophets. Some were persuaded, while others would not believe. After criticizing the Jews by quoting a passage from Isaiah 6:9-10, Paul turned from them to focus his ministry on the Gentiles.

For two full years, Paul was able to preach concerning the kingdom of God to everyone that came to him. He was completely unhindered. According to the proverbial saying, "All roads lead to Rome"—those who journeyed to Rome and heard the gospel took it back to their homelands. Soon, the gospel had reached the remotest parts of the earth (cf. 1:8). Let us continue the work begun by Jesus and the Apostles and preach the gospel to everyone we meet.

SE

Thursday

THREE MOTIVATIONS FOR THE GOSPEL
Read Romans 1

I am under obligation ... I am eager to preach the gospel ... I am not ashamed of the gospel, for it is the power of God for salvation to everyone who believes ... the righteous man shall live by faith. (1:14–17)

The most important principle for sharing the gospel may be surprising. Sure, it is necessary to know the gospel and to have some training on how to share it with others, but many people obtain this knowledge and still rarely share their faith. Joe Aldrich puts it this way: "If evangelism is accurately expressing what I possess in Christ, then edification [growing in Christ] is the key to evangelism" (*Lifestyle Evangelism*, p. 102, Multnomah, 1982). This means your church, the center for edification, and your home, the headquarters for your evangelism/discipleship in the neighborhood and city, are key! In fact, the central theme in Romans is the righteousness of God in the gospel which you receive by faith and live out by faith (v. 17).

You may be experiencing hesitation and fear in your thinking. These feelings are not unique to you, but are hindrances to every believer in proclaiming the gospel. Paul's three motivations should be our prayer for they will greatly encourage a gospel lifestyle. *First*, pray that the Spirit will convict your heart with the obligation to proclaim the gospel (v. 14). This conviction should not come from external pressures but the inward working of the Spirit through the teaching of the Word that encourages the sharing of the gospel.

Second, sometimes the obligation is there but the eagerness is not. Pray about how God can use your gifts, activities, and relationships to cultivate the eagerness to proclaim the great news of eternal life (v. 15). This strategic life change often stimulates people to consider evangelism as a lifestyle and not an event. *Third*, Paul says he is not ashamed of the gospel (v. 16). Fear is often the main culprit that shuts our mouth! Ask the Spirit to give you boldness in the gospel because it is God's dynamite which causes men of steel to crumble and cry like babies in repentance and faith in Jesus, Who died for their sins. Oh, that God would use our church and home to grant us obligation and eagerness that is not ashamed of the gospel.

SS

Friday

IS A "GOOD" PERSON SAVED?
Read Romans 2

But do you suppose this, O man, when you pass judgment on those who practice such things and do the same yourself, that you will escape the judgment of God? (2:3)

Before Paul can explain the content of the gospel that leads to salvation, he needs to demonstrate that everyone is a guilty sinner in need of that salvation. As a result, he first proves that those who have never heard the gospel are guilty (1:18–32). He later argues that Jews, those who first received the Word of God, are likewise guilty (2:17–29). But what about the one who is basically a "good person"; someone who does not commit the grave sins of our society? They often help others, donate their time and money to useful charities, and may even attend church regularly. Many of these individuals believe that their good works will outweigh their bad works. Accordingly, they expect to go to heaven when they die. Is this true?

A common problem for the moralist is their own lack of obedience to the moral standards they confess and by which they judge others. They often argue that they do not break their standards to the same degree as others. While this may be true, the fact remains that they still break their standards! They tell their children not to steal but they loaf at their job, stealing time from their boss. They condemn adulterous relationships while at the same time they lust in their heart. Thus, their own standards rise up and condemn them. God judges on His standard and He does not grade on the curve.

Morality is good. However, morality cannot earn eternal life. Our failure to meet the divine standard, no matter how minor the transgression, condemns us. God's standard is sinless perfection in thought, word, and deed throughout one's entire life. Jesus Christ, Who never sinned in thought, word, or deed in His entire life, is the only one qualified to be our substitute, to pay for our sins and lack of holiness. Salvation comes by trusting in His work for us, not by trusting in our own works! In what/whom are you trusting for your own salvation?

SS

Monday

REDEMPTION AND PROPITIATION
Read Romans 3

Being justified as a gift by His grace through the redemption which is in Christ Jesus; whom God displayed publicly as a propitiation .... (3:24-25)

A remarkable example of impartial justice is provided by Brutus, the Roman Consul. A plot was discovered, and the brave and loyal Brutus made the unfortunate discovery that his two sons were the ringleaders. His powerful natural affections as a father were overruled by his righteous duty as an impartial judge. As a result, both sons were executed. This illustration pictures to some degree the situation God faced. God is the righteous judge of the universe. His righteousness demands that He punish sin. Yet, like Brutus, God found His own sons of creation rebelling against Him. Is it possible to satisfy God's righteousness while at the same time pardoning man's sin? The answer to this question is centered around two words: *redemption* and *propitiation*.

Redemption is the act of God purchasing us out of the slave market of sin in order to be freed from bondage. An example of redemption is provided by the prophet Hosea. Hosea's wife Gomer became a harlot and was eventually sold into slavery. However, Hosea, demonstrating unconditional love, went to the slave market and purchased his wife and set her free (cf. Hos 1-3). This story serves as an illustration of what God has done. Every human has fallen into the slavery of sin. Our redemption was accomplished when Jesus Christ paid the price for our sins by shedding His blood on the cross. He purchased us out of the slave market of sin and set us free to serve Him. Since we have been bought with such a great price, let us glorify God in all we do (1 Cor 6:20).

A good synonym for the word *propitiation* is the word "satisfaction". Sin is an affront to God's holy character, thereby resulting in His wrath (1:18). The death of Christ satisfies God's wrath, resulting in our salvation. When others offend us, we should remember that we were once an offense to God. May we be slow to anger, and quick to forgive (Prv 19:11).

SS

Tuesday

THE SECURITY OF JUSTIFICATION
Read Romans 4

"For this reason it is by faith, in order that it may be in accordance with grace, so that the promise will be guaranteed …." (4:16)

No one can have access to heaven unless they are just as righteous as Jesus Christ. But there is no way anyone can do this. This means no one goes to heaven, right? This would be correct; however, there is one exception—if Jesus provides justification for the sinner. Justification is based upon Christ's death on the cross. Because of Christ's atonement all our sins may be forgiven and paid in full. As a result, God grants us the status and position of Christ's righteousness.

This promise comes by God's grace (undeserved gift) through faith and not by works so that it can be guaranteed. Martin Luther was asked one day, "Do you feel you are saved?" He answered, "No, but I'm as sure of it as there is a God in heaven." Charles Spurgeon came to a dying saint and asked her if God will let her down and not save her. She replied, "If the Lord wills, but if He does He will lose more than I will. He will lose His honor by breaking a promise and I will only lose my soul."

Since the promise is given by grace through faith and not by works or law (3:28), then our eternal inheritance does not depend upon our faithfulness, but upon the faithfulness of God's character. Consequently, the believer's eternal destiny is absolutely guaranteed. As Luther says, it is "as certain as there is a God in heaven." The question is not whether the promise is secure—it is! The question is, do you possess the secured promise of righteousness that is given to us by Jesus when we by grace believe in His justifying work on the cross? If your answer is yes, then God has credited to your account the status of Christ's righteousness. You can now abide in the security of justification and live out a life of practical righteousness as an expression of praise and thankfulness to the security of righteousness in Christ (cf. 2 Cor 5:21)!

SS

Wednesday

THE HOPE OF HIS GLORY
Read Romans 5

Therefore, having been justified by faith, ... we exult in hope of the glory of God. (5:1-2)

One of the main reasons that believers do not do well in their Christian life is their misplaced search for hope. They look for hope in all the wrong places. If your ultimate joy and hope is tied to the substance and pleasure of this life, then the Book of Ecclesiastes is correct, "Vanity of vanities, all is vanity and striving after wind" (1:2, 14). However, there is real joy and hope for every believer—"we exult in hope of the glory of God" (v. 2).

The word "hope" used here does not mean a wishful thinking. Biblical hope is the confident assurance that God will do just what He said He would do in His Word. The joyful, confident hope of the believer is to exult in the glory of God. Our lives today should be motivated, directed, and filled with the glory of God (cf. 1 Cor 10:31). This is one of the main reasons why some believers have a lack of hope and meaning in life. They do not know, they rarely seek, or they are unsure of God's glory.

God's glory may be defined as the visual or conceptual manifestation of the beauty, perfection, and excellence of the work and character of God. Meditate over this previous sentence. Most people relegate the concept of the glory of God to their time of death. Or when Christ returns and our bodies are changed and we are in His presence forever. This hope of the future glory should be part of our lives now! As 2 Corinthians 3:18 says, "But we all, with unveiled face, beholding as in a mirror the glory of the Lord, are being transformed into the same image from [one degree of] glory to [another degree of] glory, just as from the Lord, the Spirit."

The Holy Spirit is molding us to be more like Jesus Christ by taking our thoughts and desires away from the pursuit of self and satisfying us with His work and character—His glory (cf. Ps 16:11). At times, God may cause us to experience more of His glory by leading us through trials (vv. 3-5). God uses these trials to develop us, so that we might live and exult in the hope of His glory.

SS

Thursday

THE REALM OF GRACE
Read Romans 6

We know that our old man was crucified with him so that the body of sin would no longer dominate us. (6:6a; NET)

The first step in victory over sin in the Christian life is to understand the importance of our union with Christ's death. Knowing who we are makes a difference in how we act. Paul said, "we know that our old man was crucified with Him" (v. 6; NET). The "old man" is who I was in Adam—condemned sinner, lost, and dominated by the reign of sin in my life. The crucifixion of the old man is not a process, nor is it our duty. God crucified our old man when we believed in Christ. He took us out of Adam and placed us in Christ. From that time forward, we are separated from the realm and rule of the old man, which is the reign of sin.

What is the purpose of this status change? The text says, "so that the body of sin would no longer dominate us" (v. 6; NET). In other words, so that the body of sin would be made powerless. The "body of sin" refers to our fleshly body which sin tries to use as an instrument. Before salvation, we were dominated by the reign of sin. But by the grace of God we trusted Christ, and our old man was crucified. We were placed in Christ, and now sin does not reign as our master anymore. Sin still seeks to reign over the members of our body to influence us to sin. However, we now have the position and power to say "No!"

By way of analogy, if you were a slave in 1863 when the emancipation proclamation issued by Abraham Lincoln went into effect, at that moment your position changed. Your previous master was no longer your master. Your status change meant that you had been placed outside the realm of your old master—he was no longer in a position of authority over you. This is what Paul means by the "old man was crucified." You are no longer a slave to sin.

When you realize you are free, and that the Holy Spirit has given you the power to say no, you can live in the grace provided by the death of Christ. Sin is no longer your master. So live your life in light of who you are—a child of God in the realm of grace.

SS

Friday

THE STRUGGLE WITH THE FLESH
Read Romans 7

On the one hand I myself with my mind am serving the law of God, but on the other, with my flesh the law of sin. (7:25b)

A believer, who did not really know a lot about the Christian life, went off to college. There, he faced a variety of temptations coupled with a heartache from a broken relationship. The combination plunged him into a lifestyle of sin and misery. He found himself in a desperate struggle, wanting to do right, but having no power to do it. The ability to obey God and resist temptation had eluded his grasp. He was frustrated, miserable, and defeated. He wondered if he would ever be able to gain freedom from his bondage.

Paul summarizes this type of conflict in the latter part of Romans 7:25. Although our old self has been put to death (cf. 6:6), sin still dwells in us. It wages war with us, taking us captive and seeking to defeat us. Who is able to deliver us from the torment of sin? The Savior! "Thanks be to God through Jesus Christ our Lord!" (v. 25). When we trust in Christ, the Holy Spirit takes up permanent residence in our lives. He gives us the ability to resist sin and follow the new life that God has given us (cf. 8:3-4).

I will never forget the first time someone explained to me the struggle described in Romans seven and the victory found in Romans eight. You see, I was that struggling young man that I described in the first paragraph. I was saved, but I was frustrated and defeated. I was a miserable Christian. I wanted to do what God said, but the law of sin was bouncing me around like a ball in a pinball machine. Then God in His mercy and grace directed me to some believers who taught me how to walk with God through the power of the Spirit. I went to a Bible Study, and in God's providence they were studying the Book of Romans. Joy filled my heart as I read chapters seven and eight. Now I knew my problem, and God had given me the answer to my struggle. I still experience, at times, the struggle of Romans seven. We all will while we are still alive. But we don't have to live in defeat. The victory was won at Calvary, and we experience that victory when we walk in the Spirit. "Thanks be to God through Jesus Christ our Lord!" (v. 25). SS

Monday

GOD WILL WORK IT FOR GOOD
Read Romans 8

And we know that God causes all things to work together for good to those who love God, to those who are called according to His purpose. (8:28)

God works all things for good! Do you believe this? What if you lost your job, your home, or a loved one; or what if your child begins to struggle with peer groups or moral temptations? What if the doctor tells you that you have inoperable cancer and you don't have many days left? Do you really believe that God will work it for good?

It is important to note that Paul is addressing those who are saved. He describes them as "those who love God" and "those who are called according to His purpose" (v. 28). God takes everything that happens to us and works it ultimately for the good (cf. Prv 16:4; Eph 1:11). Many times we will have to wait for heaven to know how something worked out for the good. That is why believing this verse in the present is absolutely crucial. Unbelief will result in confusion, estrangement toward God, and a root of bitterness (cf. Heb 12:15).

Joseph is a classic illustration of the principle of Romans 8:28. Joseph was only seventeen years old when his brothers sinned against him. They treated him unfairly, desired to kill him, and sold him into slavery. As he served in Potiphar's house, he prospered; but then Potiphar's wife tried to seduce him. When he resisted her advances, she lied about the encounter; and Joseph, who had done what was right, was thrown into prison. Although he interpreted the cupbearer's dream and asked him to remember him when he was restored to his position, the cupbearer forgot about him. Joseph was consistently obedient to God, yet bad things kept happening to him. For thirteen years God used a series of negative events to mold Joseph into a man who could handle the powerful position of second to Pharaoh. He then used Joseph to preserve his family from famine and to fulfill the Lord's covenantal promise (cf. Gn 45:5, 7; 50:20).

Romans 8:28 is designed to be a source of great comfort. When you go through the trials of life, let this verse serve as your inspiration—God will work it for good!

SS

Tuesday

A HEART FOR THE LOST
Read Romans 9

For I could wish that I myself were accursed, separated from Christ for the sake of my brethren, my kinsmen according to the flesh. (9:3)

This chapter is famous for its juxtaposition of the unconditional election of God with man's personal responsibility for his own decisions. No matter how one understands this mystery, there is another important truth that Paul drives home in verses 1-3. How could Paul love the Jewish people when so many of them wanted to kill him because he proclaimed that Jesus is the Christ, the Son of God (cf. e.g., Acts 13-14)?

Paul's attitude is a great illustration of God's love demonstrated through a human instrument. If Paul could stand before us today he would be the first one to proclaim that God was the One Who produced in him this kind of heart for the lost. The Apostle was willing to do anything to save his countrymen. Paul revealed in verse two that he had "great sorrow" and "unceasing grief" in his heart for his brethren. He even went so far as to declare that if it were possible (which it is not possible) to be damned to hell forever in their place, he would willingly do so in order that his Jewish brothers would be saved. The Apostle's great love was simply a reflection of the love shown by the Savior. While Paul was not able to take the place of others in terms of salvation, Jesus Christ was able to do so. "Christ redeemed us from the curse of the Law, having become a curse for us" (Gal 3:13).

What kind of heart do you have for the lost? Perhaps you witness in an attempt to satisfy your guilty conscience, or so that you can look spiritual, or because some preacher challenged you to reach out to your neighbors this week. Generally speaking, these reasons are temporary and do not produce a heart like that exhibited by Paul (cf. 1 Thes 2:7-12). A heart for the lost is cultivated through the pursuit of the heart of God. By His grace and through the power of the Holy Spirit, you can cultivate a heart for the lost through the reading of the Word and prayer. Then seek opportunities every day to share the gospel of Jesus Christ.

SS

Wednesday

BEAUTIFUL FEET
Read Romans 10

How then will they call on Him in Whom they have not believed? How will they believe in Him Whom they have not heard? And how will they hear without a preacher? How will they preach unless they are sent? (10:14-15a)

Having proclaimed the means by which a person is saved, "Whoever will call on the name of the Lord will be saved" (v. 13), Paul reveals the process by which that means is accomplished. The Apostle describes the process in reverse order, using a series of four related questions that form links in a chain. The most likely reason he does this is because he wants to stress the importance of believers being sent to proclaim the gospel.

Some might object to this responsibility, believing that they are not called to be a "preacher". However, the word "preacher" in Greek simply refers to someone who proclaims—it is not a reference to an office. We need to remember that the Lord has commissioned all of us (cf. Mt 28:18-20). Accordingly, He has given us strength to be His ambassadors on earth (cf. 2 Cor 3:4-6; 5:20).

In verse fifteen, Paul quotes from Isaiah 52:7, which emphasizes the "feet" of those who bring good news. He probably does this to demonstrate that our commission will be hard work. It is something that must be done regularly. We need to be proactive—it is something we should take to people, not sit back and wait for them to come to us. I fear many believers' feet have become ugly instead of "beautiful" (v. 15) because they are sitting and enjoying their salvation, not taking the good news to others. They often use excuses such as that they are too busy, or they are afraid of losing a friend, or that evangelism will affect their job or business, or that someone else would be better able to do it.

Make a list of those individuals you see daily and ask God to give you the opportunity to share the gospel with them. Look for opportunities to steer conversations to spiritual truth, perhaps by focusing on what is happening in the news of the day or in the life of the person you know. God will soon make your feet beautiful.

SS

Thursday

THE INFINITE PLAN OF GOD
Read Romans 11

Oh, the depth of the riches both of the wisdom and knowledge of God! For from Him and through Him and to Him are all things. To Him be the glory forever. Amen. (11:33a, 36)

Sometimes life seems to have no purpose and makes no sense to our finite minds. It may appear as if God is not in control of all things. However, it should be remembered that we live in a fallen world and the presence of sin often accentuates the vanity in life. As a result, if we are to live with purpose and meaning we must rest upon the knowledge and wisdom that God's plan is best, even when it does not make sense to us. In this context, wisdom is not that we will know why God allows certain things to happen—it is the ability to trust God when we don't know the why. The ability to have faith in these types of situations starts with the knowledge of His Word coupled with learning to walk with Him in faith at all times. This confidence will help us to trust Him when things don't make sense.

The Lord sits as King of the universe and nothing happens unless He directs it. Our perspective is very limited—we live in a single city, in a single country, on a single continent, for a relatively short period of time. We cannot know how the Conductor of the universe is orchestrating the harmonies of all of life into a beautiful symphony for His glory. We may have to wait until heaven to understand His purposes; but the key is to trust God's knowledge and wisdom today.

Paul closes Romans eleven with a declaration that everything in this universe from beginning to end was created, sustained, ruled, and guided to its ordained goal by God. "For from Him"—He is the source of all things, and "through Him"—He has the means to accomplish all things, and "to Him"—the aim and goal of all things is to bring glory to God (v. 36). Although we might have many questions, practically speaking, there is one important question to answer: Will we trust in the Lord's knowledge and wisdom? "Oh, the depth of the riches both of the wisdom and knowledge of God! How unsearchable are His judgments and unfathomable His ways!" (v. 33). The more you know Him, the easier it is to trust Him.

SS

Friday

A LIVING SACRIFICE TO GOD
Read Romans 12

Therefore I urge you, brethren, by the mercies of God, to present your bodies a living and holy sacrifice, acceptable to God, which is your spiritual service of worship. (12:1)

A living sacrifice is someone who is wholly dedicated to God. This dedication includes at least three things. First, it involves a necessary and decisive act on the part of the believer. This commitment is a definite act that has continuing responsibilities. It is similar to a marriage vow or an enlistment into the armed forces. These types of commitments ought to be reviewed as many times as needed to maintain their associated responsibilities.

Second, this is not only a definite commitment, it is a total commitment. God does not just want hands or feet for His service—He wants the whole body. Paul uses the body as the totality of one's being. This commitment pictures a believer presenting himself before the altar of God as the sacrifice. As he climbs on the altar, he is saying, "I totally commit my intellect, feelings, preferences, priorities, values, plans, and purposes to the Lord." One must beware, however, because living sacrifices have the temptation and tendency to crawl off the altar. Believers need to make a decisive act of committing their whole lives to the Lord. They should also renew their commitment daily to make sure they have not crawled off the altar.

Finally, this commitment is a "spiritual service of worship" (v. 1). When believers go to church on Sunday, they go to worship corporately. But worship does not start or end in the local church. Believers should be worshipping all week long. Their entire life should be an act of worship.

This is what it takes to be a living sacrifice to God: a decisive commitment, a total commitment, and worshipful service. Are you presenting yourself as a living sacrifice to the Lord? Are you allowing Him to use you right where you are—at work, at school, in your home, in your ministry? Make a commitment to be a living sacrifice to God and then live it out for the rest of your life. It will be worth it all for He is worthy of it all.

SS

Monday

THE DEBT OF LOVE
Read Romans 13

Owe nothing to anyone except to love one another; for he who loves his neighbor has fulfilled the Law. (13:8)

Debt is almost always viewed in a negative light in Scripture, with the notable exception being the debt of loving one another. We always owe people love. However, the word "love" in verse eight is often misunderstood. The Greeks used at least four words to convey the idea of love. The first word is *eros*, which is characterized by a possessive physical love. It is a love that embodies physical passion and intense feelings. It most often deals with the idea of sexual lust. Our English term erotic is based on this word and reflects this meaning. The sole Christian application would involve a couple in a marriage relationship, which is the only situation where this kind of romantic love should be found. However, if this is the only love a couple has toward one another, theirs will be a very unhealthy marriage. This word is not found in the New Testament.

The second word is *storge*, which involves natural obligation, such as family love. This love typically overlooks the faults of others and offenses that occur due to family relationships. While the Greek term *storge* is not found in the New Testament, its negative derivative is used twice (*astorge*, meaning unloving; cf. 1:31; 2 Tm 3:3).

The third word is *philia*, which expresses the idea of affection and care in connection with friendship. This expression is based upon our particular likes and enjoyment of people. This kind of love is commonly expressed as brotherly love and is found in passages like 1 Thessalonians 4:9 and Hebrews 13:1. This love is usually good, but it can exclude people with whom we have nothing in common.

The highest form of love is expressed by the word *agape*. This love is self-giving, meeting the needs of others while expecting nothing in return (cf. 1 Cor 13:4-8). *Agape* is best expressed by God in sending His Son to die for our sins (Jn 3:16). This love is not based on feelings or emotions—it is an act of the will. *Agape* is the term used in verse eight. Are you showing *agape* to everyone? Or is there someone in your life that you refuse to *agape*? If so, you have a debt to pay.

SS

Tuesday

JUDGING ONE ANOTHER
Read Romans 14

Therefore let us not judge one another anymore, but rather determine this—not to put an obstacle or a stumbling block in a brother's way. (14:13)

The first half of verse thirteen sums up verses one thru twelve. The stronger brother, who by grace understands his liberty, should not regard the weaker brother with contempt. The weaker brother should not judge the liberty of the stronger brother. Paul tells us not to do this because we all will be brought before the judgment seat of Christ. This judgment has nothing to do with our eternal destiny, for this is determined by our belief in Christ's death for our sins. Rather, this judgment evaluates the believer's works and attitudes in order to determine whether or not rewards should be given.

In the second half of verse thirteen, Paul narrows his discussion not to the moral commands given in Scripture, but to the liberties that believers may exercise. He states that a believer should not put an obstacle before a fellow believer that hinders their spiritual progress. A believer might have the biblical liberty to do a certain activity, but must always consider whether it will hinder, confuse, or damage the spiritual growth of the weaker believer. Note that the burden is put on the believer who is more mature. A spiritually strong person is one who is humble, not asserting his rights, not insisting on his liberties, and not looking after his own interest. That person is walking according to love, constantly looking out for the interests of others (v. 15). The kingdom of God is not filled with squabbles over liberties, but rather righteousness, peace, and joy (v. 17). Believers can only exhibit these qualities by the power of the Holy Spirit (v. 17; cf. Gal 5:22-23).

As a grandparent, I often take walks with my grandchildren. We all hold hands and walk together at the pace of the youngest child. No one desires to race on ahead. Why? Because we all love the youngest and have no problem accommodating our liberties. How are you managing your liberties? Are you walking in love? Or are you looking after your own self-interests?

SS

Wednesday

THREE CHARACTERISTICS OF MATURITY
Read Romans 15

... you yourselves are full of goodness, filled with all knowledge and able also to admonish one another. (15:14)

What does maturity in Christ look like? Many Christians believe that they are mature, but how is it recognizable? Paul does not provide an exhaustive list, but he does give us three important characteristics. First, maturity is "full of goodness" (v. 14). This is not absolute goodness, for that is reserved for God alone. The goodness that Paul denotes is a consistent moral excellence in faith and lifestyle. This person seeks the welfare of others in order to meet their needs, whether physical or spiritual. When you meet others, is it your sincere desire to express God's goodness to them in word and deed? Or are you caught up with only what is happening in your own life?

Second, maturity is full of "knowledge" (v. 14). While no one can ever be fully mature without biblical knowledge, this knowledge alone does not lead to maturity, but only pride. Mature knowledge comes through humble service in love (cf. Phil 1:9–10; Col 2:2–3). This service involves submission to Christ and is lived out in acts of love toward others. Do you seek out others to serve? Or are you overly worried about having your own needs met?

Third, mature believers "admonish one another" (v. 14). Biblical admonishment is loving counsel which seeks to influence others through exhortations, warnings, and corrections (cf. Col 1:28; 1 Thes 5:14). Ideally, this admonishment should be done with those whom you know well and with whom you have a relationship. It should always be expressed with love, humility, and self-control, for you may one day be in need of admonishment (cf. Gal 6:1). Many times, we may avoid admonishment because we are afraid of the reaction of the one corrected; or because we want to avoid conflict. However, it might help to keep Proverbs 27:5-6a in mind, "Better is open rebuke than love that is concealed. Faithful are the wounds of a friend."

SS

Thursday

ESTABLISHED BY THE GOSPEL
Read Romans 16

Now to Him Who is able to establish you according to my gospel and the preaching of Jesus Christ. (16:25a)

The foundation of our lives is of absolute importance if we are to be a solid testimony in a world that is falling apart. Accordingly, Paul ends his letter where he began—with the foundation of the "gospel" (v. 25; cf. 1:1, 9, 15, 16). Paul's gospel is no different from that of any of the other apostles. It is the gospel that he received directly from the Lord (cf. Gal 1:11-12).

Paul was chosen by God to take the gospel to the Gentiles (cf. Gal 2:7-9). At the Jerusalem Council, the apostles gathered together and agreed that salvation was by grace, not by works. Peter declared, "But we believe that we [Jews] are saved through the grace of the Lord Jesus, in the same way as they [Gentiles] also are" (Acts 15:11). Strictly speaking, the gospel is centered around the death, burial, and resurrection of Jesus Christ as a penal substitute for sinners (cf. 1 Cor 15:3-4). If you do not have the death and resurrection of Christ in your gospel, then you do not have the full gospel. Furthermore, if you do not have a statement that Christ served as a substitute for sinners, then you do not have the full gospel.

Paul goes on to declare that God is able to "establish" us according to "the preaching of Jesus Christ" (v. 25). These two ideas seem to indicate that the proclamation of the church is not just the gospel. In essence, Paul is saying, "I pray that God would establish us, not just with the basic core of the gospel message, but with all the details of the doctrinal and practical teachings in the Book of Romans, which is centered on Jesus Christ."

How well do you know and understand the Book of Romans? Its doctrine is given to us so that we may have a firm, established foundation to proclaim the gospel to a unsaved world and the teachings of Jesus Christ to believers. Now more than ever we need mature believers on the front lines proclaiming these truths. Equipped with the knowledge of Romans, will you be one of those Christians who will step up and say, "Here am I, send me!" (Is 6:8)?

SS

Friday

SPIRITUAL UNITY
Read 1 Corinthians 1

Now I exhort you, brethren, by the name of our Lord Jesus Christ, that you all agree and that there be no divisions among you, but that you be made complete in the same mind and in the same judgment. (1:10)

Paul begins 1 Corinthians by reminding the church of their calling, enrichments, and gifts (vv. 2-7). The Corinthian church seemed to have had everything needed for success. Unfortunately, the church was full of divisions. These divisions were a sign of spiritual immaturity—the members were acting like they were babes in Christ as opposed to spiritually mature believers (cf. 3:1-3). Paul exhorts the church to be unified, having the "same mind" and "same judgment" (v. 10). That is the only way the church can be "made complete" (i.e., brought to spiritual maturity; v. 10).

The predicament of the Corinthian church serves as a warning to the modern church. Even with abundant resources, proven abilities, and sound doctrine, there can still be divisions amongst us. As you experience difficulties with others that threaten your spiritual unity, consider the following factors.

First, we have all been saved by placing our trust in the death, burial, and resurrection of Jesus Christ (v. 2). There is not a person, place, or circumstance that can take that away from us. We have all been set apart to live for the Lord and to love others accordingly. Our salvation and calling unify us.

Second, seek to connect with fellow saints according to the common ground of the enrichments God has given us. We have been given speech and knowledge so that we can confirm the testimony concerning Christ to the outside world (vv. 5-6).

Third, the Lord has blessed each of us with gifts (v. 7). These gifts unify us because they are all given by the same Spirit (cf. 12:4). Furthermore, these gifts are supposed to be used for the "common good" (12:7). They are for the "edification of the church" (14:12).

When you experience conflict with other believers, always remember that you are fellow saints, enriched by God, and endowed with gifts to serve and strengthen each other.

NE

Monday

EMBRACING THE MIND OF CHRIST
Read 1 Corinthians 2

For who has known the mind of the Lord, that he will instruct Him? But we have the mind of Christ. (2:16)

In this chapter, Paul contrasts the wisdom from above, which is the mind of Christ (v. 16), with the wisdom of men, which is of this world (v. 12). The wisdom from above is "taught by the Spirit, combining spiritual thoughts with spiritual words" (v. 13). The wisdom of men is full of human words (v. 13). The wisdom from above is eternal, having been "predestined before the ages" (v. 7). The wisdom of men is temporary, because the rulers of this age are "passing away" (v. 6). Have you embraced the mind of Christ? Or are you still trusting in the wisdom of men?

If you are embracing the mind of Christ you will find yourself understanding life in terms of what God has provided for us in Christ, and what is to come in the future. Your focus will be on the things above and their impact on the things of this world.

But if you are embracing the wisdom of men you will find yourself consumed with the cares, riches, and pleasures of this life. What is important to God will not necessarily be important to you. In fact, you may not even know what is important to God. You may find yourself interested only in the things that impact your worldly interests.

If you belong to Jesus Christ you have the ability to understand His will and His ways as He has given us His Spirit to reign in us. You have also been given a new heart to embrace Him, His will, and His wisdom. Unbelievers cannot understand the mind of Christ because they do not have the Spirit (v. 14).

Are you taking advantage of the remarkable gift of the Spirit, or are you taking Him for granted? Are you taking time daily to understand who you are, what you have, and what's to come from the Lord Jesus Christ? Are you taking time daily to embrace God's agenda for the world? Take time today to embrace the mind of Christ and subject yourself to Him. Do not trust in the wisdom of men—trust in the wisdom from above.

NE

Tuesday

PLANTERS AND WATERERS
Read 1 Corinthians 3

Now he who plants and he who waters are one; but each will receive his own reward according to his own labor. (3:8)

In verses 1-8, Paul rebukes the Corinthian church for exalting men rather than God. The Corinthians were declaring allegiance to individuals like Paul or Apollos, who were merely servants of the Lord—God had simply given opportunities to these men, who had been used by Him to grow His kingdom.

Because of this emphasis on human leaders, the Corinthian church was full of jealousy and strife. They found themselves comparing and contrasting Paul and Apollos to determine which one to follow. This kind of behavior demonstrated worldly wisdom (cf. 2:13). Ultimately, it was a rejection of God, Who alone is responsible for the salvation and sanctification of individuals.

Beware of comparing and contrasting and elevating one individual above another in relation to spiritual leadership. All leaders have a variety of strengths and weaknesses. Yet God uses each of these leaders according to His will and pleasure to impact lives in relation to the ministry of the kingdom. From our perspective, it might appear as if one leader is more successful or greater than another; but in reality, God is using each one to perform different tasks and roles. One "plants" and one "waters" (v. 8), but both are regarded simply as the Lord's "servants" (v. 5). And each will receive a reward for his labor (v. 8). While it is okay to honor and be grateful for those spiritual leaders who impact your life, always remember that it is ultimately God Who controls the process and is responsible for spiritual growth.

As the Lord's servant yourself, make sure you are involved in the building of God's kingdom (cf. vv. 9-15). Your life will be judged according to how you have or have not been involved in this work. Profitable work will receive a reward (v. 14); unprofitable work will result in loss (v. 15). Don't get caught up in comparing yourself with other builders. We are all simple servants building on the foundation laid by Jesus Christ (v. 11).

NE

Wednesday

FOR WHOM ARE YOU FAITHFUL?
Read 1 Corinthians 4

In this case, moreover, it is required of stewards that one be found trustworthy. (4:2)

In 4:1, Paul identifies himself as a servant of Christ and as a steward of the mysteries of God. Servants and stewards have at least two things in common. First, they both answer to a higher authority—they have masters. Their focus should be on the will of their masters, not on their own wants and desires. They ought to seek the approval of their masters, not the approval of others. Second, servants and stewards should be trustworthy. They ought to live lives of faithfulness to their masters.

How much of your time is spent seeking the approval of men rather than the approval of your Master? You can't be a bond-servant of Christ and seek to please men at the same time (cf. Gal 1:10). If you focus on the approval of men, your life will be shaped by what others think of you. Your actions and behavior will be designed to please others. However, if you focus on being a faithful servant, you will be content with what God says about you—you are "sanctified in Christ Jesus" and a saint "by calling" (1:2). Your actions and behavior will be designed to please your Master.

Are you living a life of faithfulness with your relationships, possessions, and abilities? These things were given to you by God. Paul asked the Corinthians, "What do you have that you did not receive?" (v. 7). You did not create yourself. Therefore, there is nothing about you that should lead you to believe that you can keep and sustain yourself. Everything you have, everything you are able to do, everything is a gift from God to be managed for His glory, not your own. You are not a self-made individual. You are not where you are in life because of your own abilities. It is all due to the grace of God (cf. 1:4).

When the Lord returns, He expects to find "faithful" stewards (cf. Lk 12:42-44). Will you be found "trustworthy" by your Master (v. 2)?

NE

Thursday

COMPASSIONATE CONFRONTATION
Read 1 Corinthians 5

I have decided to deliver such a one to Satan for the destruction of his flesh, so that his spirit may be saved in the day of the Lord Jesus. (5:5)

When sin goes uncorrected it can create a lot of damage within the assembly of believers. The Corinthian church was faced with this reality when they tolerated the open sin of one of their members. Rather than mourn the wicked behavior of the offender, they became arrogant, proud that they were able to accommodate his sin while believing that it was having no effect on them. Paul corrected this type of thinking by informing the church, "Do you not know that a little leaven leavens the whole lump of dough?" (v. 6). The Apostle then commanded the Corinthians to separate themselves from the offender and to no longer have fellowship with him, "Remove the wicked man from among yourselves!" (v. 13). The modern church can learn a few lessons from this unfortunate situation.

First, we must be involved in the lives of fellow Christians. We cannot ignore the sin of others as if it is none of our business. That is not a loving thing to do. The loving thing is to confront them with their sin in a compassionate, yet firm, way. "Better is open rebuke than love that is concealed. Faithful are the wounds of a friend" (Prv 27:5-6). On the other hand, we should not be rooting around in the lives of others trying to find sin behind every bush.

Second, we need to be careful with the company we keep. Professing Christians who live a life of sin will contaminate us and damage our testimony in a lost world. We need to lovingly separate ourselves from them, trusting that our action will lead them to godly sorrow and repentance.

Third, we should remember that God is a God of forgiveness. When the offender repents, we must be quick to restore them in a spirit of gentleness (cf. Gal 6:1). All believers have been delivered out of sin to live by God's grace. We should no longer continue in sin nor should we be condemned in our sin.

NE

Friday

SAINTS IN SECULAR COURTS?
Read 1 Corinthians 6

Does any one of you, when he has a case against his neighbor, dare to go to law before the unrighteous and not before the saints? (6:1)

In 6:1-8, Paul rebukes the Corinthians for taking their fellow Christians before secular courts to settle disputes. The Apostle presents three arguments to demonstrate that this type of behavior is counterproductive to the unity of the church.

First, Christians will judge the world, including angels (vv. 2-3). If believers will eventually judge the world, then certainly they have the competency to judge one another in law courts (v. 2). In fact, they already have everything they need to resolve disputes among themselves. Through the indwelling presence of the Holy Spirit, the Lord has provided believers with wisdom that is superior to the wisdom of the world (cf. 2:6-13). So why would Christians go to secular courts that are based on human wisdom?

Second, believers would never appoint unbelievers as elders in the church, so why would they allow them to judge Christians outside the church? (vv. 4-6). The Apostle shames the Corinthians by sarcastically asking, "There is not among you one wise man who will be able to decide between his brethren?" (v. 5). Believers embarrass the name of Jesus by taking family business before unbelievers. It communicates to the world that God has not provided Christians with what is necessary to handle their own disputes.

Third, it is better to be wronged or defrauded than to inflict the same on other believers (vv. 7-8). When Christians take their disputes before secular courts, they are defeated before the trial even begins. Victory comes when believers settle their differences in a loving way that brings unity to the church, always being mindful of the interests of others rather than their own personal interests (cf. Phil 2:1-4).

Instead of attempting to resolve your dispute with a fellow believer by taking them before a secular court, take your matter to the church, or at least some form of Christian mediation.

NE

Monday

SINGLE OR MARRIED, WALK IN THIS MANNER
Read 1 Corinthians 7

Only, as the Lord has assigned to each one, as God has called each, in this manner let him walk. And so I direct in all the churches. (7:17)

This chapter provides a great deal of instruction on the topic of marriage. It tells Christians how to live as single individuals as well as how to live as married couples. Unfortunately, these directives are often misinterpreted or misapplied. Rather than going through all the details of Paul's teaching, I would like to highlight three central truths.

First, whether believers are single or married, their status is a gift from God (v. 7). It is good to be single. It is good to be married. Both situations have their advantages and disadvantages. And both can be used by God for the advancement of His kingdom. Be content in whatever state you find yourself (v. 27). Don't actively seek to change your status.

Second, whether believers are single or married, they are called to live holy lives (v. 19). The goal of our lives should be holiness in whatever roles and responsibilities God has granted us. When someone is devoted to the Lord, they seek an intimate walk with Him. Fellowship with God is only possible when one is keeping His commandments (cf. 1 Jn 1:6-7).

Third, whether believers are single or married, they belong to the Lord (vv. 22-23). You are a slave to Christ. You were bought with a price. Therefore, your life should be lived for your Master, no matter your status. Your life should be characterized by a genuine pursuit to know Christ, to become like Him, and to be useful to Him. Every decision you make should be for His glory.

As you read through this chapter, ask yourself the following questions. Are you content in your current condition, or are you seeking something else? Are you living a holy life, or is your life characterized by sinful actions? Are you living as a slave to Christ, or are you seeking to please others? Whether single or married, your life should reflect your devotion to God.

NE

Tuesday

LIBERTY AND LOVE
Read 1 Corinthians 8

But take care that this liberty of yours does not somehow become a stumbling block to the weak. (8:9)

The city of Corinth was well-known for its idolatry. It was the site of the Temple of Aphrodite, which employed a significant number of sacred prostitutes to promote the worship of the goddess of love. Unfortunately, the city's idolatry greatly impacted the church. Paul had earlier warned the church about participating in prostitution by explaining that a believer's body is the temple of the Holy Spirit (cf. 6:15-20). In this chapter, Paul addresses the subject of food offered to idols and whether or not it was lawful for the church to eat it.

Paul does not answer the question with an unqualified yes or no. Instead, he approaches the subject by addressing Christian liberty. The Apostle affirms that there is only one God in the universe. As a result, the gods worshiped by the Corinthians don't really exist. So the fact that a piece of food was sacrificed in honor of one of these gods did nothing to harm the quality of that food. Unfortunately, this knowledge was not held by everyone in the church. There were many who thought eating food offered to idols was wrong. So Paul's command is that believers should limit their freedom so that it does not become a stumbling block to those who are weak.

We need to evaluate our limits and liberties in light of what God has ordained in His Word, not in light of our own wants and desires. Where God has given us freedom, let us embrace that freedom in faith. Where God has limited our behavior, we must act accordingly.

We must also recognize that fellow Christians may not share in the knowledge we have in relation to our liberties. Love for our brethren ought to lead us to restrict our behavior where it might tempt the conscience of a fellow saint. If we do not follow this pattern, we sin against God and against others, demonstrating a lack of love for both. We must never allow our liberty to override our love for other believers. As we consider our freedoms and constraints in light of God's word, let us walk in them, being ever mindful of the conscience and convictions of our fellow believers.

NE

Wednesday

YOUR RIGHTS AND THE GOSPEL
Read 1 Corinthians 9

If others share the right over you, do we not more? Nevertheless, we did not use this right, but we endure all things so that we will cause no hindrance to the gospel of Christ. (9:12)

Evidently, there were some in the Corinthian church who were critical of Paul's ministry (v. 3). Using rhetorical analysis, we can make a conjecture as to their lines of attack by examining Paul's statements in his defense. First, his detractors questioned whether Paul was in fact an apostle (v. 2). Second, they did not believe that he had the right to earn a living off of the church (vv. 4-14). Third, they viewed him as hypocritical, changing his behavior depending on whether he was ministering to Jews or Gentiles (vv. 19-22).

Paul's first defense is that the Corinthian church itself is proof of his apostleship. He also claims that he is an eyewitness of the resurrected Lord, a necessary mark of an apostle (v. 1; cf. 15:7-8). Paul's second defense is that the Lord directed that those who proclaim the gospel have the right to make their living from the gospel (v. 14). He uses several illustrations to prove his point, including those of a soldier, a farmer, a shepherd, and a Levitical priest. Paul's third defense is that he is willing to become all things to all men, so that he might save some (v. 22).

Even though Paul had a right to certain things as an apostle, he did not always take advantage of those rights for the sake of the gospel. There may be times in your life where you have rights that you can impose on others, yet for the sake of the gospel you refuse to exercise your rights. This does not mean that insisting on your rights is antithetical to the gospel. It is a voluntary course of action. Following the direction of the Holy Spirit, you need to decide the appropriate time to insist on your rights and the appropriate time to relinquish your rights. Limiting your rights is a noble thing when done for the right reasons. Make sure that your actions are performed with the wisdom that comes from above, the love of God and the love of others being your primary motivations.

NE

Thursday

WHICH CUP ARE YOU DRINKING?
Read 1 Corinthians 10

Now these things happened as examples for us, so that we would not crave evil things as they also craved. (10:6)

In this chapter, Paul uses the experiences of the nation Israel as illustrative of the issues being faced by the Corinthian church. Even though the Israelites of the Exodus generation all shared the same spiritual events, God was greatly displeased with many of them because of their evil cravings (vv. 1-6). They committed idolatry, acted immorally, tested the Lord, and grumbled (vv. 7-10). As a result, they experienced the discipline of God.

After explaining that the experiences of the Israelites are to serve as examples for their instruction, Paul encourages the Corinthians to be careful when they face temptations, reminding them that the Lord will always provide a way of escape. The Apostle then warns the Corinthians of the incongruity of partaking of the Lord Jesus Christ while craving evil things within the heart and pursuing evil things in action, "You cannot drink the cup of the Lord and the cup of demons; you cannot partake of the table of the Lord and the table of demons" (v. 21).

It is hypocritical to claim to follow Jesus Christ while at the same time pursuing that which offends Him. We must consistently evaluate our lives to see if there is anything that competes with our allegiance to the Lord. Those things make us double-minded and unstable in all our ways (cf. Jas 1:8). Why? Because we know what is right while pursuing that which is evil. This sets us up for failure in our spiritual lives. Although temptations will arise, our God will always provide a way of escape. We must be willing to follow God's path so that we do not experience the negative consequences of craving and pursuing evil things. In everything we do, we should demonstrate the greatness of God's character according to His divine power.

NE

Friday

THE LORD'S SUPPER
Read 1 Corinthians 11

Therefore when you meet together, it is not to eat the Lord's Supper, for in your eating each one takes his own supper first; and one is hungry and another is drunk. (11:20-21)

The Lord's Supper is intended to be a solemn reminder of the death of Jesus Christ that is to be observed until He returns. There is a divine order for conducting the Lord's Supper. First, individuals should examine themselves so that they do not eat and drink in an unworthy manner (vv. 27-29). Second, a prayer of thanks should be offered (v. 24). Third, individuals partake of bread representing the body of Christ (v. 24). Fourth, individuals drink wine representing the New Covenant in His blood (v. 25). These last three steps should be undertaken in a communal setting (cf. vv. 20, 33).

The Apostle does not go into much detail concerning the prayer or the partaking of bread and drinking of wine; however, he spends a considerable about of time expounding on the first step—the act of self-examination (vv. 27-32). Whoever eats and drinks in an unworthy manner is "guilty of the body and the blood of the Lord" (v. 27) and in danger of experiencing the judgment of God (cf. vv. 30, 32). Believers must confess their sins against God and others so that they can eat and drink in a state of unhindered fellowship.

Unfortunately, many modern believers take a casual approach to the Lord's Supper. For them, the meaning and value of the occasion is greatly diminished. The Lord's Supper is one of the most important and sacred events observed by Christians. Believers need to be wary of participating in it with wrong attitudes or actions. We must examine ourselves and make sure that there is nothing in our lives that will make us "unworthy" (v. 27). We should come to the Lord's Supper filled with thoughts about the Lord's work on the cross on our behalf. We should also pray for and prepare ourselves for the Lord's return. Finally, we should be considerate of those around us, ensuring that all experience the Lord's Supper in the same manner and with equality.

NE

Monday

ONE BODY, ONE SPIRIT
Read 1 Corinthians 12

But to each one is given the manifestation of the Spirit for the common good. (12:7)

Few subjects are as controversial in the modern church as spiritual gifts. The same was true for the ancient church at Corinth. In fact, Paul spends three chapters of 1 Corinthians discussing this issue. He also addresses the topic in Romans 12:4-8 and Ephesians 4:7-13. There are a variety of spiritual gifts, but they are all administered by the same Spirit (v. 4).

A spiritual gift can be defined as an endowment of grace given to a believer by God so that he or she can serve the church. While everybody has natural abilities, a spiritual gift is a special empowerment stewarded by the individual Christian. Believers discover their spiritual gifts by serving in the church. It is vitally important that saints know how they are gifted so that they can seek out situations where they can be the most effective.

God has made sure that every Christian has at least one spiritual gift (v. 7). Believers do not choose their own gifts, nor do they choose their function. Therefore, they must humbly submit to God's plan for their lives by obediently following His direction. Christians do not have the right to claim independence from other Christians. They all need each other and should learn to play their part in the building of the body of Christ (Eph 4:11-12). This requires that believers get personally involved in the lives of their fellow saints, lovingly providing instruction, correction, and compassionate care according to our God-given gifts.

Are you currently using your spiritual gifts to minister to the church? If not, I would strongly encourage you to find a God-honoring local church where you can make a contribution to the body of Christ. As you serve others, your gifts will become evident. We are one body in Jesus Christ, with many members; different gifts and different functions, but the same Spirit.

NE

Tuesday

LOVE NEVER FAILS
Read 1 Corinthians 13

Love never fails; but if there are gifts of prophecy, they will be done away; if there are tongues, they will cease; if there is knowledge, it will be done away. (13:8)

This chapter is commonly known as the love chapter. Paul's central point in this passage is that love should be the fundamental basis of all acts of service and ministry. When love is not applied to a service or ministry, that particular service or ministry is not honoring to God. Everything we do should be done in love.

Love is an attitude toward or action performed for others that seeks the highest good for their lives with no thought of reciprocation. When viewed in this way, love can be shown to everyone, even enemies. As the Lord said, "But I say to you who hear, love your enemies, do good to those who hate you, bless those who curse you, pray for those who mistreat you" (Lk 6:27-28). Love never fails (v. 8).

All Christians have roles and responsibilities in relation to others. Believers should carefully consider the manner in which they carry out their roles and responsibilities. If their actions are not carried out with love, then they are not pleasing to God. It is not enough to simply perform good deeds for others. Those good deeds need to be done with the right attitude and for the right reasons.

In whatever role you find yourself (e.g., husband, wife, parent, child, friend, etc.), you should ask yourself two key questions. First, am I doing what God has commanded me to do in this role? Second, am I doing it with the action and attitude of love? An impatient father or an unkind wife is not honoring to God, even if they perform the correct tasks associated with their roles. Many relationship problems stem from a lack of love, not necessarily a lack of service. It's not enough to simply perform your responsibilities. They must be done in love.

NE

Wednesday

EDIFICATION OF THE BRETHREN
Read 1 Corinthians 14

What is the outcome then, brethren? When you assemble, each one has a psalm, has a teaching, has a revelation, has a tongue, has an interpretation. Let all things be done for edification. (14:26)

The Book of 1 Corinthians is loaded with controversial topics, including believers' rewards, excommunication, marriage, food offered to idols, spiritual gifts, and the role of women in church. These issues have been debated in the church since Paul wrote this letter. Many Christians are eager to present the evidence supporting their views and are quick to rebuke those who disagree. The Apostle's message in the midst of all the conversation about these matters is to make sure believers recognize that the goal of his instruction is the edification of the brethren, for the benefit of the body of Christ as a whole. He wanted the Corinthian church to be unified, in doctrine and in practice.

Spiritual gifts are given to believers so that they can serve one another for the common good (v. 7). Spiritual gifts are not to be used for selfish ambition or personal gratification. Love should be the foundation of service; otherwise, other motives will emerge. Therefore, the ultimate goal of Christians should not be to seek certain gifts or to exercise them in a selfish way, but to edify others through them.

The discussion surrounding a woman's role in the church should focus on how she can best glorify God and bless others according to the order and design God has created for women. The church often misses out on significant contributions from women because it is focused on what women can't do, rather than on what women can do. The church should honor women and be edified through them as they serve in their God-given roles.

Paul's central command in this chapter is, "Let all things be done for edification" (v. 26). The form and function of the church's practice is important and must be considered if we are going to do things properly and in an orderly manner (cf. v. 40). But the goal of form and function must be to glorify God and to edify the brethren.

NE

Thursday

THE GOSPEL IN WHICH WE STAND
Read 1 Corinthians 15

Now I make known to you, brethren, the gospel which I preached to you, which also you received, in which also you stand. (15:1)

The gospel is relatively simple—Christ died for our sins, was buried, and was raised on the third day (vv. 3-4). All believers stand firm in this truth. This chapter is a wonderful reminder of what we have and what is to come. Here are a few key points to embrace.

First, if you have put your faith in the person and work of Jesus Christ, you have been delivered from your sin and placed in right standing and right relationship with God. You have a new condition on the inside—you have been regenerated. This is all due to the grace of God—it is a free gift (cf. v. 10).

Second, since Christ has been raised from the dead, we have certain hope that we also will be "made alive" (v. 22). Christ is only the first fruits of the resurrection. We are assured of a new heavenly home, and an inheritance waiting for us.

Third, when we are resurrected, we will be given a new body, one that is imperishable and immortal. Our current body is perishable and will soon die because it is without honor, weak, natural, and earthly. But we will be changed. Our resurrection body will be glorious, powerful, spiritual, and heavenly.

Finally, in light of these great truths, we ought to be "steadfast, immovable, always abounding in the work of Lord" (v. 58). Since our debt has been paid, and our life has been delivered from sin, we should live according to the blessed hope we have been given. We should live a life of love for God and others in anticipation of the blessings to come our way. The glorious gospel should be a motivator for us. As we await the return of the Lord, let us reflect on what Jesus has done for us, how it has impacted our lives, and how we can abound in the work He has given us.

NE

Friday

STAND FIRM
Read 1 Corinthians 16

Be on the alert, stand firm in the faith, act like men, be strong. Let all that you do be done in love. (16:13-14)

Paul begins the final chapter of 1 Corinthians with a discussion of the collection for the saints in Jerusalem. The church in Jerusalem was struggling mightily because of the great persecution they were facing at the hands of the Jews. The Apostle encourages the church to put aside money on the first day (i.e., Sunday) of every week so that the collection would be ready by the time of his arrival. He planned to visit Corinth after leaving Ephesus and passing through Macedonia. Paul never tells the church how much to give—but that each one should give "as he may prosper" (v. 2).

The Apostle's final exhortations for the Corinthians centered on their need to acknowledge and be in subjection to those who have devoted themselves to the ministry (cf. vv. 15, 16, 18). He singles out several by name, including Timothy (vv. 10-11), Apollos (v. 12), and the household of Stephanas (vv. 15-16). Paul's list serves as an inclusio around verses thirteen and fourteen, highlighting his commands. Undoubtedly, these courageous individuals are foremost in Paul's mind as he exhorts the church, "Be on the alert, stand firm in the faith, act like men, be strong. Let all that you do be done in love" (vv. 13-14).

The first four commands are essentially a call for courage. Courage requires us to be committed to living for the Lord no matter what might happen to us. In other words, we must have fortitude in our ministries no matter the dangers or difficulties. To test your fortitude, fill in the blanks: I will obey God if _____ or until _____. If you put something in the blanks, you are exhibiting a lack of courage. There should never be "ifs" or "untils" when it comes to our commitment to God.

In your life you will face many dangers and difficulties. It will be a challenge to stand firm in the faith. But God will be with you and will give you what you need to be strong and courageous. God will stand with you if you are willing to stand for Him.

NE

Monday

DIFFERENT ON PURPOSE?
Read 2 Corinthians 1

Paul, an apostle of Christ Jesus by the will of God, and Timothy our brother, to the church of God which is at Corinth with all the saints who are throughout Achaia. (1:1)

Has there ever been a time when being different seemed to be too much to bear, fitting in seemed an impossible task, and being liked by the majority just never materialized? Could it be that God intended a life of difference for His children—a life for His saints that, in the end, would be so much better than being liked by everyone or being a part of the popular crowd—a life that would glorify the Father in heaven.

In the first chapter of this book, Paul writes to the Corinthians and reminds them that they have been chosen by God, just as he had been. The Apostle had been sent by God to minister to this group of individuals, who were "saints by calling" (1 Cor 1:2). Yet one might ask, "Called as a saint to do what?" Unlike other proclaimers of his day, Paul was set apart to proclaim God's truth (cf. 7:14; 11:10). This truth was not popular or pleasing to the majority (cf. Acts 14:19; 21:30-32). Nevertheless, the Apostle was faithful to his calling until his death (cf. 2 Tm 4:6-8).

David Garland writes, "Saints are called to be separated from the world but then are called to go back into the world to flood it with God's light and reconciliation" (*2 Corinthians*, p. 51, Broadman & Holman, 1999). Saints are called to proclaim the gospel, which is truth (cf. Eph 1:13; Col 1:5), to a world full of falsehood and lies.

Today is a good day to reflect on your calling. Make sure that you are indeed proclaiming God's truth by presenting yourself as a saint that is in the world, but not of the world. A saint who is daily seeking to represent the Holy Father in word and deed. A saint who accepts the call to walk upright, to be holy, and to be different, in Jesus' name and for His glory (cf. 1 Thes 4:7).

VE

Tuesday

LOVE EVEN WHEN IT HURTS!
Read 2 Corinthians 2

Wherefore I urge you to reaffirm your love for him. (2:8)

"If I come up there and find that you have not done what you are supposed to do, I will be very upset and will have to ground you for the rest of the summer!" These words are typical of a general retort that can be heard in most homes with teenagers. Generally speaking, parents are deeply grieved and sorrowful when their children are found to be disobedient. In fact, many call statements like the one above the "parental response." However, this type of grief or sorrow is not limited to parent-child relationships. It can also be found in mentor to mentee, pastor to congregation, employer to employee, friend to friend, and many other relationships.

In this chapter, Paul addressed the Corinthians with great sorrow regarding his impending visit (v. 1). He reminded the church of a situation that was quite grievous to him—a situation that involved a sharp rebuke. However, this was not a self-centered rebuke; this was a rebuke flowing from a heart full of love (cf. v. 4). Paul sincerely loved the Corinthians and was deeply concerned about their spiritual well-being. Although he highlighted the need for rebuke, he also reminded the church of the need to stand ready to grant forgiveness and seek reconciliation (v. 7; cf. 5:18-19).

In this day and age many seem to struggle with the concept of rebuke. Others may struggle with the concept of reconciliation. However, in the Christian arena, these concepts are two sides of the same coin. One should naturally lead to the other. Both are necessary. And both are required.

One day you might find that you have sinned against somebody and caused them great grief. You may then be rebuked by someone who loves you. And after your earnest confession and repentance, they will probably grant forgiveness and seek reconciliation with you (cf. Lk 17:3-4). Be sure to extend the same kind of love towards someone who sins against you (causing you grief and sorrow) and seeks your forgiveness.

VE

Wednesday

FREE INDEED!
Read 2 Corinthians 3

But whenever a person turns to the Lord, the veil is taken away. Now the Lord is the Spirit, and where the Spirit of the Lord is, there is liberty. (3:16-17)

What is true freedom? Absence of trials and tribulations? Absence of financial woes and paycheck to paycheck living? Absence of harmful negative words and backstabbing friends? What about absence of physical ailments?

Although these things would be truly helpful and would really provide relief on this side of heaven, true freedom is found when individuals turn to the Lord, trusting in the work of Jesus Christ on the cross. At that point, they are liberated from the bondage of sin, death, and, for Jews, the Mosaic Law with its extensive set of rules and regulations. To highlight this idea, many Bible translations choose to use the word "freedom" instead of the word "liberty" in verse seventeen (e.g., ESV, NET, NIV, NRSV).

When the Holy Spirit draws someone to the Lord, then and only then can they really see. Their eyes are opened and the veil is taken away. Their life is eternally changed. Now the law of the Lord is forever written on their hearts (v. 3) as they are being transformed into Christlikeness by the Holy Spirit (v. 18). Immediately, there is a new relationship between God and man where obedience and love take center stage.

This transformation does not eliminate the need for and/or desire for change in one's financial, social, or physical situations. However, it elevates the need of a Savior high above all other needs or desires, because the greatest need is salvation from sin and death. Once someone is saved, other needs and desires lose much of their urgency and significance.

Have you turned to Jesus for the forgiveness of your sins? If not, today is a good day to put your faith in Him so that the veil can be lifted from your eyes. Jesus is mankind's greatest need and the only way to true freedom. If you have turned to the Lord, are you allowing the Holy Spirit to transform you into Christlikeness (cf. Rom 12:2)? VE

Thursday

A GREAT TREASURE!
Read 2 Corinthians 4

But we have this treasure in earthen vessels, so that the surpassing greatness of the power will be of God and not from ourselves; we are afflicted in every way, but not crushed; perplexed, but not despairing; persecuted, but not forsaken; struck down, but not destroyed; always carrying about in the body the dying of Jesus, so that the life of Jesus also may be manifested in our body. (4:7-10)

In this chapter, Paul continued to defend his courageous proclamation of God's great truth without deviation. He assured the Corinthians that he had not lost heart for his ministry, even though he had suffered many trials and tribulations. Through it all, God had shown mercy. However, Paul's ministry did not always bear fruit. The gospel was veiled to those who were perishing, because the god of this world (i.e., Satan) had blinded their minds so that they could not see the light of the gospel (vv. 3-4).

Paul did not take personal offense to the rejection of those who did not believe—the Apostle never preached himself, but only Christ Jesus as Lord (v. 5). Paul did not boast in his own abilities, but rather gave credit to the Father (v. 7), Who had shone the "Light of the knowledge of the glory of God" in his heart (v. 6). Paul probably used this phrase as a reference to his own experience of seeing a bright light on the Damascus Road (cf. Acts 9:3; 22:6; 26:13), where he was personally introduced to the "face of Christ" (v. 6).

The Apostle described his ministry as a "treasure" in an earthen vessel, a reference to his own human body. Paul was a physical manifestation of "the life of Christ" (v. 10). That's why he was never "crushed" or "destroyed" when he was "afflicted" and "persecuted" (vv. 8-9). The Apostle knew he carried in his body "the dying of Jesus" (v. 10).

We too have this treasure wrapped in our earthen vessels—we have been set apart to proclaim the gospel. We have no need to fear persecution—we will never be forsaken by God. And we have no need to fear rejection, or to take it personally, as long as we always preach the Son of God, not ourselves.

VE

Friday

LIVING FOREVER
Read 2 Corinthians 5

Therefore, being always of good courage, and knowing that while we are at home in the body we are absent from the Lord—for we walk by faith, not by sight—we are of good courage, I say, and prefer rather to be absent from the body and to be at home with the Lord. (5:6-8)

A doctor walked in to the examination room and delivered what he perceived to be bad news to his patient. He informed the patient that life as he knew it would immediately change due to a horrible health issue that was certain to end the patient's life. The patient looked intently into the eyes of the doctor and said, "I may not live much longer here on earth, but … I will surely live."

Here in chapter five, Paul continues a conversation of hope that he had begun at the end of the previous chapter (cf. 4:7-18). The Apostle reminds the Corinthians that their body is an "earthly tent" (v. 1; cf. 4:7, where he calls bodies "earthen vessels") that will eventually be replaced by "a building from God, a house not made with hands, eternal in the heavens" (v. 1; cf. 1 Cor 15:35-53).

The time will soon come when all believers will transition from this life into the presence of the Lord for all eternity; or, as preachers of old would say, "We will transition to the land of 'no more'—no more sickness, no more dying, no more sorrow, and no more pain." Even though the time has not yet come for each of us to transition into the arms of the Lord, we should long for His presence (v. 8). In the meantime, the Holy Spirit is currently present and living in all believers (cf. Rom 8:11).

Death is simply a transition from one life to the next. Everyone will live forever. Some will live forever in hell, eternally separated from the Savior (cf. Rev 20:10-15). But those who have believed in Christ and have put their faith in Him will live forever in eternity with the Lord (v. 8).

Today is a great day to ask yourself, "Where will I spend eternity?" For believers, their faith gives them hope that they will immediately be in the Lord's presence when they depart this life, when their mortal puts on immortal, when time and space give way to eternity.

VE

Monday

MINDFUL MINISTRY
Read 2 Corinthians 6

Giving no cause for offense in anything, so that the ministry will not be discredited. (6:3)

Do as I say and not as I do! Nobody's perfect, only Jesus was perfect! God is still working on me! Don't judge me, I'm a work in progress! At least I'm not as bad as some people! These are typical statements voiced when somebody has done something that is not in line with God's standards. They are frequently used when a person has chosen to make excuses instead of confessions.

In this chapter, Paul continues to remind the Corinthian church of his commitment to the ministry that God has granted him by grace. He urges the Corinthians to have the same level of commitment, encouraging them to consider the grace that they too have received and warning them not to treat it lightly (v. 1).

Paul explains that he has governed himself so that his ministry would not be discredited before them (v. 3). The Apostle practiced what he preached. He didn't say one thing and do another. His actions were consistent with his words.

Paul vindicates himself, providing an extensive list of various situations that he had faced while fulfilling his calling. In each case, he was a faithful servant of God who sought not to cause offense or bring dishonor to the ministry that the Lord had bestowed upon him (vv. 4-9).

Although we may face hardships and difficulties while serving in ministry, we must always remember the grace of God and seek to live a life that is pleasing unto Him—one that models the words we say. Not a life of perfection, but a life that is being perfected day by day. We may be dishonored, disrespected, spoken of with evil reports, regarded as deceivers, or otherwise abused. Nevertheless, we must not cause an offense by our heart attitudes or our ungodly verbal responses to such mistreatments.

Today, by the power of the Holy Spirit, we must strive to make sure that the ministry of Jesus Christ is not discredited. Today, let us render a blessing for a cursing (cf. Rom 12:14).

VE

Tuesday

WALKING IN HOLINESS
Read 2 Corinthians 7

Therefore, having these promises, beloved, let us cleanse ourselves from all defilement of flesh and spirit, perfecting holiness in the fear of God. (7:1)

In 2 Corinthians 6:14-7:1, Paul encourages the church to keep themselves separate from the notorious temple cults of Corinth (cf. 1 Cor 6:15-20). The "promises" referred to in verse one are those of 6:17-18; "I will welcome you. And I will be a Father to you. And you shall be sons and daughters to Me." Believers have been adopted into the family of God and have a right to call Him "Father" (Rom 8:15). Thanks to this adoption, saints have become "heirs of God and fellow heirs with Christ" who are destined to be "glorified" (Rom 8:17). As a result, believers need to remain separate from unbelievers, who are the children of Satan (i.e., Belial; 6:15). And this is especially true of those unbelievers who actively participate in the worship of idols (cf. 6:16).

Believers are commanded to strive for holiness (v. 1; cf. 1 Pt 1:15-16). They must "cleanse" themselves from all defilement of "flesh and spirit" (v. 1). The phrase "flesh and spirit" is probably a reference to both internal and external defilements. Internal defilements would include activities like idolatry and other mental sins, while external defilements would include immorality and other physical sins. The Corinthian church had significant problems in both of these areas (cf. 1 Cor 5:1, 11; 6:15-20; 10:7, 14). As a result, the church was in need of Godly repentance, which was the purpose of Paul's words of rebuke (cf. v. 8).

Today is a good day to examine your walk with God. Have you separated yourself from the things of this world that are displeasing to your Heavenly Father? Have you accepted the rebuke of a good friend and devoted your heart to godly repentance (v. 9)? Are you relying on the promises of the Lord? You are an heir of His kingdom. Live like a child of God.

VE

Wednesday

ABUNDANT GIVING
Read 2 Corinthians 8

For I testify that according to their ability, and beyond their ability, they gave of their own accord, begging us with much urging for the favor of participation in the support of the saints. (8:3-4)

"We are not called to equal giving—but to equal sacrifice" (cf. Lk 21:3-4). This statement has been made in many different churches, among many different dominations, generally during the time of the offering. The main point of the statement is that everyone should give according to what they have been given—not according to how much their neighbor gives.

Paul addresses the topic of giving in 2 Corinthians 8-9. He first references the precedent set by the churches of Macedonia. Although these churches were mired in great affliction and deep poverty, they had not simply given, they had given abundantly. Furthermore, they had given of their own accord, with great joy, because they were eager to participate in the support of the saints (vv. 2-4; cf. Rom 15:26).

Paul uses the example of the churches of Macedonia to encourage the Corinthian church in their giving. A few years earlier, the Apostle had directed the church to begin a collection for the saints (cf. 1 Cor 16:1-2). Now, as he was about to revisit the church, he wanted to ensure that their gift was ready. Paul expressed great confidence in the Corinthians, referencing their earnestness in other spiritual activities (v. 8).

Unfortunately, many modern saints need to be constantly reminded to give. I once heard a pastor say, "If we want a million dollar ministry, we must collectively give a million dollars." Believers shouldn't have to be prompted by a preacher to give—they should eagerly seek out opportunities to give. The grace of God has been given to all (v. 1); all should be given to God.

Today is a good day to evaluate your behavior as it relates to giving. Purpose in your heart to give graciously and liberally; with a joyful heart and a willing attitude.

VE

Thursday

CHEERFUL GIVING
Read 2 Corinthians 9

Each one must do just as he has purposed in his heart, not grudgingly or under compulsion, for God loves a cheerful giver. And God is able to make all grace abound to you, so that always having all sufficiency in everything, you may have an abundance for every good deed. (9:7-8)

"You Can't Beat God Giving." You may have heard this song a time or two and wondered what the phrase really means. The message of the song is that no matter how much you give to God, God has given you more.

This chapter continues Paul's conversation on the topic of giving that he began in the previous chapter. The Apostle commends the Corinthians for their readiness and zeal (v. 2) and encourages them to finish well, lest his confidence be put to shame (vv. 3-5). He also urges them to give a bountiful gift (v. 5), promising, "He who sows sparingly will also reap sparingly, and he who sows bountifully will also reap bountifully" (v. 6). This proverbial saying illustrates the biblical principle that the more someone gives to others, the more they will receive in return (cf. Lk 6:38).

Paul then shifts the conversation to a person's heart attitude while giving. He commands the Corinthians to be faithful to whatever they have purposed in their hearts (v. 7). He also encourages them to give cheerfully, not grudgingly or under compulsion, "for God loves a cheerful giver" (v. 7). Finally, the Apostle urges the church to be thankful for what God has given them, just as their gifts are producing thanksgiving in the hearts of those saints whose needs are being met (vv. 11-15).

Today is a great day for each of us to be faithful to what we have purposed in our hearts as it relates to our giving patterns. We should also evaluate our heart attitude. Are we giving cheerfully, or under compulsion? Always remember what we have been given by God. He gave His precious Son for the redemption of our sins. We will never beat God giving!

VE

Friday

AUTHORITY UNDER GOD
Read 2 Corinthians 10

For even if I boast somewhat further about our authority, which the Lord gave for building you up and not for destroying you, I will not be put to shame, for I do not wish to seem as if I would terrify you by my letters. For they say, "His letters are weighty and strong, but his personal presence is unimpressive and his speech contemptible." (10:8-10)

In this chapter, Paul returns to the central subject of the book, i.e., a defense of his authority, his ministry, and his actions as they relate to the Corinthian church. The Corinthians do not seem worried about Paul's impending visit, believing that the Apostle is bold and strong with his writings, but timid and weak in person. As a result, they are reluctant to change their sinful lifestyle because they believe Paul lacks the courage to confront them when he interacts with them face to face.

Paul responds to the church's criticism with a thinly veiled threat, "Let such a person consider this, that what we are in word by letters when absent, such persons we are also in deed when present" (v. 11). This threat echoes that of 1 Corinthians 4:19-21, "But I will come to you soon, if the Lord wills, and I shall find out, not the words of those who are arrogant but their power. For the kingdom of God does not consist in words but in power. What do you desire? Shall I come to you with a rod, or with love and a spirit of gentleness?"

The Apostle possesses both the authority and ability to confront the Corinthian church. Nevertheless, his approach will be entirely dependent upon the attitude exhibited by the congregation. If they change their behavior in Godly repentance, then he will treat them with love and a spirit of gentleness. However, the church should not take this approach as a sign of weakness. For if the Corinthians refuse to repent, their disobedience will be punished (v. 6).

Like Paul, you will face critics in your ministry. But don't let them discourage you. Always remember that the Lord is the ultimate judge Who will examine you (cf. 1 Cor 4:4). He has granted you whatever authority you possess. Wield it with godly wisdom. Sometimes you need to be forceful; sometimes you need to be gentle.

VE

Monday

PASTORAL PERSEVERANCE
Read 2 Corinthians 11

I have been on frequent journeys, in dangers from rivers, dangers from robbers, dangers from my countrymen, dangers from the Gentiles, dangers in the city, dangers in the wilderness, dangers on the sea, dangers among false brethren; I have been in labor and hardship, through many sleepless nights, in hunger and thirst, often without food, in cold and exposure. Apart from such external things, there is the daily pressure on me of concern for all the churches. (11:26-28)

Spiritual leaders, especially pastors and missionaries, face enormous pressures. Many encounter ridicule and persecution from unbelievers. Others are abused by Christians who are choosing to submit to their flesh instead of walking by the Spirit. All are under attack from the adversary, Satan (cf. 1 Pt 5:8).

In this chapter, Paul reminds the Corinthians of the many dangers and hardships he had faced while faithfully fulfilling his ministry. At times, his very life was in peril. Despite these great difficulties, Paul never lost his affection and concern for all the churches (v. 28). The Apostle exhibited true pastoral care for them, putting their interests above his own.

Many modern religious organizations select leaders based on their speaking abilities, or their effectiveness in growing ministries or increasing church membership, or their skill in raising money or generating large offerings. They often value education and experience. Some may even put stock in a person's clothing, or the car they drive, or whether or not they possess the requisite swagger or charisma. These may all be fine qualities, but a love for God's people and a willingness to suffer for the sake of the gospel should outweigh them all.

Spiritual leaders often suffer great hardship as they selflessly strive to feed, lead, and watch over their flocks. They need your prayers. Today is a good day to pray for your spiritual leaders. Pray that, like Paul, they will persevere in their ministries no matter the dangers or difficulties. Pray that they will fight the good fight, finish the course, and keep the faith (cf. 2 Tm 4:7).

VE

Tuesday

APPRECIATION FOR AFFLICTION?
Read 2 Corinthians 12

Because of the surpassing greatness of the revelations, for this reason, to keep me from exalting myself, there was given me a thorn in the flesh, a messenger of Satan to torment me—to keep me from exalting myself! (12:7)

Have you ever been sick and tired of being sick and tired? Perhaps you have faced many physical ailments or trials in your life and are near the breaking point. You just want to give up or give in. You wonder when your suffering will end.

Paul suffered from a "thorn in the flesh" for an unknown length of time, but probably many years, perhaps even his entire life (v. 7). On three different occasions the Apostle implored the Lord to take it away from him (v. 8). To his dismay, the Lord repeatedly refused to grant him his request (v. 9). Nevertheless, God offered him a solemn promise, "My grace is sufficient for you, for power is perfected in weakness" (v. 9).

Scholars have debated the nature of Paul's affliction. Perhaps it was a physical ailment that affected his eyesight (cf. Gal 4:13-15). Maybe it was a particular recurring temptation (cf. Rom 7:14-25). It's possible that he was referencing the continual persecution he suffered at the hands of his antagonists (cf. e.g., Acts 14:19; 21:30-32).

Although an interesting topic of conjecture, it is not really necessary to know the exact nature of Paul's distress. The focus should rather be on the Apostle's acknowledgement that it had been given to him by God so that he would not become prideful because of the "surpassing greatness of the revelations" (v. 7; cf. vv. 1-4). Paul chose to focus on the positive aspects of his affliction.

Today is a good day to thank God for the many things he has allowed in your life, even those that have caused suffering. Evaluate whether you have allowed your "thorn in the flesh" to produce a "root of bitterness" in you (Heb 12:15). Or has it produced a humble spirit of gratitude? God's grace is sufficient for you. His power is perfected in your weakness.

VE

Wednesday

CARING CONFRONTATION
Read 2 Corinthians 13

This is the third time I am coming to you. Every fact is to be confirmed by the testimony of two or three witnesses. (13:1)

Modern culture is consumed with personal preferences, quick accusations, perceived offenses, and unconfirmed indictments. Unfortunately, these attitudes and behaviors have also infiltrated our churches.

In the final chapter of 2 Corinthians, Paul informs the church that he is coming to confront them because of their sinful actions. He is not going to spare anyone (v. 2). Referencing the Mosaic Law, he acknowledges that his accusations must be confirmed by two or three witnesses (cf. Dt 17:6; 19:15). David Garland explains, "The assumption behind the law is that it is better for someone who is guilty to go unpunished because of a lack of the requisite number of witnesses than to harm an innocent person's reputation with reckless charges" (*2 Corinthians*, p. 540, Broadman & Holman, 1999).

Although confrontation of sin and proper rebuke is an integral part of the Christian life, one must also remember that the Bible has much to say about false accusations (cf. Ex 23:1, Lv 19:16, Mt 5:11, Lk 3:14). Today is a good day for you to consider the manner in which you confront those who sin against you. Yes, as Paul indicates, confrontation must take place. Nevertheless, you must take care that you have all of the facts and that the details can be confirmed by reliable and trustworthy witnesses. This is especially true if the accusation is presented against those in positions of spiritual authority (cf. 1 Tm 5:19).

Holding one another accountable to God's biblical standards is an act of love. "Better is open rebuke than love that is concealed" (Prv 27:5). It should always be done with a spirit of gentleness, lest one day you are in need of rebuke (cf. Gal 6:1).

VE

Thursday

JESUS IS LORD
Read Galatians 1

Grace to you and peace from God our Father and the Lord Jesus Christ. (1:3)

The Apostle Paul, formerly a fierce persecutor of Christians (v. 13; cf. Acts 9:1-2), addresses this letter, probably his first, to the churches in Galatia. Like many modern churches, the Galatian churches experienced their fair share of controversy, including a challenge to Paul's apostleship and authority. Nevertheless, Paul greets his readers with his customary greeting, "grace to you and peace" (v. 3; cf. e.g., Rom 1:7; 1 Cor 1:3; Eph 1:2).

Although Paul begins many letters in this way, the greeting should never be taken for granted or casually overlooked. These terms have great significance for believers. "Grace" is unearned, undeserved kindness or favor before the Lord. "Peace" has its roots in the Hebrew concept of *shalom*, which generally meant wellness, wholeness, and completeness, and it characterizes the freedom that grace brings (George, Timothy, *Galatians*, p. 85, Broadman & Holman, 1994).

Paul continues by noting the source of grace and peace—"God our Father and the Lord Jesus Christ" (v. 3). These words hint at the Trinity of God, Who exists from eternity as Father, Son, and Holy Spirit (4:6; cf. Mt 28:19; 2 Cor 13:14; Eph 1:1-14). Because He is fully God, no one can receive grace or peace apart from Jesus Christ.

Paul identifies Jesus Christ as "Lord" (v. 3). Other apostles make this same declaration. Soon after Jesus' resurrection, Thomas addressed his Master as "my Lord and my God" (Jn 20:28). In his speech at Pentecost, Peter revealed that God had made Jesus both "Lord and Christ" (Acts 2:36). Christ's lordship is indisputable and unassailable. All authority, in heaven and on earth, belongs to Him (cf. Mt 28:18). One day every knee will bow and every tongue confess, either voluntarily or involuntarily, that Jesus is Lord, and this will be done to the glory of the Father (cf. Phil 2:10-11).

Does your life exhibit evidence that you recognize Jesus as Lord? Are you living in submission to your Master?

BBH

Friday

LIVING BY FAITH IN THE SON OF GOD
Read Galatians 2

The life which I now live in the flesh I live by faith in the Son of God, Who loved me and gave Himself up for me. (2:20b)

Prior to his conversion, Paul characterized himself as a righteous Jew who lived in strict accordance with Jewish Law (1:13-14). The Law itself is "holy" (Rom 7:12), because it came from a holy God Who commanded His people to be holy, just as He is holy (cf. Lv 11:44; 19:2; 1 Pt 1:16). Since the Law reflects God's perfect standard, anyone who breaks it, either by commission or omission, stands guilty of being a breaker of the Law (cf. Jas 2:10-11). Only the God-Man, Jesus Christ, has fully kept the Law's righteous standards. For that reason, Paul maintains that sinners become "justified" (or "declared righteous") not by keeping the Law but by having faith in Christ Jesus (v. 16).

However, some in the Galatian churches, commonly identified as Judaizers, taught that Christians still needed to adhere to the Law, particularly in the area of circumcision, in order to be saved (cf. Acts 15:1). Paul argues forcefully against this assertion, because it counters the doctrine of salvation by grace—a salvation that cannot be earned by human effort. Paul declares that if anyone preaches a "different gospel" that requires adherence to the Law, then it is no gospel at all; and the propagator of such teaching is to be accursed (1:6-9).

We may not face literal Judaizers today, but all of us are prone to rely on our own works rather than on the grace of God. In those moments of self-reliance, we must turn to Christ. The eternal Son of God took on human flesh (cf. Jn 1:1, 14) and gave Himself for our sins (v. 20). Make no mistake—good works are important. We were created for good works (cf. Eph 2:10), and our faith ought to produce good works (cf. Jas 2:17, 20). However, it is only faith in Jesus that can ultimately save us (v. 16).

Upon whom/what are you relying for your salvation? Are you trusting in yourself and your own works; or is your confidence placed in the power of the risen Christ, Who loves you and gave Himself up for you?

BBH

Monday

JESUS IS REDEEMER
Read Galatians 3

Christ redeemed us from the curse of the Law, having become a curse for us—for it is written, "Cursed is everyone who hangs on a tree." (3:13)

In Genesis 12:1-3, the Lord called Abram (later named Abraham; Gn 17:5) and promised that all the families of the earth would be blessed through him. Then, in Genesis 15:5-6, the Lord established a covenant with Abram and promised that Abram's descendants would be as numerous as the stars in the heavens. When the Lord made these promises to Abram, the patriarch believed God, and he was credited with righteousness (Gn 15:6).

Christ's work of redemption on the cross made it possible for Gentiles (i.e., non-Jews) to become the promised offspring of Abram when they have faith and believe in the promises of God. But how exactly was this accomplished?

The act of redemption is the process of acquiring a slave or captive by paying a ransom and then setting that slave or captive free. For the Christian, it refers to our transfer from the kingdom of sin and death to the kingdom of life in Christ. Because God is righteous, He cannot simply ignore our sin. Everything comes at a cost. According to the Law, the blood of another had to be shed in order to deal with sin (Lv 17:11). The Law also states that anyone who hangs on a tree is cursed (Dt 21:23). Jesus hung on a tree (i.e., cross) at a place called Calvary and shed His own blood in order to pay our ransom. By doing this, the perfect Son of God became a curse, on our behalf, so that we would never experience the curse of God. When we have faith in God, like Abram, and believe in the power of Jesus to save, then He credits us with His perfect righteousness.

Thousands of years ago, the Lord promised Abram that all the families of the earth would be blessed through him. If you are a believer, then you are living proof that God keeps His promises. And it has all been made possible because of the redemptive work of Jesus Christ on the cross. Take a moment and thank the Lord for His gift of salvation. You have been redeemed!

BBH

Tuesday

AN HEIR THROUGH GOD
Read Galatians 4

Therefore you are no longer a slave, but a son; and if a son, then an heir through God. (4:7)

According to Hebrews 1:2, God has appointed His Son, Jesus Christ, as the "heir of all things." Therefore, as the heir, Christ possesses supreme authority over everything (cf. Ps 2:8; Mt 28:18; Eph 1:20-22). Scripture also teaches that Jesus is the "firstborn among many brethren" (Rom 8:29). How it is possible that believers become brothers to Jesus and heirs through God?

As Adam's descendants, we are born into sin; and we are under its power and control. Because of our sin, we are spiritually dead (Eph 2:1). We are children of wrath who naturally follow Satan, "the prince of the power of the air" (Eph 2:2). But the Father, who is rich in mercy, made us alive together with Christ (Eph 2:4-5), and adopted us as His children through Jesus (Eph 1:5).

Because Jesus is fully human and fully God, He is the only mediator between God and man (1 Tim 2:5). Because of His perfect life, His death on our behalf, and His victorious resurrection, only He can secure our adoption into God's household. When Christ redeemed us, He didn't just bring us *from* something, He also brought us *to* something. Christ brought us *from* darkness *to* light and *from* the power of Satan *to* the kingdom of God (Acts 26:18). Christ's perfect work allows repentant sinners to enter the family of God as heirs (cf. Jn 1:12-13; Mt 12:49-50). We are no longer slaves to our natural father, the devil (cf. Jn 8:44). Now we are the children of God by faith in Jesus Christ. Our natural father has no claim, no right, and no authority over us. None!

As believers, we are not defined by our relationships, our possessions, or even our own thoughts and feelings. We are defined by our Father. He declares that we are adopted heirs who are sealed by the Spirit of the Eternal Son. We are brothers of Christ and children of God. When others look at your life, do they see the family resemblance?

BBH

Wednesday

WALKING BY THE SPIRIT
Read Galatians 5

But I say, walk by the Spirit, and you will not carry out the desire of the flesh. (5:16)

As believers, there is a tug-of-war taking place in each of our lives. On one side is the Holy Spirit, Who lives in us. On the other side is our sinful flesh in which we were born. The two are in opposition to each other (v. 17). A believer's life serves as a sort of scorecard. To know which side is winning, simply look at a person's thoughts and deeds. If a saint's life is characterized by immorality, strife, and jealousy, then the flesh is winning (vv. 19-21). If a saint's life is characterized by love, joy, and self-control, then the Holy Spirit is winning (vv. 22-23).

In light of this spiritual battle, Paul exhorts his readers to "walk by the Spirit" (v. 16). "Walk" was a common way of saying "live". In other words, Paul is saying "live your life under the control of the Spirit." Notice that the Apostle's words are in the form of a command. Living by means of the Spirit should not be viewed as a suggestion—it is an order. As God's covenant people, we must live in a way that honors and glorifies Him, not ourselves.

The Father has given us the indwelling Holy Spirit to guide us in truth (cf. Jn 14:16-17). The Spirit helps us to "walk" by convicting us of sin (Jn 16:8), sanctifying us (Rom 15:16), helping us to pray as we ought (Rom 8:26), teaching us (1 Cor 3:12-13), and endowing us with gifts (1 Cor 12:7-11).

Are you walking by the Holy Spirit? Are you praying according to His guidance (Eph 6:18)? Do you get spiritual nourishment by feeding on the Word that He inspired (2 Pt 1:21)? Are you unified with other believers (1 Cor 12:13)? Are you using your spiritual gifts for the benefit of the body (1 Cor 12:7)? If not, you are quenching the Spirit (1 Thes 5:19). Be filled with the Spirit (Eph 5:18) and walk by His power.

BBH

Thursday

DO NOT GROW WEARY
Read Galatians 6

And let us not grow weary of doing good, for in due season we will reap, if we do not give up. (6:9; ESV)

In the final chapter of his letter to the Galatians, the Apostle Paul provides a series of guidelines for how believers ought to conduct themselves in the "household of the faith" (v. 10). Given the turmoil that existed in the Galatian churches, and in our own, it is not difficult to see how believers might grow weary in ministry. As we serve, it is easy to become discouraged, particularly when we do not see obvious fruit from our labor. However, we serve for the glory of the Lord and for the good of His people, not for our own satisfaction. God is worthy of all that we do.

In verse nine, Paul urges the Galatians to not become weary of doing good. He reminds his readers that their work is not in vain because they will reap a harvest. In the ancient world, "farmers were dependent upon the seasons to know when to harvest their crop. Plowing for winter crops usually did not begin until the arrival of early autumn rains. Fields were fertilized with dung, and the rain and sun brought different crops to maturity at different times" (Achtemeier, Paul J., ed., *Harper's Bible Dictionary*, p. 304, Harper & Row, 1985). In other words, the timing has to be right. Our ministries are not according to our own calendars—we are on God's schedule. Just as the Father knew the right time to send forth His Son (cf. 4:4), He knows the proper time for His people to yield a harvest.

Note that reaping comes with a condition, "If we do not grow weary" (v. 9). We must persevere in our ministries (cf. 2 Tm 4:7). All of us have a race to run (cf. 1 Cor 9:24; Heb 12:1). It is easy to run when we are in great shape and when we can see the finish line; it is much more difficult to run when we are weary and the end is far away. When we are hurting, struggling, doubting, or tired, we must keep running. The Holy Spirit will help us cross the finish line. He gives us strength every day (cf. Eph 3:16). He will reward us, in due season, if we do not grow weary.

BBH

Friday

OUR HEAVENLY RICHES
Read Ephesians 1

Blessed be the God and Father of our Lord Jesus Christ, Who has blessed us with every spiritual blessing in the heavenly places in Christ. (1:3)

In the modern world, there is a great deal of attention paid to the acquisition of material goods. From a very young age children learn what money can buy. Teenagers focus on obtaining the latest media devices and fashionable clothing. And adults, as Jesus said, are building ever larger barns in which to store wealth that they may never even use (Lk 12:18).

The first chapter of Ephesians speaks of another type of wealth—riches that far exceed the value of physical possessions. In verses 3-14, Paul writes what is commonly called "the long sentence", because it is the lengthiest such structure in the New Testament. The size of the sentence betrays its profound importance. It is the spiritual wealth of the Christian that occupies Paul's mind throughout the writing of this sentence. And he is determined to communicate these truths to the Ephesians, no matter how long it takes, so that they might understand what they possess by virtue of their faith.

The long sentence begins and ends with proclamations of praise to God ("blessed be the God," v. 3; "to the praise of His glory," v. 14) for the immeasurable wealth afforded every Christian. Three major asset classes are described that begin in eternity past and endure throughout all eternity, linked by an unbreakable chain of blessings during a believer's lifetime. The Father chose His children before time began (vv. 4-6), in time He redeemed them through the work of His Son, Jesus Christ (vv. 7-10), and beyond time He promises them an everlasting inheritance, which is sealed with the indwelling Holy Spirit (vv. 11-14).

Material goods are not inherently bad, for we are told to manage them wisely and store them up for uncertain days (cf. Prv 6:6-8). But when we are the recipients of kingdom wealth, worldly wealth loses its luster. The Christian walk becomes a form of asset management, as a believer uses those immense riches to further the kingdom, to bless others, and to glorify God.

RC

Monday

FROM DEATH TO LIFE
Read Ephesians 2

And you were dead in your trespasses and sins. (2:1)

One of the remarkable advantages of the Christian faith is that it offers explanations for many of the imponderable mysteries of life. Science certainly has its benefits, answering a few of the "what" problems about the physical universe, but it falls short concerning many of the most profound "why" questions that gnaw at the human heart.

In Ephesians two, Paul addresses one of the most obvious and unrelenting problems in life—why do we do bad things? How do we explain the history of man's inhumanity to man, the local and international crimes on our daily news, and the personal challenges we face in trying to make good decisions while inevitably finding ourselves unable to do so? Most of us want to live better lives, but how can we accomplish this?

The phrase "dead in your trespasses and sins" (v. 1) speaks of the current nature of man, which was inherited when Adam and Eve were enticed into sin (cf. Gn 3:1-7; Rom 5:12). That single act cast a long shadow over all of us, and we find ourselves in an inexorable tide of sin and wrongdoing. We are "by nature children of wrath" (v. 3). "By nature" means that we do what we do because we are fundamentally wired to do so. In other words, we sin because we are sinners.

But this bad news is immediately followed by good news. Believers are made "alive" in Christ (v. 5). They are given a new nature. The dead nature that led to inevitable wrongdoing is reversed by faith. Paul summarizes this concept in 2 Corinthians 5:17—"Therefore if anyone is in Christ, he is a new creature; the old things passed away; behold, new things have come."

Not only does the Bible explain our penchant for wrongdoing, it offers a solution—we have been saved by grace (v. 5). Death that reigned in Adam has now been reversed; those who receive the gift of righteousness will reign in life through Jesus Christ (Rom 5:14-18). Praise God for His amazing "gift" (v. 8).

RC

Tuesday

BEYOND WHAT WE ASK OR THINK
Read Ephesians 3

Now to Him Who is able to do far more abundantly beyond all that we ask or think, according to the power that works within us. (3:20)

What is the best way to pray for others? There are many important items we could pray for, including physical healing, meeting daily needs, and any number of general requests. These are legitimate prayer concerns, for we are told to pray for these things (Mt 6:11; Phil 4:6; Jas 5:14).

However, when Paul had a chance to pray for the recipients of this letter he chose different themes. In 1:15-23, he focused on the benefits of salvation, including the "surpassing greatness of His [God's] power" (1:19). In 3:14-19, he focused on spiritual growth in hopes that the Ephesians would be "strengthened with power through His Spirit in the inner man" (v. 16). The second prayer complements the first as both refer to divine power.

Immediately after the second prayer, Paul concludes the first half of the epistle by reciting a doxology that praises God for His ability to answer such prayers (vv. 20-21). Verse twenty has a pyramid structure in which one concept is built upon another for purposes of emphasis. The point is to reflect God's ever-increasing ability to answer prayer and bless His people in the inner person.

The pyramid begins with the assertion that God is "able." Next, Paul reveals that God is able to do "far more." If this were not enough, the Apostle adds that God is able to do far more "abundantly." He then continues with "beyond all." Paul is not done, he builds on his statement with the clarifying phrase "that we ask." Finally, the Apostle tops off the pyramid by adding "or think." The doxology ascends to dizzying heights. God can bless beyond our wildest dreams.

Many Christians are of the belief that if God could only grant them their own ideas, that would be sufficient. Yet God is able to exceed human notions. His divine power is able to do far, far more!

RC

Wednesday

AT PEACE WITH OTHERS
Read Ephesians 4

Being diligent to preserve the unity of the Spirit in the bond of peace. (4:3)

Individuals who experience conflict with others often pay a heavy toll. Such disputes can dissolve marriages and families, lead to loss of friends, cause problems at work, threaten our health, and create many other difficulties. Unresolved conflict can be destructive, to say the least!

Paul wants believers to resolve conflicts by showing tolerance for one another so as to maintain unity (v. 2). He bases his appeal on the fact that Christians have a common "calling" (vv. 1, 4), one unifying "Spirit" (vv. 3, 4), one corporate "body" (v. 4), and one "hope" (v. 4). Saints have one "Lord" (v. 5), one "faith" (v. 5), one "baptism" (v. 5), and one "God and Father of all" (v. 6). Because Christians are unified in so many ways, this unity should manifest itself with believers living in peace and harmony with others.

Paul commands his readers to be "diligent" (v. 3). This term emphasizes the intense effort that should be put forth in achieving unity. The word implies that the process is not an easy one. How many of us have faced this kind of difficulty, perhaps feeling that a broken relationship is beyond healing? Many times we stand at odds with another person, neither of us willing to give an inch. Persistent effort towards resolution is required.

The phrase "preserve the unity of the Spirit" adds insight as to the supernatural basis by which conflict is resolved and unity is achieved. It is not so much that we create unity with other believers; rather, we maintain what we already have by virtue of our faith. The unifying Spirit of God indwells each Christian.

Not all conflicts can be resolved (cf. Rom 12:18). After all, it takes two to tango. Jesus Himself experienced a great deal of unresolved conflict, as did His disciples and apostles. However, this fact should not be used as an excuse to give up too quickly. We should always attempt to link the desires of the Spirit Who indwells us with the same Spirit Who indwells those with whom we experience conflict.   RC

Thursday

BEING AN IMITATOR OF GOD
Read Ephesians 5

Therefore be imitators of God, as beloved children. (5:1)

When you were a child, did you ever try to imitate someone? If you are like most, you probably tried to imitate one of your parents or siblings; or perhaps when you grew older, a sports star or celebrity.

In Ephesians 5:1, we are told to imitate God. The Greek term "imitator" occurs six times in the New Testament. It means to mimic or to follow the example of someone or something. The usages beyond Ephesians involve imitation in contexts of suffering and needed endurance (1 Cor 4:16; 11:1; 1 Thes 1:6; 2:14; Heb 6:12). These passages include calls to imitate Paul (and the other apostles), inasmuch as Paul imitates Christ (1 Cor 11:1). Imitation of others is a good thing, assuming they are positive examples of the life of faith. For if we imitate godly believers, we are ultimately imitating God.

The phrase "as beloved children" (v. 1) refers to the underlying motivation to imitate God. Since God's children are beloved, they have a natural inclination to imitate their Father, from Whom they feel love. Love is a prominent theme in Ephesians, with some form of the word being found about twenty times. Love is used in reference to God's love for humans (e.g., 2:4), believers' love for Christ (e.g., 6:24), and the love that Christians should have for one another (e.g., 1:15). In 5:1, "beloved" is used to denote the demonstrated affection that God has for His children. Accordingly, those children are commanded to imitate the One Who so deeply loves them.

If we imitated a parent when we were children, it was probably because of the love we felt from that parent. As we felt their love, we longed to mimic the one loving us. In a similar way, as we are the recipients of God's unwavering affection through Jesus Christ, we should have every motivation to imitate our heavenly Father. As we love others, we reflect God's love for them.

RC

Friday

PREPARING FOR BATTLE
Read Ephesians 6

Put on the full armor of God, so that you will be able to stand firm against the schemes of the devil. (6:11)

In the Book of Ephesians, Paul emphasizes the spiritual assets of Christians (chapters 1-3) and the corresponding life that should take place as a result of those blessings (chapters 4-6). Although believers are already the recipients of immeasurable spiritual wealth, there remains the challenges of this life and the immense difficulties that come from living in a world of darkness (cf. 6:12).

When Paul wrote this epistle, he was bound in "chains" (v. 20). Undoubtedly, he found himself guarded by Roman soldiers. Accordingly, in 6:11-17, Paul uses a soldier as a metaphor for the Christian life. The metaphor highlights many of the themes of the epistle. Six elements illustrate a believer's protection: belt of "truth" (v. 14), breastplate of "righteousness" (v. 14), feet shod with the gospel of "peace" (v. 15), shield of "faith" (v. 16), helmet of "salvation" (v. 17), and "sword of the Spirit" (v. 17).

"Truth" is probably best taken as a reference to the gospel (cf. 1:13), though it may also refer to speaking truth to others (cf. 4:15, 25). "Righteousness" describes the "new self" (4:24), which replaces the "old self" that is "corrupted with the lusts of deceit" (4:22). "Peace" refers to the good news that believers have been reconciled to God (cf. 2:15-17). "Faith" is a reference to saving faith in Jesus Christ (cf. 1:15; 2:8). "Salvation" describes a believers emancipation from sin (cf. 1:13). "Sword of the Spirit" refers to the revelation given to apostles and prophets by means of the Holy Spirit (cf. 3:5; see also Is 49:2 and 2 Pt 1:21).

As believers, we need to take advantage of our armor. "For our struggle is not against flesh and blood, but against the rulers, against the powers, against the world forces of this darkness, against the spiritual forces of wickedness in the heavenly places" (v. 12). We cannot be victorious in the Christian life relying on our own power and might. Spiritual battles require spiritual weapons.

RC

Monday

REJOICING IN PRISON?
Read Philippians 1

Now I want you to know, brethren, that my circumstances have turned out for the greater progress of the gospel. (1:12)

The Apostle Paul's circumstances at the time he wrote this letter were not ideal. Paul used to be a man of renown in the Jewish community—he was the person in charge of persecuting Christians. However, now Paul finds himself being persecuted. He used to put others in prison, and here we find him imprisoned. Interestingly, instead of pitying himself, we see that Paul was able to recognize God's hand in the midst of his persecution. Many were hearing and receiving the good news of the gospel because of his imprisonment (v. 14).

In a similar way, you may feel you once had it all. Perhaps you had a great job, but then you lost it and now you find yourself reminiscent of the prestige and authority you once had. Perhaps you previously had more freedom and less responsibility, and now you find yourself just trying to make it through each day with the little energy you have left because you are carrying so many burdens.

Be encouraged! In the same way that Paul was a child of God, so you also are a child of God. Your difficult circumstances are not permanent or indicative of your life as a whole. God "causes all things to work together for good to those who love God, to those who are called according to His purpose" (Rom 8:28). As a result, I encourage you to envision your trials as opportunities for God to be glorified.

When you encounter suffering, find an opportunity to radiate God's grace, peace, love, and forgiveness to those around you. Others are drawn to God when they see you reflect His character in the midst of your difficult circumstances. So next time you find yourself in the midst of turmoil, remind yourself: let's make God shine! (cf. Ps 34:5).

LC

Tuesday

SELFISH OR SELFLESS?
Read Philippians 2

Do nothing from selfishness or empty conceit, but with humility of mind regard one another as more important than yourselves. Do not merely look out for your own personal interest, but also for the interests of others. (2:3-4)

In the context of this passage, Paul is dealing with certain individuals who were sharing the gospel with wrong motives; they were seeking glory for themselves rather than God. Paul writes that *selflessly* serving in ministry ought to take precedence over our own *selfish* ambitions and interests, despite the fact that it may result in our persecution, imprisonment, or even death!

It is doubtful that the self-seeking people Paul wrote about were willing to go through the same sufferings Paul himself went through for the sake of the gospel. They were probably seeking handouts, taking advantage of the kindness and generosity of the saints. Paul contrasts the *selfish* choices of these people with the servant-like attitudes of Timothy, Epaphroditus, and even Jesus Christ, as they are all examples of *selfless* servanthood and sacrificial love towards the saints (cf. vv. 5-11, 19-30).

The significance of a person's eternal destiny or spiritual growth should be enough of an incentive for us to minister to others, regardless of whether it results in the loss of our luxuries, health, freedom, or even our lives! Many pastors and missionaries are no strangers to this kind of sacrificial love, for they often suffer greatly while serving on the mission field or at home. Paul encourages us to hold them in high regard (v. 29).

When was the last time you served the saints sacrificially or shared Christ with someone in spite of the negative consequences? Be bold, because in your boldness to *selflessly* and lovingly serve and share Christ, you are viewing others as more important than yourself. In this way you are honoring Christ and bringing the gospel to a world in need.

LC

Wednesday

THE GIFT OF RESURRECTION
Read Philippians 3

But whatever things were gain to me, those things I have counted as loss for the sake of Christ. In order that I may attain to the resurrection from the dead. (3:7,11)

In his youth, Paul's spiritual reputation among the Jews was absolutely impeccable (cf. vv. 5-6). He was blameless as it related to the righteousness found in the Law. He had obeyed every commandment. He had done everything possible to attain a form of spiritual perfection in the eyes of his peers. But what he was lacking was spiritual perfection in the eyes of God.

Paul's experience on the road to Damascus changed everything. He quickly came to the realization that the only way to attain spiritual perfection in God's eyes was by placing his faith in the Lord Jesus Christ. And it was only through Christ that he could obtain true righteousness—the sort of righteousness necessary to secure resurrection from the dead (vv. 9-11).

All those things that Paul had previously considered good and worthy of awe were now deemed by him to be "rubbish" (v. 8). They could never compare to the "surpassing value of knowing Christ Jesus" as Lord (v. 8) and the gift of eternal life through the resurrection (v. 11).

As believers, we have all been granted this same gift. It is impossible to obtain this gift through human effort. If it were, then Paul would have done so. And no other human can ever give you this gift. It can only be acquired through faith in Christ.

What a comforting thought! This promise should carry you through the hardest circumstances in your life. Your world may one day fall apart. Someday you might lose everything that you have struggled so hard to achieve—a good reputation, a nice job, earthly possessions, meaningful relationships, etc. But in the end, all of these things will be worthless in comparison to the incredible gift of eternal fellowship with the Lord. He will wipe away all of your tears and take away all of your fears. This certainty is why Paul was able to rejoice always, even in the midst of persecution and imprisonment.

LC

Thursday

THANKFUL SPIRIT = GENTLE SPIRIT
Read Philippians 4

Let your gentle spirit be known to all men. The Lord is near. Be anxious for nothing, but in everything by prayer and supplication with thanksgiving let your requests be made known to God. (4:5-6)

As one reads Paul's letter to the church in Philippi, one can't help but notice the pattern of thankfulness exhibited by the Apostle. He is thankful that the gospel is being preached (1:12-18). He is thankful for the ministry support of Timothy and Epaphroditus (2:22-25). He is thankful because God healed Epaphroditus (2:27). He is thankful for the salvation provided by grace, and for his fellowship with Christ (cf. 3:7-10). He is thankful that his citizenship is in Heaven (3:20). And he is thankful for all the provisions sent by the Philippians (v. 18).

Paul was thankful for so many things, despite the fact that he was in prison and otherwise persecuted by those who sought to cause him distress (v. 17). His attitude of thankfulness is why Paul exhibited so much joy and such a gentle spirit. His joy and gentleness were by-products of his thankfulness.

We should follow the example set by Paul. When we dwell on the things we don't have, we become bitter. Envy and jealousy consume us. And envy and jealousy naturally lead to conflict and strife. However, when we focus our thoughts on what God has so graciously provided (e.g., salvation, Christian fellowship, loving relationships, basic necessities, etc.), then we develop an attitude of thankfulness. We are able to exhibit a "gentle spirit" to others (v. 5) because we are focused on their interests (cf. 2:4). Our anxieties dissipate and we begin to let our requests be made known to God (v. 6), trusting that He will supply all our needs according to His riches in glory (v. 19).

As you reflect on the Book of Philippians, consider the many things the Lord has given you. Thank Him for each and every one. Your attitude of thankfulness will soon manifest itself to others through your gentle spirit.

LC

Friday

JESUS IS THE IMAGE OF GOD
Read Colossians 1

He is the image of the invisible God. (1:15a)

The Apostle Paul wrote the Book of Colossians during his first Roman imprisonment (cf. 4:3, 10, 18). Paul wrote to the church at Colossae to address the false teaching that had arisen in the church, particularly regarding the deity of Christ. In 1:15-20, Paul records a hymn that directly refutes this heresy. It is unknown if Paul composed this hymn himself or if he borrowed it from another source because it perfectly suited his purpose.

The hymn begins by noting that Jesus is "the image of the invisible God" (v. 15). An image bears a likeness or resemblance to something or someone else. When Jesus asked whose image was on a denarius, the response was "Caesar's" because the image of Caesar was imprinted on the coin (Lk 20:24).

Human beings were made in the image of God (Gn 1:26-27). When others see us, they should see the reflection of God in us. However, the presence of sin has marred and perverted our divine image, and it has separated us from God (cf. Is 59:2). Now when others see us, they see a false representation of God. Humans have become false image-bearers.

Unlike fallen human beings, the sinless God-Man, Jesus Christ, resembles His Father perfectly and completely. If you want to see the Father, just look at Jesus (cf. Jn 14:9). Jesus makes God known (Jn 1:18), and in Him "all the fullness of Deity dwells in bodily form" (2:9). He radiates the Father's glory and is the "exact representation of His nature" (Heb 1:3). While Scripture is clear that Jesus is fully human (cf. Jn 1:14; Gal 4:4; Heb 2:6-18), Scripture is just as clear that Jesus is fully God (cf. Jn 1:1; 2 Pet 1:1).

As believers, we must know Who Jesus is. He is a human being with a mother and brothers and sisters (cf. Mk 3:31; 6:3). He is also the eternal God and the only way to the Father (Jn 14:6; cf. Acts 4:12). But it is not enough to just know about Jesus. We need to know Him, and know Him intimately, for in such knowledge lies eternal life (Jn 17:3).

BBH

Monday

MADE ALIVE WITH CHRIST
Read Colossians 2

When you were dead in your trespasses and the uncircumcision of your flesh, He made you alive together with Him, having forgiven us all our trespasses. (2:13)

Zombies tend to be a popular subject on television and in movies and books. They are meant to reflect something unnatural—a physically dead person who still walks and functions, albeit at a greatly reduced level.

Interestingly, sin works in a similar way. Sin has not just disfigured or hardened humans—it has killed them, just as the Lord said it would (Gn 2:17; cf. Rom 6:23). Like zombies, the spiritually dead can walk, talk, eat, and work. Many people don't even realize that they are dead. But Scripture is clear—humans are dead in their sins and trespasses (v. 13; Eph 2:1). Humans have no spiritual pulse, and they are in a hopeless state spiritually—but God ….

Because of His rich love and mercy, God "made us [those who believe] alive together with Christ" (Eph 2:4; cf. 2:13). Just as He raised Jesus from the dead (Gal 1:1), He raises believers from spiritual death (Eph 2:6).

When human beings sinned, they offended an infinite, holy God. He cannot allow their rebellion to go unpunished, so humans must suffer the consequences. An infinite violation results in an infinite debt—a debt that fallen human beings can never repay. Only one who is fully man (who represents the offending party) and one who is fully God (who represents the offended party) can satisfy such a significant debt and serve to reconcile both parties. Jesus is that debt-payer and reconciler (cf. 2 Cor 5:18-19).

For believers, Christ's death on our behalf satisfied God's wrath against sin and effectively canceled our debt (cf. Rom 3:25). With the debt cancellation comes the forgiveness of all trespasses (vv. 13-14). He died in our place so that we could have life; and when He rose from the dead, Jesus brought us with Him into resurrection life. We have moved from death to life. We are forgiven and debt-free. We have been redeemed.

BBH

Tuesday

IMAGE RESTORATION
Read Colossians 3

Do not lie to one another, since you laid aside the old self with its evil practices, and have put on the new self who is being renewed to a true knowledge according to the image of the One Who created him. (3:9-10)

Throughout this chapter, Paul provides several statements on how we ought to live in light of our redemption. Since we have been raised with Christ, we should set our minds "on the things above, not on the things that are on earth" (v. 2). Because we are alive with Christ, we should not live like we did when we were spiritually dead (vv. 5-9). Since we have been chosen by God, we should exhibit spiritual characteristics such as compassion, forgiveness, and love (vv. 12-14). Because we are one body with Christ, we should let the "peace of Christ" and the "word of Christ" richly dwell within us as we continually express thankfulness (vv. 15-17). The Holy Spirit has breathed life into us, and Paul commands us to walk in that newness of life (Rom 6:4).

Human beings were created in the image of God (Gn 1:26-27), but sin tarnished and distorted the divine image in us. In order to restore our divine image, we were indwelt by the Holy Spirit when we believed (1 Cor 6:19; 2 Tm 1:14). Since the Spirit lives in us, He causes us to be conformed to the image of Christ (Rom 8:29; Gal 2:20), Who is the perfect image of the Father (1:15). Day by day, God is restoring His image in us through the transforming power of the Holy Spirit because we are in Christ (1:27-28; 2:6-7).

We serve a God Who wants to be known (Jer 9:24; Jn 17:3); and Jesus makes God known (Jn 1:18). The more that we know Jesus, the more that we will be shaped and transformed by His Spirit. And this transformation produces the restoration of the divine image—"But we all, with unveiled face, beholding as in a mirror the glory of the Lord, are being transformed into the same image from glory to glory, just as from the Lord, the Spirit" (2 Cor 3:18).

Are you allowing the Holy Spirit to transform your life (cf. Rom 12:2; 1 Thes 5:19)? When others look at you, do they see a mirror reflection of the image of God?

BBH

Wednesday

GRACIOUS SPEECH
Read Colossians 4

Let your speech always be with grace, as though seasoned with salt, so that you will know how you should respond to each person. (4:6)

"Sticks and stones can break my bones, but words will never hurt me." Many of us are familiar with this old saying; and we can also attest to its lack of truth. Physical wounds often heal, but words can leave battle scars for the rest of a person's life. James offers a sharp warning concerning the use of the tongue (Jas 3:2-12). He explains that the tongue is impossible to tame because it is "a restless evil and full of deadly poison" (Jas 3:8). It is used to bless God and curse people, "who have been made in the likeness of God" (Jas 3:9). It "ought not to be this way" (Jas 3:10).

Since we have been made in the image of God (Gn 1:26-27), our speech should be pleasing to Him. "The Lord is gracious and merciful; slow to anger and great in lovingkindness" (Ps 145:8). Just as the Lord is gracious, so must our speech be full of grace (v. 6). Grace is unearned, underserved kindness or favor. We should always remember that God has shown us grace as we speak with grace to others.

Our speech should also be "seasoned with salt" (v. 6). Salt is a preservative. It is used to keep food fresh, not allowing it to become rotten. At times, our speech may need to be forceful and direct. However, the goal of our speech should never be to tear down another person; it must always be to preserve and to edify.

Just as the Lord is slow to anger toward us, we should be slow to speak and eager to listen, particularly when we are angry (Jas 1:19). We should never forget that we will one day have to give an account for everything we say (Mt 12:36-37). Anger will be no excuse for our careless words when we stand before the Lord. We must put aside "anger, wrath, malice, slander, and abusive speech" from our mouths (3:8). As we follow the guidance of the Holy Spirit, we will know how we should respond to each person—with grace, and seasoned with salt (v. 6).

BBH

Thursday

THE POWER OF EXAMPLE
Read 1 Thessalonians 1

Constantly bearing in mind your work of faith and labor of love and steadfastness of hope in our Lord Jesus Christ in the presence of our God and Father. (1:3)

Fair or not, our reputation forecasts what people will believe about us, even in advance of our presence. Reputations precede us wherever we go. And they are often difficult to change. In this sense, reputations have a tendency to be sticky.

Thankfully, the church in Thessalonica had a sterling reputation. Paul had first visited the city during his second missionary journey—with Silas and Timothy (cf. Acts 17:1-14). This group had just been released from prison in Philippi and had made their way southward to evangelize Thessalonica. Unfortunately, the Jews of the city were hostile to the new converts and persecuted them extensively. Paul wrote this epistle primarily to comfort and encourage the church, which was persevering in the midst of persecution.

As we read chapter one, we see that this trait of perseverance was actually passed on to them from Paul and his companions. The church had witnessed this missionary group persevering in their ministry, despite extensive persecution and imprisonment, and had become imitators of them (v. 6). The church itself then became an "example" to all the believers in Macedonia and in Achaia (v. 7).

Note Paul's use of the word example in this verse. Reputation and example are not synonyms. Reputation is what others think of you. Example, on the other hand, reflects who you actually are, because it is based on your conduct. While a reputation might impress others, an example has the power to transform others.

Reputation might be sticky, but example is downright contagious. "For the word of the Lord has sounded forth from you, not only in Macedonia and Achaia, but also in every place your faith toward God has gone forth, so that we have no need to say anything" (v. 8).

Are you worried more about your reputation or your example? Your reputation may not influence others to change their behavior, but your example should inspire them in positive and godly ways.

MA

Friday

IMAGES OF SERVANT LEADERSHIP
Read 1 Thessalonians 2

For we never came with flattering speech, as you know, nor with a pretext for greed—God is witness—nor did we seek glory from men, either from you or from others. (2:5-6a)

We are all familiar with leaders who constantly remind others of their position and title in order to intimidate them or to secure their submission. Though possessing the highest possible title and authority, Jesus chose to demonstrate a higher form of influence—that of servant leadership. His leadership style proved that when individuals who possess the right to lead through title also earn the right to lead through trust, then true leadership is expressed. And instead of merely submitting, their followers tend to be transformed.

In this chapter, Paul describes his own servant leadership. The underlying premise of servant leadership, not using one's authority for personal gain, is found in the phrase "even though as apostles of Christ we might have asserted our authority" (v. 6). He then uses three images to illustrate this kind of loving influence.

The first image is a nursing mother—"But we proved to be gentle among you, as a nursing mother tenderly cares for her own children. Having so fond an affection for you, we were well-pleased to impart to you not only the gospel of God but also our own lives" (vv. 7-8). Servant leaders love those they lead.

The second image is a faithful worker—"For you recall, brethren, our labor and hardship, how working night and day so as not to be a burden to any of you, we proclaimed to you the gospel of God" (v. 9). Servant leaders work hard and earn credibility.

The third image is a concerned father—"Just as you know how we were exhorting and encouraging and imploring each one of you as a father would his own children" (v. 11). Servant leaders share a compelling vision with those they lead.

Paul chose this form of leadership due to the outcome that only it could produce—"So that you would walk in a manner worthy of the God Who calls you into His own kingdom and glory" (v. 12). As you lead others, will you choose the path of servant leadership?

MA

Monday

COMFORT THROUGH COMMUNITY
Read 1 Thessalonians 3

For this reason, brethren, in all our distress and affliction we were comforted about you through your faith; for now we really live, if you stand firm in the Lord. (3:7-8)

Years ago, I went to a hospital to visit a man who was near death. On the way, I prayed for God to use me to bring him comfort and hope. However, during the visit this man spoke about his joy in Christ and the deep gratitude he felt for all that God had blessed him with during his long life. He expressed peace and assurance about his eternal home. When I left, I realized that I was the one who had been ministered to. I was the one who had been filled with hope and inspiration because of the visit. Have you ever gone to encourage someone only to leave as the one encouraged? This very thing happened to the Apostle Paul.

This chapter continues Paul's review of his interaction with the Thessalonians (cf. 2:1-20). The Apostle reflects back to a time when he was distanced from them and therefore concerned that they had possibly lost faith and the courage to endure. To ease his anxiety, he had dispatched Timothy to embolden and strengthen them (vv. 2-5).

However, when Timothy returned to Paul, the Apostle learned that the church was actually thriving. Their faith and courage were strong. Their love and longing for Paul had endured as well (v. 6). The news greatly lifted Paul's spirit (v. 9) as he explained, "In all our distress and affliction we were comforted about you through your faith" (v. 7).

The chapter ends with a beautiful benediction revealing Paul's great love for the church (vv. 11-13). The Apostle prays that the Lord would allow him to return to Thessalonica. He also prays for the Thessalonians, that their love for others would increase and that God would establish their hearts in holiness until the coming of Christ.

There is great strength and comfort in authentic Christian community. Are you building the kind of relationships with other believers where you can encourage them as well as be encouraged by them? May God provide for all of us this kind of biblical community!

MA

Tuesday

A DIFFERENT KIND OF GRIEF
Read 1 Thessalonians 4

But we do not want you to be uninformed, brethren, about those who are asleep, so that you will not grieve as do the rest who have no hope. (4:13)

In the classic movie The Wizard of Oz, Dorothy wished herself back home by clicking her heels and chanting the words, "There's no place like home." Almost everybody would agree. Because for most of us, our home is a place of comfort and peace, filled with the presence of loved ones.

In an effort to comfort the suffering Thessalonians, Paul describes the hope of eternity. While admitting that believers still grieve for a loved one who is "asleep" (v. 13; a euphemism for dead), the Apostle explains that believers should grieve in a unique way. They should not grieve like unbelievers, "who have no hope" (v. 13); rather, they should grieve with hope, knowing that their ultimate home is in heaven. To prove this point, Paul describes the basis for this hope.

First, this hope is based on the death and resurrection of Jesus. His death made payment for sin; His resurrection conquered death. "For if we believe that Jesus died and rose again, even so God will bring with Him those who have fallen asleep in Jesus" (v. 14).

Second, this hope is based on the word of the Lord, Who speaks truth (cf. Jn 1:14; 8:45; 14:6). "For this we say to you by the word of the Lord, that we who are alive and remain until the coming of the Lord, will not precede those who have fallen asleep" (v. 15).

Third, this hope is based on the promise of the immanent return of Christ. "For the Lord Himself will descend from heaven with a shout, with the voice of the archangel and with the trumpet of God, and the dead in Christ will rise first" (v. 16).

Paul concludes the passage by encouraging believers to "comfort one another with these words" (v. 18).

For believers, there really is no place like home—a home prepared and promised by the Lord Himself (cf. Jn 14:2-3). This reality should comfort you when you lose a loved one who is a believer. It should also cause you to grieve differently—to grieve with hope.

MA

Wednesday

THE DAY OF THE LORD
Read 1 Thessalonians 5

Now as to the times and the epochs, brethren, you have no need of anything to be written to you. For you yourselves know full well that the day of the Lord will come just like a thief in the night. (5:1-2)

Having just mentioned the return of Christ (4:16-17), Paul begins the final chapter of this letter by providing more details regarding this climactic event. He describes the unpredictable nature and impact of Christ's coming—it will happen suddenly, "like a thief in the night" (v. 2), and will be full of "destruction" (v. 3). It will take place when people don't expect it; rather, they think they are at peace and therefore safe (v. 3). In the following verses, the Apostle outlines the proper response to the Second Coming.

Paul commands saints to be "alert" (v. 6) and "sober" (vv. 6, 8); the opposite characteristics of those who "sleep" and get "drunk" (v. 7). The Greek word for "alert" means "to be awake" while the word for "sober" means "to abstain from alcohol." In using these terms, Paul was probably imagining a soldier on guard duty. Accordingly, he reminds saints of their spiritual armor—"the breastplate of faith and love, and as a helmet, the hope of salvation" (v. 8; cf. Eph 6:11-17).

Paul also commands the church to continue to encourage and build up one another with brotherly kindness (vv. 11, 14-15), with special emphasis on their spiritual leaders (vv. 12-13). These spiritual leaders are worthy of honor, respect, and appreciation as they fulfill their ministries of guiding and teaching the congregation.

The Apostle closes the section with a list of general responsibilities. He commands the church to rejoice always, pray without ceasing, and to be thankful in everything (vv. 16-18). He also admonishes believers to be responsive to the leading of the Holy Spirit (vv. 19-20) and to hold fast to that which is good, abstaining from every form of evil (vv. 21-22).

The letter concludes with a doxology and appropriate salutations (vv. 23-28). These words include a final reminder of the certainty of the Second Coming—"Faithful is He Who calls you, and He also will bring it to pass" (v. 24). Are you prepared for the Lord's return?

MA

Thursday

DEFENDING THOSE WE LOVE
Read 2 Thessalonians 1

For after all it is only just for God to repay with affliction those who afflict you, and to give relief to you who are afflicted and to us as well when the Lord Jesus will be revealed from heaven with His mighty angels in flaming fire. (1:6-7)

I was raised with two younger brothers. Although we loved each other, we often teased and argued and fought amongst ourselves. However, even though we picked on each other, none of us would allow other boys to do the same. When one of us was harassed, the others would immediately come to his defense. There is a natural tendency for humans to defend the ones we love.

Paul's first letter to the Thessalonians revealed just how deeply he loved the people of this church (cf. e.g., 1 Thes 2:8-11; 3:6-12). By the time he wrote 2 Thessalonians, the situation in the church had not changed much—they were still facing intense persecution. So the Apostle writes a second letter to once again encourage them in their suffering and in their Christian walk (vv. 4-12; 2:13-3:15) and to correct misunderstandings concerning the Lord's return (2:1-12).

The first chapter begins with a declaration of Paul's thanksgiving for the faith, love, and perseverance of the Thessalonians (vv. 3-4). He reminds the church that their suffering is a plain indication that they will be "considered worthy of the kingdom of God" (v. 5).

The Apostle's tone abruptly changes beginning in verse six. He rises up with indignation toward those who would dare persecute his beloved children in the faith. He announces that the God of justice will repay those who afflict the Thessalonians with affliction of their own (v. 6). Their fate will be "the penalty of eternal destruction, away from the presence of the Lord and from the glory of His power" (v. 9). To comfort the church, Paul reveals that God will provide relief for those afflicted. He also reminds the church that he is praying for them—that God will count them worthy of their calling (v. 11).

If you find yourself in a state of affliction, take comfort in your suffering. God will rise to your defense and give you aid. The Lord defends the ones He loves.

MA

Friday

MAN OF LAWLESSNESS
Read 2 Thessalonians 2

Now we request ... that you not be quickly shaken from your composure or be disturbed either by a spirit or a message or a letter as if from us, to the effect that the day of the Lord has come. (2:1-2)

By way of a false teacher (probably several), the Thessalonians were influenced to believe something about the return of Christ that was not only inaccurate, it also disturbed them to the point of shaking their composure and undermining their security and peace (v. 2). The false teacher had convinced the church that the Day of the Lord had come. The congregation feared they had missed the rapture—"the coming of our Lord Jesus Christ and our gathering together to Him" (v. 1). To comfort the church, Paul supplied three proofs that the Day of the Lord had not yet come.

First, the "apostasy" had not yet taken place (v. 3). The Greek word simply means "departure." Bible scholars debate whether this term refers to the literal departure of the church (v. 1; cf. 1 Thes 4:14-17; Rv 3:10) or a spiritual departure from the faith (vv. 7-12; cf. 1 Tm 4:1-3; 2 Tm 4:3-4).

Second, the "man of lawlessness" had not yet been revealed (v. 3). While the ultimate identity of this person is unknown, the Apostle provided a number of characteristics to distinguish him from ordinary men (vv. 3-4, 8-10). Most significantly, he will oppose and exalt himself "above every so-called god or object of worship" and display himself as God (v. 4; cf. Dn 11:36-37). This person is probably to be identified as the Antichrist (cf. 1 Jn 2:18, 22).

Third, the one "who now restrains" had not yet been "taken out of the way" (v. 7). This is almost assuredly a reference to the Holy Spirit, Who will be taken out of the way with the rapture of the church. Just as the church age began with the coming of the Holy Spirit (Acts 2:2-4), so it will end with the departure of the Spirit.

In light of these proofs, Paul commanded the church to stand firm and hold fast to the traditions they were taught (v. 15). When we are confronted by false teaching, let us remain steadfast, secure in the knowledge of sound doctrine (cf. 1 Tm 4:6; Ti 1:9; contra Eph 4:14).

MA

Monday

RESPONSE AND RESPONSIBILITY
Read 2 Thessalonians 3

We have confidence in the Lord concerning you, that you are doing and will continue to do what we command. (3:4)

Paul's final words to the Thessalonian church are a call for response. That response is one of Christian responsibility. This chapter outlines some very specific and practical ways for believers to act.

First, Paul commands believers to "keep away from every brother who leads an unruly life and not according to the tradition which you received from us" (v. 6). This command was designed to protect the church from negative influence.

Second, Paul commands believers to act in a disciplined manner as it relates to labor and hardship (vv. 7-13). Evidently, many in the church were taking advantage of the generous support of their fellow believers, especially in the area of food. They were not working and were instead "acting like busybodies" (v. 11). As a result, they had no right to eat the bread of others without paying for it (v. 12; cf. v. 8).

Third, Paul commands believers to remove themselves from willfully disobedient believers in hopes that this disassociation would compel the offenders to repent because of their shame (vv. 14-15). However, believers must be careful to not treat an offender as an enemy, but instead to "admonish him as a brother" (v. 15).

Paul concludes the book with a request that the Lord would grant the church "peace" (v. 16) and "grace" (v. 18). These references serve as an inclusio with 1:2, "Grace to you and peace from God our father and the Lord Jesus Christ." The Apostle also assures the church that he had written the final greeting with his own hand, as was his custom (v. 17). Silvanus or Timothy had probably written the rest of the book under Paul's direction (cf. 1:1).

Paul's second letter to the church in Thessalonica is one of great instruction and inspiration. Paul's love for these believers who are enduring in the midst of persecution is evident. As we reflect on the book, we should allow it to comfort and encourage us as well. "May the Lord direct your [our] hearts into the love of God and into the steadfastness of Christ" (v. 5)!

MA

Tuesday

LEADING WITH A CLEAR CONSCIENCE
Read 1 Timothy 1

But the goal of our instruction is love from a pure heart and a good conscience and a sincere faith. (1:5)

Fixing the leadership problems at Ephesus appears to be the principle reason the Apostle Paul wrote this letter to Timothy, his young disciple in the faith. Paul, having gone on into Macedonia, left Timothy in charge at Ephesus to halt the influence (i.e., leadership) of those who were teaching false doctrines.

The false teachers were motivated by questions related to the Old Covenant; questions that, even if they were stimulating and engaging, were not central to the gospel (cf. v. 4). These questions may have been exciting and new, and thus interesting, but they weren't useful in advancing God's work of making disciples. Pursuing these questions doesn't turn people from their sin and towards Jesus, which is the purpose of the Law (Old Covenant). Paul, by contrast, was motivated by his appointment by Jesus to be an apostle, in spite of his own sinfulness. Therefore, he reminded Timothy of the prophecies about his ministry so that these might continue to motivate his leadership.

The Ephesians were caught up in "fruitless discussion" and speculations (v. 6), primarily due to the false teachers' blasphemous doctrine. By contrast, proper teaching of the Law should lead those in sin to lives of faith, putting away their disobedience and replacing it with behavior that is consistent with sound doctrine (vv. 8-9, 15).

The false teachers had corrupted their own faith and poisoned their own hearts, leaving them vulnerable to Satan's torment. Paul calls Timothy to persevere in keeping his conscience clear, being faithful to God Who called him.

In this age of reason coupled with advances in Bible tools, it is easier than ever to explore deep theological truths, desiring to lead others in doing the same. While the pursuit of theological truth is essential, it should never take precedence over personal holiness. Effective leaders should prioritize their own holiness and faithfulness, teaching others to do the same, out of love both for God and for those they lead.

MM

Wednesday

PEACE AND QUIET AIDS THE GOSPEL
Read 1 Timothy 2

This is good and acceptable in the sight of God our Savior, Who desires all men to be saved and to come to the knowledge of the truth. (2:3-4)

The Apostle Paul wanted Timothy to rid the Ephesian church of all distractions from the gospel. Unfortunately, the freedom that the gospel brings to a person's life appears to have been motivating the Ephesian believers to behave in ways that would both distract them from spiritual growth and hinder unbelievers from coming to faith.

Perhaps the Ephesian believers began to rebel against government and other societal authorities. Since they now belonged to the kingdom of heaven, they may have become contemptuous of earthly kings. Instead, Paul encouraged them to pray for social leaders so that they would not interfere with or oppress the Ephesian church. The resultant lack of government interference, combined with godly and dignified behavior from the Ephesians, would encourage unbelievers to acknowledge Jesus as their Lord and Savior.

Similarly, as the female Ephesian believers understood themselves to now be equal in value before God to their brothers in Christ, it is likely that they began to rebel against the social norms requiring them to remain in the background or even dependent on men. Paul does affirm an order to the role of pastoral authority (men to women, not vice versa; vv. 12-13); however, his primary concern appears to be that women remain godly in their behavior (vv. 9-10). Instead of drawing attention to themselves, whether through their role in the church or through their attire, believing women are to let their good works draw others' attention to God.

Modern Christians should likewise keep their focus on removing whatever distracts from peaceful and quiet living. An unhealthy quest for discovery, self-determination, and self-expression can lead to rebellion against social norms, society's leaders, and sound doctrine. If that is what the world sees when viewing Christians, they will have to meet Jesus in spite of us rather than through us.

MM

Thursday

IS YOUR LEADER(SHIP) SETTING A GOOD EXAMPLE?
Read 1 Timothy 3

... so that you will know how one ought to conduct himself in the household of God... (3:15)

It is no wonder that Christians, including the women of the Ephesian church, might aspire to lead in the church (cf. 2:11-12). Paul reveals that the office of overseer is a noble one. Linked to the previously-ordained offices of prophet and priest, the overseer has the privilege of drawing nearer to God and to all His goodness. This is the overseer's full-time vocation (cf. 5:17-18); they should not be distracted by other responsibilities, just as Mary and Martha learned from Jesus (Lk 10:39-42). However, to whom much is given, much is required (cf. Lk 12:48), and Paul details those requirements to Timothy.

Rather than go through the list individually, think about the list as a whole. Paul provides seventeen different characteristics (depending on how one counts them). *Seventeen!* Most people have trouble just keeping the Ten Commandments, or even the greatest and second greatest commandments (cf. Mt 22:36-40). Similarly, deacons must meet nine characteristics, and their wives four. The problem for many who aspire to be overseers is that they haven't committed to building the character that a person must exhibit to be qualified for the job. They want the privileges of the office, but haven't yet become the type of person able to fill it.

Why is this so important? Because it is the proper way to protect and proclaim the mystery of Jesus Christ. God has ordered both creation and the Law so as to reveal Himself to the world (cf. Rom 1-2). He has given the church this same purpose (v. 15). Its very procedures, including the qualities of the persons conducting its activities, are ordered so as to tell the world about Jesus.

Believers do well to aspire to the offices of overseer and deacon. But they do better to aspire to exhibit a character that reflects Christ, regardless of their responsibilities in the church.

MM

Friday

THE ANTIDOTE TO FALSE TEACHING
Read 1 Timothy 4

In pointing out these things to the brethren, you will be a good servant of Christ Jesus, constantly nourished on the words of the faith and of the sound doctrine which you have been following. (4:6)

The influence of false teachers had sent the Ephesian believers off course. They apparently began practicing a religion based on works, especially works that required them to abstain from the good things of life—certain foods, marriage—that God has given us to enjoy (vv. 3-5, cf. Eccl 2:24; 5:18-20). The false teachers themselves may even have been victims of deceitful spirits and the teachings of demons, spread by those who knowingly lead people astray (v. 1).

The antidote to false teaching is sound doctrine from a godly teacher, who in this case was Timothy. Paul reminds Timothy of three attributes to his leadership that will help him resolve the leadership problem in the Ephesian church. First, Timothy was solidly grounded in sound doctrine, having been trained in God's Word from childhood (v. 6; cf. 2 Tm 3:15). Timothy lived out this doctrine though godly speech, conduct, love, faith, and purity. And this in spite of his youth—younger folks are more prone to foolishness (cf. Prv 22:15). Second, Timothy had been gifted by the Holy Spirit, probably with the ability to teach (v. 14; 2 Tm 1:14). Third, Timothy had been called to this work by Paul himself and by God (2 Tm 1:6). Note that other leaders—the council of elders—had recognized and confirmed Timothy's gifting and calling (v. 14). While Timothy may have felt this gifting and calling, Paul used the confirmation of these elders to motivate Timothy to stay firmly affixed and devoted to the difficult task of leadership.

While many may aspire to lead (and that is a good thing; cf. 3:1), Christians who know sound doctrine, live godly lives, are called by others to lead, and are recognized as gifted in teaching and leading *should* eagerly seek leadership in the church. Thus, they will fill the leadership vacuum that false teachers will so eagerly try to exploit.

MM

Monday

KEEP CHURCH FINANCES PURE
Read 1 Timothy 5

… and the church must not be burdened, so that it may assist those who are widows indeed. (5:16)

Jesus talked a lot about money (it plays a prominent role in eleven of thirty-nine parables). So it is not surprising that Paul addressed church finances in his so-called "Church Manual" to Timothy and the Ephesian church.

Paul's instructions on finances integrate neatly with James' description of pure and undefiled religion: "to visit orphans and widows in their distress, and to keep oneself unstained by the world" (Jas 1:27). Paul first singles out widows who are "widows indeed," that is, those widows who have no one to care for them and are truly in need of assistance. He then moves on to ministry leaders—those who get paid to do ministry—who have helped their congregants live holy lives. Both groups are to be supported using church finances.

Paul provides two reasons why widows and gospel workers are worthy of assistance. First, they may be completely dependent on the church for their daily provision. The widow that has Christian family members, or could through remarriage, is dependent first on her family, who should support her in obedience to God's command (vv. 4, 14; cf. Ex 20:12; Jn 19:26-27). The gospel worker has voluntarily surrendered any vocation other than the work of the ministry.

The second reason widows and gospel workers are worthy is from exemplary service. Paul labels this church assistance as an "honor" (vv. 3, 17), similar to a decoration in recognition of something that is to be exalted, given higher rank, or is deserving of greater privilege. This may be why Paul addresses this honor amidst discussion of dishonorable behavior and how Timothy is to handle those who continue in sin (v. 20).

The way a person handles their finances gives evidence of their values and priorities. Christians should carefully monitor how their church manages its finances, praying and helping to keep that handling pure and undefiled.

MM

Tuesday

HOW TO GET RICH OFF THE GOSPEL
Read 1 Timothy 6

But godliness actually is a means of great gain when accompanied by contentment. (6:6)

Having opened his letter addressing the central problem of false teachers at Ephesus, the Apostle Paul now closes the letter by revealing the central motivations of the false teachers—gaining fame, allegiance, and wealth. The false teachers accomplished this by creating an "us" vs. "them" mentality. The false prophets claimed to know more than "them", slandered "them", made "us" jealous of "them" and covetous of "their" privilege. This tension and controversy proved to be very effective, attracting those prone to willful depravity, who willingly enrich those who affirm them. And all of this was done under the guise of ministry, which was nevertheless revealed to be false because of its divergence from sound doctrine and through the ungodly behavior of those who fell prey to the false teachers.

The funny thing is that one can actually gain great wealth from the gospel itself. It's just that gospel wealth is not necessarily of this physical world, but rather belongs to the eternal world that believers enter after death. For Paul, this is what believers should strive after (cf. Col 3:2). All that is needed of this world is that which is needed in this world: food, clothing, and basic necessities (v. 8). When believers strive after anything more, they open themselves to being led away from the gospel, ultimately finding ruin and destruction (v. 9).

But what of believers who do achieve earthly wealth? Their focus should remain the same: *heavenly* not earthly treasure. While these believers have the additional challenge of remembering that God, not their wealth, is their security (v. 17), they also have the additional opportunity to give generously (v. 18), like the believer who furnished the upper room for the Last Supper (Mk 14:14-15).

The desire for the wealth of this world led astray the Ephesian false teachers and their followers. Godly believers should instead strive for spiritual treasure both in this world and the next.

MM

Wednesday

ENTRUSTED WITH TREASURE
Read 2 Timothy 1

Guard, through the Holy Spirit Who dwells in us, the treasure which has been entrusted to you. (1:14)

Imagine you had one last opportunity to write a letter to your closest friend or brother or sister in the Lord before you left this world. What would you write? What would be your focus?

In 2 Timothy, the Apostle Paul had such an opportunity. Yes, his letter was divinely inspired by the very Spirit of God. Yet it reveals the humanity and passion of a man who truly believed the gospel is a priceless treasure. It also reveals a man concerned for his spiritual son in the faith who was facing hardship for that gospel (cf. v. 8; 2:3). Paul wanted Timothy to understand that the resurrection hope we have in Christ is worth any difficulty, any hardship, and any persecution we may face in this lifetime in His service. Accordingly, he exhorted Timothy to persevere in serving Christ.

Thus, the aged Apostle—facing his final hardship (i.e., awaiting execution for his faith)—commanded his beloved friend to "guard … the treasure" (v. 14). The preceding verse makes it clear that this "treasure" is the gospel message. Paul had previously written: "O Timothy, guard what has been entrusted to you, avoiding worldly and empty chatter and the opposing arguments of what is falsely called 'knowledge'" (1 Tm 6:20).

The world system and its leader—Satan (cf. 2 Cor 4:4)—want people to turn away from the conviction that the Word of God is absolute truth. Our enemies want us to turn elsewhere to find solace and hope in the midst of difficulty. Paul wanted to encourage Timothy and all believers to persevere and guard the priceless treasure of the Word.

Do you believe that the Word is a priceless treasure? Are you willing to defend its purity and sufficiency? Guard the Word. We do this by reading it, by living obediently in light of its commands, and by telling others what it says and means. In a word—we believe it.

May God strengthen you today to guard the treasure He has entrusted to you.

WB

Thursday

A SACRED TRUST
Read 2 Timothy 2

The things which you have heard from me in the presence of many witnesses, entrust these to faithful men who will be able to teach others also. (2:2)

Paul wrote the words cited above to Timothy approximately 2000 years ago. You are reading these words today because they were obeyed and applied by generations of believers. Faithful teachers taught faithful students who themselves became faithful teachers—year after year, decade after decade, century after century. And because of the faithfulness of God's Word through these diligent believers, we are now beneficiaries of the glorious news of salvation in Jesus Christ.

Paul was nearing the end of his earthly journey as he wrote 2 Timothy. His protégé, Timothy, was going to face opposition and difficulty, and within a few decades he too would finish his race. But he would be faithful to place the truths of God's Word before trustworthy believers, who would in turn place them before other trustworthy believers to carry on the sacred trust.

As those who believe that the God-Man, Jesus Christ, has risen from the dead to save sinners (cf. v. 8), we too have a responsibility to guard and pass on this life-changing news. It is our primary earthly mission for the glory of our risen Savior.

Every Christian has a unique gift (cf. 1 Pt 4:10). Timothy was Paul's representative in Ephesus. He served in a role perhaps roughly comparable to a modern pastor. We may not all be apostolic delegates or pastor-teachers, but we all have a gift by which we serve. We are all called to be disciples and to make disciples by teaching them to observe the commandments of the Lord (cf. Mt 28:18-20).

Whether you are a pastor or parent or simply as a peer, you have the responsibility to share what you have learned from God's Word. As you do, the sacred trust is carried forward, and saved men and women from every tribe, tongue, and nation will be gathered to praise our wondrous Savior and Lord forever. Be faithful to your sacred trust!

WB

Friday

~~DEATH~~ PERSECUTION AND TAXES
Read 2 Timothy 3

Indeed, all who desire to live godly in Christ Jesus will be persecuted. (3:12)

You have probably heard the old saying, "There are only two things in life that are sure—death and taxes." But biblically speaking, it may be better to replace "death" with "persecution". The Bible teaches that some will escape death at the rapture (cf. 1 Cor 15:51-54; 1 Thes 4:17). But here in verse twelve, Paul makes it clear that no one who truly desires to live for Christ in this world will escape persecution.

In this epistle, the Apostle encourages Timothy to stand firm and to be faithful to the truth of God's Word, even in the face of false teaching and false teachers. Like Timothy, we live in the difficult days of the last times (v. 1)—the New Testament era. Many people hold to a form of godliness, but deny its power (v. 5). Grace instructs in godliness (cf. Ti 2:11-12). But false teaching promotes religious learning that is ultimately compatible with love of self, love of money, and love of pleasure rather than the love of God (vv. 2-4).

Paul commands Timothy to continue in the things he had learned—the truth of God's Word (vv. 14-15). Since the Scriptures are God-breathed, they are sufficient to instruct us, to tell us where we are wrong, to show us what is true, and to train us in doing what is right (v. 16). If we are going to stand firm in the face of false teaching and false loves, we must continue in God's Word. We should not be surprised if we are persecuted while we seek to genuinely love like Christ.

Persecution in some cultures means imprisonment, physical torture, and perhaps even death. In other cultures it may simply consist of the laughter of others and the ridicule that you are just a little too radical in your faith. But make no mistake about it—persecution is more sure for the faithful believer than death and taxes.

Give yourself to the Scriptures and the Holy Spirit will equip you for every good work that God has called you to accomplish for Jesus' sake.

WB

Monday

LOOKING TO THE CROWN
Read 2 Timothy 4

In the future there is laid up for me the crown of righteousness, which the Lord, the righteous Judge, will award to me on that day; and not only to me, but also to all who have loved His appearing. (4:8)

As Paul penned this epistle, he knew that his earthly life was nearing its end—he would soon offer up his life's blood to God as an offering (v. 6). He could now say that he had fought the good fight, finished the course, and kept the faith (v. 7). But his sustaining hope was not in the fight itself—for fighting without something to gain is futile. Rather, the Apostle looked forward to God's crowning gift in glory (v. 8).

Notably, Paul widened the application beyond his own personal hope. The crown of righteousness was not Paul's personal reward—it was for "all who have loved [Christ's] appearing." In ancient times, the term "crown" was associated with a victor's wreath given to the winner of a race or competition. The crown of righteousness may then be understood to be the perfect righteousness of Christ that we now possess in position, but will fully receive in Christ's presence when we see Him face to face (cf. 1 Jn 3:2).

The ultimate motivation for remaining steadfast while facing difficulty in the Christian life is the privilege of perfectly reflecting the glory and righteousness of the One Who is infinitely worthy—the One Who has given us His righteousness. Imagine how wonderful it will be to never again fail in our actions or attitudes to honor and love Jesus Christ as He deserves! We will never again fail to love others. All that we think and do will be right and righteous—just as Jesus is righteous.

Paul encouraged Timothy that until that day, he was to "be sober in all things, endure hardship, do the work of an evangelist" and "fulfill [his] ministry" (v. 5). We too have a ministry to fulfill—people to talk to about Christ, difficulties to face in our faith, and stray thoughts to bring under subjection to the truth of the Scriptures. Live today in light of the crown of righteousness that awaits you as you longingly look forward to the appearing of Jesus Christ.

WB

Tuesday

CHOSEN OF GOD
Read Titus 1

Paul, a bond-servant of God and an apostle of Jesus Christ, for the faith of those chosen of God. (1:1a)

The fact that believers are "chosen" (v. 1) is an amazing theological concept. The Bible is full of stories of individuals who were chosen by God before they were even born. While in their mother's womb, Jacob was chosen over Esau, "For though the twins were not yet born and had not done anything good or bad, so that God's purpose according to His choice would stand, not because of works but because of Him Who calls, it was said to her, 'The older will serve the younger'" (Rom 9:11-12; cf. Gn 25:23). God selected and appointed Jeremiah before his birth to be His prophet, "Before I formed you in the womb I knew you, and before you were born I consecrated you; I have appointed you a prophet to the nations" (Jer 1:5). John the Baptist, who was "filled with the Holy Spirit while yet in his mother's womb" (Lk 1:15), was selected and set apart to be the forerunner of the Messiah prior to his birth (Lk 1:13-17). And, of course, the Savior, Jesus Christ, was appointed to be a sacrificial "lamb" to save people from their sins "before the foundation of the world" (1 Pt 1:19-20; cf. Mt 1:20-21).

This concept is summed up in Paul's words to Timothy, "Who has saved us and called us with a holy calling, not according to our works, but according to His own purpose and grace which was granted us in Christ Jesus from all eternity" (2 Tm 1:9). Accordingly, as Paul writes to Titus, those chosen of God have "the hope of eternal life, which God, Who cannot lie, promised long ages ago" (v. 2).

This concept encouraged Paul to persevere in his ministry, "For this reason I endure all things for the sake of those who are chosen, so that they also may obtain the salvation which is in Christ Jesus and with it eternal glory" (2 Tm 2:10).

This concept should also encourage us to persevere in our ministries. We have been chosen by God. Therefore, we have the hope of eternal life, which was promised by Him—"Faithful is He Who calls you, and He also will bring it to pass" (1 Thes 5:24).

MS

Wednesday

ZEALOUS FOR GOOD DEEDS
Read Titus 2

In all things show yourself to be an example of good deeds. (2:7a)

Sound doctrine is designed by God to produce good works. Accordingly, Paul charged Titus to admonish the various groups within the church to adhere to that general principle. Titus was to preach "the things which are fitting for sound doctrine" (v. 1). These included the responsibility to be "sound in faith" (v. 2) and "sound in speech" (v. 8).

Titus himself was to provide the Cretan believers with "an example of good deeds" (v. 7) in life, doctrine, and speech, so that "the opponent will be put to shame" (v. 8). "Opponent" is probably a singular reference to the collective "those who contradict" in 1:9 (cf. 1:10-16). These individuals "profess to know God, but by their deeds they deny Him, being detestable and disobedient and worthless for any good deed" (1:16).

Paul knew that a proper understanding of sound doctrine would correct the wrong behavior of these Cretans. He wrote, "For the grace of God has appeared, bringing salvation to all men, instructing us to deny ungodliness and worldly desires and to live sensibly, righteously, and godly in the present age" (vv. 11-12). A correct view of the grace of God should manifest itself in godly behavior, such as that demonstrated by the elders of the church (cf. 1:5-9). Correspondingly, an incorrect view of the grace of God will probably manifest itself in ungodly behavior, such as that demonstrated by the "rebellious" individuals in the church (1:10; cf. 1:16).

Jesus Christ died "to redeem us from every lawless deed, and to purify for Himself a people for His own possession" (v. 14). We who have been purchased by the Lord are "His workmanship, created in Christ Jesus for good works, which God prepared beforehand so that we would walk in them" (Eph 2:10). In light of the fact that we have been redeemed by Christ, let us please our Savior by being "zealous for good deeds" (v. 14)!

MS

Thursday

FROM GRACE TO GODLINESS
Read Titus 3

He saved us, not on the basis of deeds which we have done in righteousness, but according to His mercy. (3:5a)

Using five infinitives, Paul commanded Titus to remind the believers of their responsibilities toward civil authorities and the unsaved. First, they were to be "subject to rulers" (v. 1). Second, they were to be "obedient" to authorities (v. 1). Third, they were to be "ready for every good deed" (v. 1). Fourth, they were to "malign no one" (v. 2). And fifth, they were to be "peaceable, gentle, showing every consideration for all men" (v. 2).

The reason why believers should be respectful and considerate of unbelievers is because they acted just like them prior to their salvation, "For we also once were foolish ourselves, disobedient, deceived, enslaved to various lusts and pleasures, spending our life in malice and envy, hateful, hating one another" (v. 3). Just as God was able to save the Cretan believers apart from any moral reformation on their part, so He is also able to save the Cretan unbelievers in spite of their wicked deeds (cf. vv. 4-7). However, those who have been saved must subsequently "be careful to engage in good deeds" (v. 8).

Paul then instructed Titus to avoid those types of dialogue that are spiritually unprofitable and cause divisions, "But avoid foolish controversies and genealogies and strife and disputes about the Law, for they are unprofitable and worthless" (v. 9). Those who engage in these activities are to be rejected if they do not respond to multiple warnings (v. 10).

After some personal remarks, Paul closed the epistle with a challenge that is still applicable for modern believers. "Our people must also learn to engage in good deeds to meet pressing needs, so that they will not be unfruitful" (v. 14; cf. Jas 2:15-16).

Good deeds are necessary to demonstrate our faith to unbelievers (vv. 1-8), to promote unity among believers (vv. 9-11), and to meet the needs of others (v. 14). Let us "deny ungodliness and worldly desires" and strive to "live sensibly, righteously, and godly in the present age" (2:12)!

MS

Friday

THE COST OF BEING A LITTLE CHRIST
Read Philemon

But if he has wronged you in any way or owes you anything, charge that to my account. (18)

Philemon is the shortest of Paul's epistles, and it is the only letter that does not mention the death and resurrection of Jesus. In this letter, Paul asks Philemon, a prominent leader of the church at Colossae, to accept back Onesimus, a runaway slave who likely stole from Philemon. Paul met Onesimus in prison and discipled him as a son (v. 10).

Paul's request would have seemed radical to his first century audience—the Apostle asks a prominent slave owner (Philemon) to regard Onesimus (Philemon's slave) as not only an equal, but as a "beloved brother" (v. 16).

This epistle is likewise potentially offensive to a modern American reader in the wake of Christian abolitionism and the twentieth century civil rights movement. Surprisingly, Paul's epistle never explicitly prohibits the institution of slavery in the church. In fact, Paul actively avoids making a command of any kind in this letter (v. 8) because he knows that Jesus's "new commandment" (Jn 13:34) was a law of love, not legalism. Paul encouraged Philemon to make the decision by his "own free will" (v. 14) as he stressed the change in Onesimus since his conversion—he is now "useful" whereas he was formerly "useless" (v. 11). Paul anticipates that Philemon will do even more than what he asks (v. 21).

In this book, Paul takes on the status of a "little Christ" (cf. Acts 11:26), essentially challenging Philemon to follow his example (cf. 1 Cor 4:16; Phil 3:17). Paul *himself* even offers to redeem Onesimus in order to reconcile the relationship between these two men. Paul's appeal to "charge that to my account" (v. 18) embodies the very nature of Christ, who took on the sin of all humanity in order to reconcile us with a holy God.

We are called to be Christ to others, and Paul's example with Onesimus shows one way we can do just that. How can you exemplify God's love and Christ's sacrifice to actively participate in reconciling a broken relationship?

BH

Monday

EVEN THE ANGELS WORSHIP HIM
Read Hebrews 1

And when He again brings the Firstborn into the world, He says, "And let all the angels of God worship Him." (1:5)

The Book of Hebrews was written to Jewish Christians who were considering reverting back to the Mosaic Covenant to avoid suffering and persecution at the hands of their fellow Jews. The author emphasized the superior person, institution, and life Christ offers to encourage these believers to persevere instead of experiencing the negative consequences of reverting back to Judaism.

The opening chapter begins with an argument for the supremacy of the revelation of the Son over the revelation given through the Old Testament prophets. While God spoke in a variety of ways through prophets in ages past (v. 1), in these last days He has spoken through His Heir, Jesus Christ, Who is the exact representation of His divine nature (vv. 2-3). In other words, Jesus Himself is the revelation of God (cf. Jn 14:9; Col 1:15). Seeing God in person is better than hearing Him speak through His prophets.

The author then presents his next argument—that Jesus is "better than the angels, as He has inherited a more excellent name than they" (v. 4). That name is the very name of God Himself—God the Father addresses the Son with the title "God" in verse eight. And because the Son is God, the Father commands the angels to worship Him (v. 6; cf. Phil 2:10). The next time someone knocks on your door and denies that Jesus is God, show them this passage. God the Father calls the Son God and demands that the angels worship Him.

If the God of the universe commands His angels to worship Jesus as God (v. 6), then we should worship Him as well. If the God of the universe calls Jesus Lord (v. 10), then we should submit to His lordship. If Jesus loves righteousness and hates lawlessness (v. 9), then we should act accordingly. Praise God that He has given us His Son, Who is greater than even the most powerful of angels. When Satan tempts us to sin, let us rely on the power of the Son to defeat him (cf. 2:14; Eph 6:10-11).

JP

Tuesday

DRIFTING AWAY
Read Hebrews 2

For this reason we must pay much closer attention to what we have heard, so that we do not drift away from it. (2:1)

This chapter continues the theme of chapter one, i.e., the supremacy of Jesus over the angels. The chapter begins with a reminder that angels were the means by which the Mosaic Law was delivered (v. 2; cf. Acts 7:53; Gal 3:19). The author then argues that if the revelation provided by these inferior angels, who are simply ministering spirits to humans (1:14), proved steadfast, then certainly the superior revelation provided by the Son, which is able to grant salvation, would prove steadfast as well (vv. 2-3). Therefore, believers should pay even closer attention to the revelation brought by the Son (v. 1; cf. v. 3) than they did to the revelation brought by the angels (i.e., the Mosaic Law). If believers fail to do so, then they are in danger of drifting away (v. 1). The Greek word that is translated "drift" in verse one was often used of a ship that was drifting without an anchor to secure it in place. The author later reveals that a believer's hope in the promises of God, Who cannot lie, serves as an anchor to their soul, thereby making it "sure and steadfast" (6:19).

Steve Sullivan, a professor at the College of Biblical Studies, often warns his students that an individual's major sinful failure is rarely an unexpected blowout—instead, it is usually the result of a small leak. A believer rarely goes from being a faithful spouse to committing adultery in a single day. Typically, there are many small transgressions along the way that lead to the climactic sinful act.

Every move that the original audience made towards returning to Judaism brought them further and further away from Christ. And those who committed such transgressions were not going to be able to "escape" the judgment of God (v. 14). If the simple act of picking up wood on the Sabbath could result in a person's death (cf. Nm 15:32-36), then surely God will judge those who turn their backs on His Son.

Believers are either tied securely to the revelation of God or they are drifting away. Make sure your anchor is sure and steadfast.

JP

Wednesday

THE DANGER OF SIN'S DECEIT
Read Hebrews 3

But encourage one another day after day, as long as it is still called 'Today,' so that none of you will be hardened by the deceitfulness of sin. (3:13)

By demonstrating that Jesus was superior to the Old Testament prophets and the angels (chapters 1-2), the author of Hebrews was ultimately arguing that Jesus was superior to the Mosaic Covenant.

In this chapter, the author of Hebrews shows that Jesus is a superior leader for the Jewish people—even greater than Moses. Jesus, the Apostle and High Priest (v. 1), is greater than Moses because of His superior position and role. Moses was indeed faithful as a servant of God (v. 5). But Jesus is faithful as a Son (v. 6). And a servant will never be greater than a Son.

In light of His superior position, the author of Hebrews encourages the audience to maintain their confidence in Jesus and His promised reward until the end, as opposed to reverting to Judaism (v. 6). To emphasize the urgency of the command, the author quotes from Psalm 95:7-11 (vv. 7-11). This quotation is used to warn the audience that they should not harden their hearts like their ancestors did when they faced trials (v. 8). As a result of their unfaithfulness, the Israelites were forced to wander for forty years and ultimately were not allowed to enter the Promised Land, where they had the opportunity to finally experience rest (vv. 9-11).

The author then warns his audience against exhibiting a similar "evil, unbelieving heart" (v. 12). Instead, they should encourage each other daily, so that they will not become "hardened by the deceitfulness of sin" (v. 13). When individuals choose to wait to repent from their sin, they open themselves up to its deceitful qualities. The sin that once offended an individual slowly becomes more tolerable, then it becomes a normal part of their life, and eventually they endorse the transgression.

Has the Lord been pricking your conscience about a specific sin in your life? Respond today, before you become so deceived that you no longer feel conviction, and before you experience divine discipline. JP

Thursday

THE COMPASSIONATE HIGH PRIEST
Read Hebrews 4

For we do not have a high priest who cannot sympathize with our weaknesses, but One Who has been tempted in all things as we are, yet without sin. (4:15)

This chapter begins with a discussion of the rest that had been mentioned at the end of the previous chapter (vv. 1-13; cf. 3:18-19). However, in verse fourteen the author starts a new argument based on the fact that Jesus serves as a High Priest. The author had previously identified Christ as the "Apostle and High Priest of our confession" (3:1). In 3:2-19, the author focused on the "Apostle" designation, showing that Jesus is superior to Moses. Beginning in 4:14, the focus shifts to Aaron as Jesus is shown to be a greater "High Priest" than the first Levitical priest. In the intervening verses, the author demonstrates Christ's superiority to Joshua (vv. 1-13).

Joshua was supposed to provide the Israelites with rest as he led the conquest of the Promised Land. However, he was ultimately unable to provide that rest because of a lack of faith on the part of the Israelites. The audience of Hebrews probably felt that by returning to the Mosaic Covenant they would be able to avoid persecution, but what they were really doing was jeopardizing their potential rest.

What is that rest? In his sermon entitled "The Promise of Rest", Don Soula provides a list of the essential elements associated with the Old Testament idea of rest: 1) God's presence with His people (Ex 33:14); 2) living in the Promised Land (Dt 12:9-10); 3) Israel ruling over the land (Dt 28:13); 4) the removal of Israel's enemies (Dt 12:10); and 5) a righteous king on the throne (2 Sm 7:12-16). Soula ultimately concludes that the rest referred to in this passage is a promise made in Exodus 33:14, not fully experienced today, that will be fulfilled when Jesus returns to earth.

The good news is that we can experience a spiritual rest by living a life of faithful obedience. This is possible because Jesus is our High Priest. He was tempted just as we are. As a result, He is able to sympathize with our weaknesses (v. 15). Let us cling to our compassionate High Priest today, so that we can receive mercy and grace (v. 16).

JP

Friday

GROWN BABIES
Read Hebrews 5

For though by this time you ought to be teachers, you have need again for someone to teach you the elementary principles of the oracles of God, and you have come to need milk and not solid food. (5:12)

In 4:14, the author began to demonstrate that Jesus is superior to Aaron, who is representative of the entire Levitical priesthood. Whereas other high priests are beset with weakness (v. 2), Jesus is sufficient. Even though other priests received their calling from God (v. 4), Jesus was given a unique calling as the Son of God. Many Jews in the original audience would have questioned Jesus' qualifications to be a priest since He was not from the tribe of Levi (cf. Nm 3:6-10). To answer this objection, the author shows that Jesus was a priest according to the superior order of Melchizedek, the mysterious high priest to whom Abraham gave a tithe (vv. 6, 10; cf. Gn 14:18-20).

The author wants to explain the relationship between Jesus and Melchizedek in more detail, however, he finds it difficult to continue, because his audience has become "dull of hearing" (v. 11). This designation continues the author's indictment of his readers. In 2:1, he warned them about drifting away from what they had heard. In 3:13, he warned them about the deceitfulness of sin. And here in this passage, he says that they have to relearn the "elementary principles of the oracles of God" (v. 12). By the time of this letter, the original audience should have been full of mature believers who were capable of teaching others (v. 12). However, they still resembled spiritual infants because they were not discerning between good and evil (v. 14).

Dave Anderson, pastor of Faith Bible Church, often says "Light accepted brings more light and light rejected brings more darkness." The point is that we are usually growing or diminishing in our faith—we rarely stay the same. The difference between a baby and an adult is that a baby needs someone to feed them while an adult can feed themselves (and others). If you are a spiritual baby, then it is natural that you find yourself in need of nourishment. But if you have been saved for a number of years, then you should be teaching others. Seek the maturity that is found in learning and obeying God's Word.

JP

Monday

SIMILAR SOIL, DISSIMILAR RESULTS
Read Hebrews 6

For ground that drinks the rain which often falls on it and brings forth vegetation useful to those for whose sake it is also tilled, receives a blessing from God; but if it yields thorns and thistles, it is worthless and close to being cursed, and it ends up being burned. (6:7-8)

In the previous chapter, the author rebuked his audience, declaring that they needed someone to once again teach them "the elementary principles of the oracles of God" (5:12). In this chapter, the author provides several examples of these elementary doctrines (vv. 1-2): 1) repentance from dead works; 2) faith toward God; 3) instruction about washings; 4) laying on of hands; 5) the resurrection of the dead; and 6) eternal judgment. The author urges his audience to leave these elementary doctrines and press on to maturity (v. 1).

Verses four through six are often used as a proof text by those who believe that Christians can lose their salvation. However, if this passage does teach that someone can lose their salvation, then it also says that it is impossible to get it back (v. 6). This view is also at odds with a number of passages that strongly support eternal security (e.g., Jn 10:27-29; Rom 8:26-39; Eph 1:11-14; 1 Pt 1:3-5).

Another common argument is that these individuals were never believers to begin with. However, the descriptive phrases in verses four and five do not support that position. The Greek word translated "enlightened" is used in 10:32 to describes individuals who have a "lasting" possession (10:34). The word translated "tasted" means to fully experience something when it is used to describe Jesus tasting death in 2:9. And the word translated "partakers" is used to describe holy brethren that are destined for heaven in 3:1.

Using an agricultural illustration, the author shows that similar soil can receive the same rain with dissimilar results (vv. 7-8). The soil that produces fruit receives blessings while the soil that produces thorns and thistles is burned. A farmer burns soil to increase its fruitfulness. The same Greek word translated "burned" is used in the Septuagint translation of Isaiah 4:4 to describe divine discipline on Israel. Are you producing fruit or thorns? Will you be blessed or disciplined? JP

Tuesday

NEW LAW, NEW PRIEST
Read Hebrews 7

For when the priesthood is changed, of necessity there takes place a change of law also. (7:12)

After the digression of 5:11-6:20, the author returns to the subject of Jesus as "a High Priest according to the order of Melchizedek" (5:10). The priesthood was of crucial importance to the Mosaic Law, and, as such, to the Jewish people as well. But a change of law required a change in high priest (v. 12). Jesus was not a descendent of Levi; therefore, he could not meet the qualification needed to be a Levitical priest (cf. Nm 3:6-10). However, Jesus could qualify as a priest according to the order of Melchizedek (vv. 15-17).

The Melchizedekian priesthood was superior to the Levitical priesthood in several ways. First, the Melchizedekian priest was eternal and righteous (vv. 2-3, 24, 26), as opposed to the temporary and sinful Levitical priests of the Mosaic Covenant (vv. 23, 27). Second, Levitical priests had to offer up sacrifices daily (v. 27) while Jesus offered up a single sacrifice that lasted forever (v. 27). Third, Levitical priests were never able to make anyone perfect (vv. 11, 19), in contrast to the Son, Who was made perfect forever (v. 28). Fourth, Abraham (and, by proxy, Levi) demonstrated the superiority of the Melchizedekian priesthood when he offered tithes to Melchizedek (vv. 4, 6-7, 9-10; cf. Gn 14:20).

The church is not required to submit to the requirements of the Law as a rule of life. As Tony Evans observed in one of his sermons, "Christians are to honor the revelation of the Mosaic Law without having to submit to all of its requirements" (cf. Rom 10:4). Unfortunately, some denominations try to require Christians to submit to cherry-picked aspects of the Mosaic Law, whether it be tithing, or observing a Saturday Sabbath, or adhering to dietary restrictions. As the author of Hebrews observes, these stipulations were never able to make anyone perfect (v. 19).

Are you trying to be made perfect by keeping the requirements of some man-made list of obligations? Or are you drawing near to your High Priest, Who lives to make intercession for you (v. 25)?

JP

Wednesday

NEW COVENANT, SAME RECIPIENTS
Read Hebrews 8

"Behold, days are coming," says the Lord, "when I will effect a new covenant with the house of Israel and with the house of Judah." (8:8b)

This chapter describes how the New Covenant is superior to the Mosaic Covenant. The fact that Jesus "has taken His seat at the right hand of the throne of the Majesty in the heavens" (v. 1) has resulted in a "more excellent ministry" (v. 6). This is primarily due to His new role as "mediator of a better covenant" (v. 6).

The author quotes Jeremiah 31:31-34 to show that the Old Testament had predicted that a New Covenant would replace the Mosaic Covenant. If it had been possible for the Israelites to have been made perfect by the Mosaic Covenant, then there would have been no need for a New Covenant (v. 7). However, because of the deficiencies of the Mosaic Covenant, it was replaced by the New Covenant. When it was replaced, the Mosaic Covenant became "obsolete" (v. 13).

The New Covenant promises were given to "the house of Israel" and "the house of Judah" (v. 8; cf. Jer 31:31). These two entities (Northern and Southern Kingdoms) compose the reunited nation of Israel—the same national group that had been given the Mosaic Covenant (v. 9; cf. Jer 31:32). The New Covenant includes both spiritual blessings (e.g., laws written on hearts [v. 10; cf. Jer 31:33], knowledge of God [v. 12; cf. Jer 31:34], forgiveness of sins [v. 12; cf. Jer 31:34]) and physical blessings (e.g., rebuilt Jerusalem [Jer 31:38], expanded Jerusalem [Jer 31:39], divine protection for Jerusalem [Jer 31:40]).

The New Covenant can only be fulfilled when Israel receives all of the aforementioned blessings. The church is a beneficiary of the covenant, even though it is not the direct recipient. When I married my wife, I promised to love her for better, for worse, in sickness and health, until death do us part. If I fail to do all of those things, then I have not fulfilled my covenant. When my son gets married, I have no covenant obligation to his wife, but she will benefit from the covenant I made with my wife. In the same way, the church benefits from the New Covenant by virtue of our marriage to Christ. But God will still fulfill His covenant promises to His wife—Israel (cf. Is 62:4-5).

JP

Thursday

BETTER BLOOD
Read Hebrews 9

And according to the Law, one may almost say, all things are cleansed with blood, and without shedding of blood there is no forgiveness. (9:22)

This chapter describes why the death of Jesus was necessary—to accomplish the forgiveness of sin.

The Mosaic Covenant contained a number of regulations to make divine worship in an earthly sanctuary possible (v. 1). It required a Tabernacle consisting of an outer section and an inner section, called the Holy of Holies (vv. 2-5). Priests routinely entered the outer section to perform the duties associated with the sacred service (v. 6). However, the High Priest alone entered the Holy of Holies once a year on the Day of Atonement to offer blood for himself and the sins of the nation (v. 7).

Unfortunately, the work performed in the Tabernacle was unable to cleanse the conscience of the worshiper (vv. 9-10). In contrast, Jesus Christ, the superior High Priest, entered into the greater heavenly tabernacle with His perfect blood, once for all, thus securing eternal redemption (vv. 11-12). It was only through the work of Christ that a worshiper could attain a clean conscience (v. 14). As a result of His sacrificial act, Christ became the mediator of a New Covenant (v. 15), because His death had made the Mosaic Covenant "obsolete" (8:13). This New Covenant guarantees believers an eternal inheritance (v. 15).

Christ's death was necessary in the same way that a will is not in effect until the one who made it dies—a covenant necessitates the death of the testator (vv. 16-17). Just as the Mosaic Covenant was inaugurated with blood (vv. 18-21), so must the New Covenant be inaugurated with blood (vv. 23-24).

Verse twenty-two makes the specific point that, according to the Mosaic Law, forgiveness for sin usually required a blood sacrifice. The lone exception was the flour offering of the poor who could not afford two turtledoves (Lv 5:11). Yet even then the blood of Jesus was necessary for the expiation of that sin. If God takes sin seriously enough to require blood to forgive it, shouldn't we do the same with our sin? JP

Friday

EVERY SAINT IS PERFECT
Read Hebrews 10

For by one offering He has perfected forever those who are being sanctified. (10:14; NKJV)

We have all heard the statement, "Nobody's perfect." Most Christians would probably modify that statement to say "Only Jesus is perfect." However, these statements directly contradict the truth of Hebrews 10:14. In this verse, the author makes the argument that Christ "has perfected" (Greek perfect tense which indicates a completed action in the past with results continuing into the present) those who are "being sanctified" (Greek present passive participle). This verse provides believers with a beautiful picture of how Jesus has positionally perfected them through His blood with His imputed righteousness while He continues to progressively sanctify their attitudes and actions to reflect His holiness. As a result, Christians can live their lives with the knowledge that they are already considered perfect judicially before God while Jesus continues to perfect their actions.

In this chapter, the author continues the theme of the benefits of the once-and-for-all sacrifice Christ made by the perfect sacrifice of His own blood (vv. 1-14; cf. 9:11-28). This sacrifice provides believers with direct access to God. Because their hearts are cleansed and their bodies washed, believers can boldly approach the throne of grace with a clean conscience (vv. 15-22).

Unfortunately, the audience was struggling to resist the temptation to return to Judaism, which would result in their forsaking assembling with other believers (vv. 23-25). Because the sacrifice of Jesus had made the Mosaic Law "obsolete" (8:13), there no longer remained an offering for sin (vv. 18, 26). The ritual sacrifice of bulls and goats would not be able to prevent the judgment and discipline that awaited those believers who chose to disregard the sanctifying blood of Jesus (vv. 26-29). Thus, the author encouraged these believers to endure by focusing on their eternal possession (vv. 30-39).

The Christian life is difficult and painful. But we can confidently and boldly approach the throne of grace to get the strength to endure whatever difficulties and temptations come our way.

JP

Monday

THE GREAT REWARDER
Read Hebrews 11

And without faith it is impossible to please Him, for he who comes to God must believe that He is and that He is a rewarder of those who seek Him. (11:6)

Growing up in the Catholic church, I often got the impression that God's goal was to make my life as difficult and painful as possible. And while the Christian life is certainly difficult (cf. 10:32-34), an important element of faith is the belief that God rewards those who seek Him (v. 6). This doctrine can certainly be taken to an extreme (e.g., prosperity theology), but Christians make a theological error when they act as though God does not reward faithfulness in this life or the next.

At this point, the author of Hebrews has demonstrated that Christ is superior to the angels (chapters 1-2), Moses (chapters 3-4), and Aaron (chapters 5-10). The final three chapters of the book describe the superior life that Christ provides. Collectively, these thirteen chapters were designed to encourage the original audience to resist the temptation to return to Judaism in order to avoid persecution.

In this chapter, the author shows that the history of faith was always one that was focused on a certain, future, unseen reward. He reviews the lives of great forefathers like Abraham, Joseph, Moses, and David while also commending the faith of people we would not necessarily expect to see on the list (e.g., Gideon, Barak, Samson, and Jephthah). Many times these lives of faith meant enduring incredible difficulties, including mockings, scourgings, imprisonments, stonings, gruesome deaths, and a variety of other afflictions (vv. 36-38). Even though these individuals gave outward evidence of the faith that resided within them, they still did not receive what had been promised to them (v. 39). It is not until the Second Coming (10:34-37) that they will be made perfect together with the church (v. 40).

As you reflect on your own life, have confidence that God will greatly reward your faithfulness. Think about those individuals you have encountered who have modeled a life of faith and thank the Lord that He has placed them in your path. JP

Tuesday

THE FATHER'S LOVING DISCIPLINE
Read Hebrews 12

For those whom the Lord loves He disciplines, and He scourges every son whom He receives. (12:6)

The Bible is full of interesting opposites. In the Book of Hebrews, the author uses both the carrot and the stick to encourage his readers to persevere in the midst of their persecution. At the end of the previous chapter, the author reminded his audience of the great reward they have to look forward to at the Second Coming (11:40; cf. 10:36-37). In this chapter, the author warns his audience concerning the discipline they will receive from God if they are not faithful.

Hebrews twelve transitions from the great heroes of the faith in the Old Testament to Jesus, Who also endured hardship in this life for the greater eternal reward in the next (vv. 1-2). Jesus endured continuous persecution from the commencement of His ministry until His death. Thus, He serves as the ultimate example for the audience, who had not yet experienced that level of persecution (vv. 3-4).

To motivate his audience, the author quotes Proverbs 3:11-12 regarding the discipline of the Lord. He encourages them not to regard the discipline of the Lord lightly nor to become discouraged because this discipline is a sign of God's love for them. As a parent, if my child is doing the same disobedient thing that one of his or her friends is doing, I may not say anything directly to the friend, but my child can be certain that their own disobedience will be addressed. Why? Because the friend is not under my direct authority. However, my child is my responsibility and is under my authority.

When believers experience God's discipline, it may seem unfair to them, especially when they see unbelievers doing the same thing and seemingly getting away scot-free. However, believers must remember that unbelievers will ultimately receive their just penalty in hell. The discipline God provides to believers is not for our ultimate harm, but for our ultimate good, so that we can be partakers in His holiness (v. 10). The goal is to produce the fruit of righteousness (v. 11).

Be thankful, not resentful, when you experience divine discipline. God is treating you as His child, whom He loves (v. 7).

JP

Wednesday

HONOR MARRIAGE
Read Hebrews 13

Marriage is to be held in honor among all, and the marriage bed is to be undefiled; for fornicators and adulterers God will judge. (13:4)

In the final chapter of the Book of Hebrews, the author exhorts his audience to live obediently in a variety of different areas in light of all they have learned. Those who read this letter are encouraged to continue in their firm love for the brethren, especially those who are prisoners (vv. 1-3), to honor the marriage bed (v. 4), to avoid greed (vv. 5-6), and to imitate the faith of those who spoke the Word of God to them (v. 7). The author then reminds his audience that Jesus Christ is unchanging so that they would not be carried away by false teaching (vv. 8-9). He charges them to continually offer up spiritual sacrifices to God based on the sacrifice of Christ (vv. 10-16). He admonishes them to obey their leaders and submit to them (v. 17). He concludes the book with a number of personal remarks (vv. 18-25).

An essential aspect of obeying God is loving one's spouse. Marriage should be held in great honor. It is to be highly valued because it is precious, unique, and ordained by God (cf. Gn 2:20-24; Mal 2:10-16). Unfortunately, we live in a society where many do not fully appreciate marriage. They minimize the value of marriage by engaging in divorce, adultery, and sex outside of the marital relationship between a husband and wife.

The author of Hebrews identifies two sins that defile the marriage bed: fornication and adultery (v. 4). This list covers sexual sins committed by single, unmarried, individuals as well as sexual sins committed by those who are married. Singles are to keep their marriage bed pure by not engaging in any sexual activities prior to marriage. These activities constitute fornication. Married couples are to keep their marriage bed pure by avoiding all forms of adultery, including lusting after others (cf. Mt 5:28). Those who commit sexual sin will inevitably bring God's judgment upon themselves (v. 4).

Are you honoring your future (in the case of singles) or present (in the case of married couples) marriage bed? If not, confess your sin and repent. For God will surely judge fornicators and adulterers.

JP

Thursday

WORSHIP HIM BY ASKING FOR WISDOM
Read James 1

But if any of you lacks wisdom, let him ask of God, Who gives to all generously and without reproach, and it will be given to him. (1:5)

Someone has said that the mark of a wise man is that he knows that he isn't. Understanding one's need for wisdom is perhaps the first step toward finding wisdom. And more often than not, we come to recognize our need for wisdom while in the midst of difficult circumstances.

The Book of James was written to help believers discern the difference between heavenly wisdom and earthly wisdom (cf. 3:13-18). Here in chapter one, James reveals that heavenly wisdom can be found in the midst of earthly trials simply by asking God (v. 5).

Saints will often ask God for wisdom, while in reality they don't really want to persevere in faith and joy in the midst of a difficulty (cf. vv. 2-6). They actually want to escape or bypass the difficulty altogether. James bluntly states what these believers can expect from their faithless prayers—"For that man ought not to expect that he will receive anything from the Lord, being a double-minded man, unstable in all his ways" (vv. 7-8).

But when a saint prays with confidence, asking that God supply the wisdom necessary to endure with joy, then "it will be given to him" (v. 5). The Father will give generously, not reluctantly. And He will not scold His children for having to ask Him for help. He is eager and lavish in His provision of wisdom—so that believers might know and enjoy Him more, even in the pain of trials.

Are you struggling to find joy in the midst of your difficulties? Ask your Father for the practical skill to take your thoughts captive and rejoice in the reality that your trials are making you more like His Son. Do you sometimes wonder how best to approach a certain situation for the glory of Christ? Ask God for the will and strength to persevere in honoring Him while that trial persists.

As we await the crown of life, which the Lord has promised to all who love Him (v. 12), our Father is pleased to give us the help we need during difficult times. Worship Him by asking for wisdom.

WB

Friday

ARE YOU JUSTIFIED BY FAITH OR WORKS?
Read James 2

You see that a man is justified by works and not by faith alone. (2:24)

At first glance, the startling assertion by James that a man is not justified by faith alone (v. 24) seems to be at odds with Paul's declaration in Galatians 2:16—"knowing that a man is not justified by the works of the Law but through faith in Christ Jesus, even we have believed in Christ Jesus, so that we may be justified by faith in Christ and not by the works of the Law; since by the works of the Law no flesh will be justified." However, the key to harmonizing these two statements is to understand the larger contexts surrounding them.

In Galatians, Paul was unpacking one of the core doctrines of the gospel, namely, salvation by grace. In doing so, He used the term "justified" in a legal sense. In other words, previously guilty sinners are judicially declared innocent with the result that they are now found to be in right standing with God based on their faith in Christ Jesus alone, not by performing the works of the Law.

James, however, was making a practical argument that heavenly wisdom calls believers to live in light of their profession of faith. He contends, "What use is it, my brethren, if someone says he has faith but he has no works?" (v. 14). He later adds, "But someone may well say, 'You have faith and I have works; show me your faith without the works, and I will show you my faith by my works'" (v. 18).

As can be seen, Paul was writing in doctrinal and theological terms, whereas James was writing in practical and relational terms. James was essentially saying, "Talk is cheap; if you claim to believe in Christ, the only way to justify or validate that claim so that others can see it is through your works."

Paul wanted believers to understand that they are vindicated before God by faith alone in Christ alone (as a gift of grace alone). James wanted believers to realize that their claims of faith are validated before men by the deeds that flow from their faith.

Praise the Lord that we are justified by faith alone, for we can do nothing to earn judicial righteousness before God. And may our praise be justified before men as we live out the life of faith.

WB

Monday

TEACH YOUR TONGUE SELF-CONTROL
Read James 3

With it we bless our Lord and Father, and with it we curse men, who have been made in the likeness of God; from the same mouth come both blessing and cursing. My brethren, these things ought not to be this way. (3:9-10)

The purpose of the Book of James is to help persecuted believers persevere in their faith by pointing them to heavenly wisdom. In this chapter, the author focuses on taming the tongue.

According to Proverbs 18:21, "Death and life are in the power of the tongue." The tongue is diminutive in size, but deadly in strength (vv. 5, 8). The world's wisdom says to lash out and take what you think is yours—even if it means tearing down others. However, God's wisdom commands believers to bridle their tongues (v. 2).

When facing difficult circumstances, a person's lips can produce praise or poison. Sadly, even the speech of believers is often a mixture of praise directed toward the Godhead coupled with poison directed toward those individuals that cause headaches, even though they "have been made in the likeness of God" (v. 9).

James gets to the heart of the matter in the following chapter. He says the root problem is one of heart desires and allegiances (4:1-4). We want things; and when we don't get our way, we lash out. We love what the world loves—not what God loves.

If a person's speech reveals that bitter water is tainting the fresh (v. 11), then how can that individual purify their well? The answer is found in humility and repentance (4:6-10). James says, "Draw near to God and He will draw near to you. Cleanse your hands, you sinners; and purify your hearts, you double-minded" (4:8). In short, we can only teach our tongues self-control when we are willing to repent of wanting what we want more than what God wants for us.

Ask God for the grace of humility before Him and others. Draw near to Him in your thoughts through His Word. When you do, your words will be Spirit-filled and your fountain will turn from bitter to sweet. Your praise will no longer be tainted by the contamination of pride.

WB

Tuesday

TRUSTING IN TOMORROW
Read James 4

Come now, you who say, "Today or tomorrow we will ...." Yet you do not know what your life will be like tomorrow. Instead, you ought to say, "If the Lord wills, we will live and also do this or that." (4:13, 14a, 15)

It is almost overwhelming to think about how many things we do every day without giving the slightest thought to God's providence. When the alarm clock goes off, we make our coffee, brush our teeth, drive to work, and go about our lives—all too often never really grasping the truth that these mundane activities, as well as those we deem to be important, are all in the hands of our sovereign Savior.

The Lord Jesus Christ "upholds all things by the word of His power" (Heb 1:3). Proverbs 16:33 reads, "The lot is cast into the lap, but its every decision is from the Lord." In Christ "all things hold together" (Col 1:17). In other words, whether or not we are able to make coffee, brush our teeth, and drive to work depends on the wisdom, faithfulness, and sovereign power of Jesus Christ.

In the flow of thought of this chapter, James has moved from a discussion of quarrels and conflicts (vv. 1-5) to the solution of humility before God (vv. 6-10), and on to the related subjects of condemning others (vv. 11-12) and boasting in tomorrow (vv. 13-17). These last two subjects are related because we all have the propensity to subtly think *we* are sovereign. We condemn others who don't agree with our supreme designs and we assume that we will be able to accomplish the plans we have for ourselves.

Few believers would admit to these tendencies because most would agree that God alone is sovereign. But in practice we often live as if we are the judge and as if we control what happens tomorrow. Instead, we should submit to God's sovereignty. He alone is Judge and He alone determines what the future holds.

Yes, we make real decisions that have real consequences—good and bad. But God is sovereign over them all. So trust that the Lord will judge others in His wisdom and sovereign timing. Trust that He will direct your steps as you make plans. Don't trust in tomorrow—but trust Christ with tomorrow. And enjoy His peace today!

WB

Wednesday

PERSPECTIVE, PERSEVERANCE, PRAYER
Read James 5

Therefore be patient, brethren, until the coming of the Lord. The farmer waits for the precious produce of the soil, being patient about it, until it gets the early and late rains. (5:7)

In this chapter, James highlights the importance of having the proper perspective, persevering in trials, and praying in every circumstance.

James begins by confronting a wrong perspective on wealth (vv. 1-6). Trusting in one's wealth, hoarding riches, and treating others with contempt will result in a miserable eternity.

James then discusses the idea of perseverance with the proper perspective—i.e., looking to the return of the Lord as the ultimate treasure (vv. 7-12). A farmer works and waits patiently for the proper time to harvest and enjoy the fruit of his labors (v. 7). The prophets of God patiently suffered while waiting for His kingdom (v. 10). And Job—the epitome of a faithful man suffering in a fallen world—patiently endured until God's compassion was revealed (v. 11).

Putting your hope in wealth ends in judgment and misery. Putting your hope in Christ ends with compassion and comfort. In the meantime, believers will surely face sadness and joy—times of sickness and health. How then are we to live in light of heaven's wisdom while persevering until the return of Christ?

"Is anyone among you suffering? Then he must pray" (v. 13a). "Is anyone cheerful? He is to sing praises" (v. 13b). If anyone is weak, he should ask mature believers to pray for him (v. 14). Prayer in every circumstance is the key to living out heavenly wisdom. Don't trust in earthly power and pensions—trust in God through prayer and praise. Just as Elijah prayed and the Lord revealed His glory and power (vv. 17-18), so too our prayers can accomplish much for His glory.

Ask the Lord to grant you a heavenly perspective about life in this fallen world (vv. 1-6), to strengthen you to persevere while waiting for Christ's return (vv. 7-12), and to inhabit your praise and ennoble your prayers as you seek to live for Him (vv. 13-18). Finally, remember to always seek the welfare of others (vv. 19-20). Do these things and the harvest of heavenly wisdom will surely come.

WB

Thursday

THIS WORLD IS NOT MY HOME
Read 1 Peter 1

In this you greatly rejoice, even though now for a little while, if necessary, you have been distressed by various trials. (1:6)

On the night Jesus was betrayed, He warned His disciples that after His departure they would face difficulty and trouble in this world. Yet Jesus also encouraged His disciples to be courageous, because He had overcome the world (cf. Jn 16:33). Approximately thirty years later, the Apostle Peter wrote to the elect believers in Asia Minor to encourage them in the midst of their suffering. Following the pattern of Jesus, Peter reminded his readers of the living hope they have in Christ. This living hope sustains believers in the midst of their suffering and the various trials they face (cf. 5:10).

Peter begins chapter one with a reminder to believers that they are aliens in this temporal world (v. 1). He further reminds them that they are "born again to a living hope through the resurrection of Jesus Christ from the dead" (v. 3). Accordingly, believers have a permanent heavenly inheritance that will never decay, be defiled, or be destroyed (v. 4). These foundational realities are the basis for their living hope.

These truths are also the basis for great rejoicing—even in the midst of the griefs, sorrows, and trials of life (v. 6). These trials, no matter how severe, are temporary—believers will only suffer "for a little while" (v. 6). But a believer's inheritance is permanent.

Believers will only experience trials "if necessary" (v. 6). The sovereign God, Whose power protects their inheritance and guarantees their salvation (v. 5), will only allow what His perfect wisdom deems "necessary" for each believer's "good" (Rom 8:28). God does not promise believers freedom from trials; rather, He uses trials to test believers so that they can demonstrate the proof of their faith with great joy (vv. 7-8).

If you're in the midst of a fiery trial, ask the Lord to fill you with the "joy of [His] salvation" (Ps 51:12). Keep your focus on your eternal home (cf. Phil 3:20). This will compel you to "greatly rejoice with joy inexpressible and full of glory" (v. 8).

ZB

Friday

ACTING LIKE BABIES?
Read 1 Peter 2

Like newborn babies, long for the pure milk of the Word, so that by it you may grow in respect to salvation. (2:2)

After reminding the suffering believers in Asia Minor of the greatness and glory of their eternal salvation in chapter one, the Apostle Peter calls on them to live in light of that great salvation here in chapter two.

Since the Word of God was the means of their salvation through the new birth (1:23), Peter commands his audience to "long for the pure milk of the Word" (v. 2). He adds the clarifying phrase "like newborn babies" to illustrate the degree of hunger and passion believers should have for the Scriptures. Nursing babies are most satisfied and content when nestled in their mother's arms, drinking eagerly of the milk that enables them to grow. In a similar way, to grow and mature spiritually, believers must diligently crave the nourishment provided by the Word of God.

As believers grow in their faith, they serve as "living stones" in a "spiritual house" that is being built "for a holy priesthood" (v. 5). As priests (v. 9), believers "offer up spiritual sacrifices acceptable to God through Jesus Christ" (v. 5). These spiritual sacrifices consist of the fruit produced by a believer's godly lifestyle (vv. 11-12). Mature believers are then able to "proclaim the excellencies" of God as His chosen witnesses (v. 9).

The Word of God informs and encourages a believer's worship of God. It trains believers to submit to those in positions of authority, knowing that they are the representatives of God as the ultimate authority (2:13-3:7). Through holy living and showing honor to all people, believers find favor with God.

Set aside time every day to read God's Word so that you can grow and thrive in your relationship with Christ. Put aside influences and attitudes that keep you from spending time in the Word. Ask the Holy Spirit to increase your appetite to know the Scriptures. As it relates to the desire to know God through His Word, thirsting like a newborn baby is not only acceptable, it is commanded!

ZB

Monday

THE HOPE THAT IS IN YOU
Read 1 Peter 3

But sanctify Christ as Lord in your hearts, always being ready to make a defense to everyone who asks you to give an account for the hope that is in you, yet with gentleness and reverence. (3:15)

Peter continues his discussion of godly submission (cf. 2:13-14, 18) by focusing on marital relationships (vv. 1-7). He encourages wives to have a "gentle and quiet spirit" (v. 4) as they conduct themselves in a "chaste and respectful" manner (v. 2). Husbands are commanded to be "understanding" with their wives and to show them "honor" (v. 7). These submissive, humble relationships reflect Christ's submission and humility as He obediently performed the will of His Father (cf. Phil 2:3-8).

Spirit-filled relationships that are "harmonious, sympathetic, brotherly, kindhearted, and humble" (v. 8) are unique in our broken world. Even more unique are the qualities of self-restraint, graciousness, honesty, and righteousness, especially when suffering hardship and persecution (vv. 9-14). As believers pursue these qualities, Christ's love and the hope they have in Him will radiate to those with whom they come into contact.

Therefore, Peter urges believers to always be ready to make a defense and to give an account to everyone who asks about their hope (v. 15). A believer's hope is alive, because Jesus is alive and their inheritance is eternal (cf. 1:3-5). The living hope of believers compels them to be humble in the midst of suffering, because their Savior not only suffered, but through forgiveness of their sins reconciled them back to God (cf. 2:21-25).

Do your life and actions give evidence of your hope in Christ? If you are living a submissive, humble life of faith, those around you will ask you about your living hope. You will have many opportunities to share your hope with others, but always be mindful to do so with "gentleness and reverence" (v. 15). You can defend the faith and endure persecution without being defensive. Ask God to help you communicate to others—by how you live and what you say—that Jesus is your living hope and peace in the midst of life's difficulties.

ZB

Tuesday

SUFFERING, SUBMISSION, AND SERVICE
Read 1 Peter 4

As each one has received a special gift, employ it in serving one another as good stewards of the manifold grace of God. (4:10)

When we are suffering, we are often tempted to withdraw and protect ourselves. This is very natural and in some sense proper. But if we are to stand firm in the true grace of God (cf. 5:12), we need to pursue something that might seem counter-intuitive when going through difficulty—using our God-given spiritual giftedness to serve others (vv. 10-11).

Unfortunately, many believers struggle to believe that they are specially gifted. Perhaps they are even unaware as to the nature of this type of giftedness. But Peter's words are clear—every believer has received a gift (v. 10). And every believer is a steward of that gift, which is a product of the "manifold" grace of God (v. 10). The term "manifold" means "many colored"—God's gifts are as varied as God's people.

Spiritual gifts are designed to be used in service to others (v. 10) "so that in all things God may be glorified through Jesus Christ, to Whom belongs the glory and dominion forever and ever" (v. 11). When believers use their gifts (e.g., "speaking the utterances of God" or serving others) in God's strength, they do so for the glory of their great Savior (v. 11).

Notably, even when believers serve others for the glory of God, they may experience fiery trials (v. 12). These trials should not come as a surprise; rather, they are to be expected (v. 12). Believers should rejoice in the midst of these trials because they provide an opportunity to share in the sufferings of Christ and will ultimately lead to blessing (vv. 13-14). Instead of relying on human effort and sinful means to alleviate these trials, believers are called upon to simply entrust themselves to their faithful Creator (v. 19).

If you are not currently experiencing suffering or trials, praise the Lord! But you will eventually. If you are suffering, submit yourself to God, and serve others with the gifts and strength He provides. In doing so, you will glorify your Savior.

ZB

Wednesday

STAND FIRM AGAINST THE DEVIL
Read 1 Peter 5

Be of sober spirit, be on the alert. Your adversary, the devil, prowls around like a roaring lion, seeking someone to devour. But resist him, firm in your faith ... I have written to you briefly, exhorting and testifying that this is the true grace of God. Stand firm in it! (5:8-9a, 12b)

Peter begins his final chapter with a list of exhortations for the spiritual leaders in his audience. He urges his fellow elders to shepherd their congregations voluntarily, with eagerness, and as examples to their flocks (vv. 2-3). He then reminds them of their future reward for faithful service—"an unfading crown of glory" (v. 4). These shepherds help protect their flocks against roaring lions (cf. v. 8).

There are two common mistakes believers make as it relates to spiritual warfare. They either underestimate the reality that the devil is an actual being, exceedingly hostile to God and His people, or they overestimate his power and become preoccupied with speculations that are not revealed in God's Word.

Peter addresses and corrects both mistakes. The commands to "be of sober spirit" and "be on the alert" are clear calls for believers to take their enemy seriously (v. 8). They need self-control in their thinking and actions and they need to be spiritually awake. The devil is depicted as a roaring lion on the hunt wanting to destroy the faith and witness of believers (v. 8).

But the devil is not omnipotent—he can be resisted. Instead of calling on believers to fight Satan with words or offensive actions, Peter commands them to take up a defensive position, "Resist him, firm in your faith" (v. 9). Trusting in the Word of God is the key to victory in the spiritual battle. It involves knowing that "no temptation has overtaken [believers] but such as is common to man" and that "God is faithful" and "will not allow [believers] to be tempted beyond what [they] are able" to endure—He will always provide a "way of escape" (1 Cor 10:13). Victory does not come by attacking the devil, but by standing firm, trusting in God's faithfulness.

Always be alert to the schemes of the devil. When you face temptations, stand firm, knowing there will always be a way of escape.

ZB

Thursday

PERFECT PROVISION
Read 2 Peter 1

Seeing that His divine power has granted to us everything pertaining to life and godliness, through the true knowledge of Him Who called us by His own glory and excellence. (1:3)

As Peter wrote what he knew would be his final inspired letter to believers, he chose to remind his audience of things they already knew (v. 12; cf. 3:1), so that they would be on guard against error and grow in the grace and knowledge of Christ (3:18).

The first chapter of the book is a reminder concerning the faith. All believers have the same essential faith as the apostles (v. 1). And all are responsible to actively live out their faith in a way that culminates in love (vv. 5-7). Believers are to use this epistle, along with the rest of the Word of God, as a guide as they pursue their life of faith (vv. 13-21).

As Peter reminds his readers, believers already have everything they need to live this life of faith (v. 3). This includes both their present possession (v. 4) and their future inheritance (v. 11). There is nothing lacking—believers have been "made complete" in Christ (Col 2:10).

This divine provision has been given to believers as a gift from their all-powerful Lord. It is accessed "through the true knowledge of [God]" (v. 3). When believers were regenerated, they were given spiritual life and illumination by the Holy Spirit. They were then able to see the glory and excellence of Christ with faith-filled eyes. Their access to everything they need to live a life of godliness for their Savior comes through that same focus on His splendor and perfections—which are revealed in the Word of God.

As you strive for godliness in your own life, don't look to emotional gimmicks or religious rituals. Instead, look to the Word of God, which reveals the beauty and majesty of Jesus Christ. Ponder His glory and excellence, and fix your eyes on Him, the "author and perfecter of faith" (Heb 12:2). You will then be useful and fruitful (v. 8), you will have spiritual vision (v. 9), and you will "never stumble" (v. 10).

RK

Friday

NOAH ... AND LOT?
Read 2 Peter 2

... the Lord knows how to rescue the godly from temptation, and to keep the unrighteous under punishment for the day of judgment. (2:9)

Can a believer lose their salvation? This chapter helps answer this critical question. In this passage, Peter reminds his audience that false teachers would soon infiltrate the church (v. 1). He describes their character as corrupt, and warns many will be deceived by their teaching (vv. 2-3). Yet, in the midst of this warning, Peter cited two examples of God's faithfulness in preserving believers from the future judgment of unbelievers. Notably, he chose Noah and Lot (vv. 5-8).

Both Noah and Lot lived in societies that were ripe for divine judgment. And indeed, judgment came—through a flood (Gn 7), and through fire from heaven (Gn 19:24-25). Yet, God preserved His own. We might have expected Noah to be delivered, since he was a righteous man, both in his faith and in his actions (Gn 6:8-9).

Lot, however, is a much more complicated character. He left Abram's land for the greener pastures of the valley near Sodom (Gn 13:1-11). He initially lived close to (Gn 13:12), but then in Sodom (Gn 14:12), a city known for its great wickedness (Gn 13:13). Accordingly, he was captured by the city's enemies (Gn 14:1-12). Amazingly enough, once he had been rescued by Abram (Gn 14:13-16), he returned to live in Sodom, even occupying a position of honor by sitting in the gate of the city (Gn 19:1). By returning, Lot exposed his daughters to grave dangers before the depraved men of the city (cf. Gn 19:8). In fact, Lot even agreed to allow his daughters to marry some of the men of Sodom (Gn 19:14). And this doesn't even account for his later sexual relations *with* his daughters (Gn 19:31-38).

Despite these actions, Peter twice called Lot "righteous" (vv. 7-8). Why? Because Lot believed the Lord (Gn 19:14; cf. Gn 15:6; Rom 4:5). And, because he believed, God graciously protected Lot from divine judgment. Our Lord rescues all those who believe in Him—no matter whether they are faithful (Noah) or less than faithful (Lot).

Praise God for His grace and faithfulness! False teachers will certainly lead many astray, but all those who truly believe in Christ will be delivered from the destruction to come. RK

Monday

LIVING IN LIGHT OF THE DAY OF THE LORD
Read 2 Peter 3

Know this first of all, that in the last days mockers will come with their mocking, following after their own lusts, and saying, "Where is the promise of His coming? For ever since the fathers fell asleep, all continues just as it was from the beginning of creation." (3:3-4)

As the Apostle Peter's earthly life was coming to a close, he wrote to believers to remind them of certain essential truths they needed to keep in mind in order to grow in the Christian life. They had everything they needed to keep the *faith* (chapter one). They were responsible to be on guard against the error of *false teachers* (chapter two). And they must continue to live in light of the *future coming of Christ* to judge the world (chapter three).

To prepare his audience for the last days, Peter warned them that many will mock the promise of Christ's return (vv. 3-4). These mockers will point to the fact that generation after generation has come and gone and life has remained largely as it has always been. So, they reason, life will continue as it always has. In response, Peter points out that they believe this because it suits their own "lusts" (v. 3)—they want the world to continue without divine accountability.

Believers, however, must remember that the delay is not due to divine impotence, indifference, or inactivity—but rather because God is exercising divine patience and mercy toward sinners (v. 9). The Lord takes no pleasure in the death of the wicked; He would rather see them repent and live (cf. Ez 18:23).

Peter then emphatically declares that the Day of the Lord will surely come. For many, it will come unexpectedly—"like a thief" (v. 10). When He returns, Christ will destroy all that has been corrupted by sin and not redeemed by His blood (vv. 10, 12). He will then create new heavens and a new earth where righteousness dwells (v. 13).

Are you prepared for the coming of Christ and the judgment to follow? Since His return is certain, be diligent to be found "spotless and blameless" (v. 14). Live out your faith "in holy conduct and godliness" (v. 11). "Guard" against error (v. 17). And "grow in the grace and knowledge of our Lord and Savior Jesus Christ" (v. 18).

RK

Tuesday

FELLOWSHIP WITH GOD AND OTHERS
Read 1 John 1

What we have seen and heard we proclaim to you also, so that you too may have fellowship with us; and indeed our fellowship is with the Father, and with His Son Jesus Christ. (1:3)

Although 1 John does not contain a statement of authorship, the early church overwhelmingly assigned it to the Apostle John. One reason why is because this letter repeats several key words and themes introduced in John's Gospel (e.g., beginning, light, darkness, love, truth, Father, Son, etc.). Assuming John is the author, it is likely that the recipients were the same churches addressed in Revelation 1-3 (cf. Rv 1:11). John's overarching goals are to encourage his readers to remain faithful in fellowship with one another and with God and to combat false teaching concerning Christ.

Beginning in the earliest years of the church, false teachers denied the truth about Jesus. One heresy in particular, Docetism, a form of Gnosticism, taught that Jesus was a spirit in human form—He appeared human, but did not actually take on human flesh. This heresy was threatening a core tenet of the faith—the humanity of Christ. As a result, John opened his letter, not with a traditional greeting, but with a strong declaration that he and the other apostles had personally witnessed the humanity of Jesus. In fact, they had physically touched Him with their own hands (v. 1).

One of the core beliefs of Gnosticism is the denial of the effects of sin because of their distinction between a person's spirit, which is good, and body, which is evil. John addresses this misconception in his opening chapter. He reveals that sin separates a person from God (vv. 6-7). Instead of denying their sins (vv. 8, 10), believers must confess their sins so that they can be forgiven and renew their fellowship with God (v. 9). When believers turn from sin, they can participate fully and joyfully in community with other believers (v. 7).

Is there a sin in your life that is hindering your fellowship with God and with other believers? If so, confess your sin. God is faithful to forgive. You will be cleansed with the blood of Jesus and your fellowship with God and others will be restored.

MM

Wednesday

DILIGENT IN RIGHTEOUSNESS
Read 1 John 2

If you know that He is righteous, you know that everyone also who practices righteousness is born of Him. (2:29)

In this chapter, the Apostle John reminds believers that they should practice a lifestyle of righteousness because of Christ's sacrifice.

John explains that Christ's sacrifice frees believers from the penalty of sin (justification) because God's wrath is propitiated (satisfied) by the death of Jesus (v. 2). If for gratitude alone, the believer should endeavor to live a life free from sin. Yet believers receive divine help even in terms of sanctification. The Holy Spirit abides in believers and teaches them about all things (v. 27).

Believers have the responsibility to help other believers to avoid sin, thereby demonstrating love to one another (v. 10; cf. 3:11, 23; 4:7, 11, 12). Believers helping other believers is a direct contrast to the work of the "antichrists" (v. 18). These folks were once part of the early church community, but had since departed, following false doctrines about Jesus (v. 19). These antichrists surely attempted to persuade others to leave the community as well, thereby trying to pull people away from their fellowship with God. John encourages believers to reject these antichrists because they are liars (v. 22).

These antichrists are not the only ones who deceive believers in an attempt to hinder their walk with God. John reveals that the collective world continually entices people to lust after the physical, material, and social pleasures it offers (vv. 16). John warns believers that they should not love the world because its benefits are fleeting, while divine benefits are eternal (v. 17).

Yet another reason for believers to stay vigilant in their spiritual walk is the imminence of the Lord's return (v. 28). Modern believers must not allow the passage of almost two millennia to lull them into a lax adherence to sound doctrine and righteous living. It is much better to be like the wise maidens who, because of their extra oil, could be confident and ready for the arrival of the Bridegroom, rather than the foolish maidens who were ashamed and absent, and therefore left out because their oil was lacking (Mt 25:1-13).

MM

Thursday

GOD'S LOVE VERSUS SATAN'S HATRED
Read 1 John 3

We should love one another, not as Cain, who was of the evil one and slew his brother. And for what reason did he slay him? Because his deeds were evil, and his brother's were righteous. (3:11b-12)

The Apostle John wanted to give his early church audience the clearest picture of the righteous life of love that believers in Jesus Christ are called to live. So he contrasted the ways of the children of God (vv. 1-2, 9) with the ways of the children of the devil (v. 8).

The devil's ways begin with a rejection of God's revelation. Note the devil's claim in the Garden of Eden—"the beginning" in John's words (1:1; cf. Jn 1:1)—"You surely will not die!" (Gn 3:4). Oh, the destructive power of that little adverb when added to God's words.

Those who reject God's laws grow murderously jealous of those whose righteous behavior reveals their own sinfulness. Yet they still seek God's approval. That's why John references Cain's slaying of Abel. Abel's righteous sacrifice revealed Cain's unrighteousness. So Cain, as if to eliminate Abel's good sacrifice and thereby force God to accept his bad one, murders his own brother out of jealous hatred. John's audience had their own example of this type of behavior. That same generation of self-righteous religious leaders who had been murderously jealous and hateful of Jesus' righteousness felt and acted with the same murderous hatred towards the early church believers.

As a result, John advised his readers, "Do not be surprised, brethren, if the world hates you" (v. 13). Believers should follow the example of Christ, acting in obedience to God's laws and loving one another. This contrast in behavior is apparent to all—faithful believers, the lawless world, and, of course, God Himself (v. 10).

Unfortunately, those who reject God's laws choose not to sacrifice what God requires; but instead they choose to sacrifice the people who actually do what God requires. How different, then, is the example of Jesus. Out of love He became the sacrifice for the world. Choosing which path to follow is a choice that each person must make. Praise God that His way secures His favor both today and for eternity (cf. vv. 2-3)!

MM

Friday

SECURE IN GOD'S LOVE
Read 1 John 4

By this, love is perfected with us, so that we may have confidence in the day of judgment; because as He is, so also are we in this world. (4:17)

In helping his readers to deal with the false teaching infecting their community, the Apostle John continues his study in contrasts. In this chapter, he addresses a believer's assurance of God's love, explaining what signifies the enjoyment of, or lack of, divine approval.

While John had implicitly referenced the doctrine of the false teachers at the beginning of the book (cf. 1:1), he now names it clearly (v. 3). The heresy taught by these individuals was that Jesus was not fully human. They believed that Jesus could not have been made of flesh because they considered it to be corrupt. Therefore, Jesus existed only in spirit. Those who adopt this belief gain the world's approval (v. 5), but are sure to lose out on God's (vv. 2-3). As a result, these false teachers, and those who follow them, should be fearful of the day of judgment when God judges all humanity (v. 17).

Believers overcome false doctrine, and disbelief in general, when they reject it for sound doctrine as taught by those moved by the Holy Spirit (cf. 2 Pt 1:21). Believers ought to listen to the testimony of the apostles and other eyewitnesses (1:1; cf. 2 Pt 1:16) rather than those who reject the revelation of God.

Believers provide evidence that they are approved by God through the presence of the Holy Spirit (v. 13), Whom God has given to guide believers in truth, and by the love (and other fruit produced by the Spirit [cf. Gal 5:22-23]) that they demonstrate towards others (vv. 7-8, 12). As a result, believers can have "confidence in the day of judgment" (v. 17) and need not fear punishment (v. 18).

Those who claim to love God, yet hate their brethren, are liars, "for the one who does not love his brother whom he has seen, cannot love God whom he has not seen" (v. 20). Believers ought to love others, because they are themselves the recipients of God's love (v. 19).

In what ways are you demonstrating love to those around you? Seek God's approval, not that of the world.

MM

Monday

FAITH MAKES THE CHOICE EASY
Read 1 John 5

For whatever is born of God overcomes the world; and this is the victory that has overcome the world—our faith. (5:4)

The false teachers, who were trying to lure away the early church believers, probably added to their claim that Jesus was only a spirit the claim that the righteous life is impossibly hard, full of unnecessary sacrifice and self-denial. The Apostle John counters this claim with the declaration, "His commandments are not burdensome" (v. 3).

Perhaps John was invoking his own experiences before the religious leaders in Jerusalem (cf. Acts 3:1-4:31; 5:17-42). He and the other apostles stood firm in their righteous disobedience, declaring, "We are witnesses of these things" (Acts 5:32). They could resist the religious leaders' commands to stop preaching because they knew the truth about Jesus' identity and mission, having seen it for themselves. Their faith turned being "flogged" (whipped) into a joyous privilege (Acts 5:40-41).

But someone might say, "We aren't eyewitnesses." Responding as though he had heard that rebuttal, John counters with the encouragement to believe the Holy Spirit, because His testimony is true (v. 6). Believers can look to the divine testimony concerning Jesus. Christ's death and resurrection, referred to as His "blood", is the ultimate proof of His humanity and deity (v. 6). The false teachers did not believe that Jesus could die because they believed He was only a spirit. As a result, Christ's death served as a proof of his humanity.

John and the apostles testified to the humanity of Christ (cf. 1:1). The Holy Spirit testifies that Christ came by "water and blood" (v. 6). And God the Father testified concerning Christ's humanity by raising Him from the dead. Against such a mountain of evidence, how could one support the view that Christ was not fully human?

The one who chooses to believe in the Son of God has life; the one who denies the Son of God does not have life (vv. 11-13). The choice is easy—choose life (cf. Dt 30:19).

MM

Tuesday

JESUS UNDERSTANDS US
Read 2 John

For many deceivers have gone out into the world, those who do not acknowledge Jesus Christ as coming in the flesh. (1:7a)

Throughout his ministry, the Apostle John reaffirmed several times and very adamantly the truth that God in Jesus Christ, "became flesh, and dwelt among us" (Jn 1:14; cf. Jn 6:51-56; 1 Jn 1:1; 4:2). Unfortunately, as we read this letter we learn that some deceivers had infiltrated the various churches and were preaching a false gospel, which was diametrically opposed to the gospel that John and the other apostles had proclaimed. These deceivers refused to "acknowledge Jesus Christ as coming in the flesh" (v. 7).

The problem with this heretical teaching, called Docetism, is that it presents Jesus as a God Who never really became fully human, and Who is therefore incapable of understanding our humanity, our weakness, and our suffering (contra Heb 2:18; 4:15). Unfortunately, when the European Catholic missionaries traveled to Latin America, they preached this form of Docetism. Some scholars believe this is the primary reason that many indigenous converts preferred praying to Mary and the saints rather than to Christ, because, in their eyes, these saints were more human than Christ, and therefore, more relatable and sympathetic to their suffering. This doctrine portrays a God who is only transcendent—always far away from us and therefore unable to understand our pain and suffering.

Contrary to this false teaching, the doctrine of Christ's humanity is reaffirmed throughout Scripture. Jesus Christ is God in the flesh. He is one hundred percent human, one hundred percent divine. As a result, we can trust that Jesus Christ understands our pain and suffering. He understands each one of our trials and tribulations. He understands what it means to be human. Accordingly, we can draw near to Him with confidence that He will give us mercy and grace, and that He is able to sympathize with us in our weaknesses, because He has experienced the same struggles that we experience (Heb 4:15-16). When you face difficulties, boldly approach the throne of grace, so that you can find help in your time of need.

LC

Wednesday

IMITATING THE GODLY
Read 3 John

Beloved, do not imitate what is evil, but what is good. The one who does good is of God; the one who does evil has not seen God. (1:11)

In this letter, the Apostle John compares and contrasts three individuals: Gaius, Diotrephes, and Demetrius. Gaius, the recipient of the letter, is praised for "walking in truth" (v. 3) and for faithfully showing hospitality to traveling evangelists (vv. 5-6). Diotrephes is criticized for his desire to be first among the brethren (v. 9), for his refusal to listen to the elders (v. 9), for his "wicked words" (v. 10), and for his lack of hospitality (v. 10). Demetrius is praised for his "good testimony" among everyone (v. 12).

To highlight the characteristics of these three, John contrasts those who do "good" with those who do "evil"—those who do good are of God while those who do evil have not "seen" God (v. 11). The word translated "seen" is often used metaphorically with the meaning of "experienced". Those who do good have experienced God while those who do evil have not experienced God. As one would expect, John urges his readers to "imitate" (v. 11) those who do good (e.g., Gaius and Demetrius), not those who do evil (e.g., Diotrephes).

In my life, I have had the pleasure of working alongside many godly individuals. One had served on the mission field for many years without electricity and through many trials and tribulations. In the midst of an antagonist population in an area dominated by mosques, he was able to bring many to the knowledge of the truth. Many others exemplified lives of sacrifice and commitment, manifesting cheerful attitudes, shepherding hearts, and godly character. These individuals, who are always seeking to grow in the knowledge of the truth, serve as examples for me to imitate in my life.

Think about those individuals in your life who have consistently modeled a life of faith; those who ultimately have become imitators of Christ. Commend them and seek to imitate their example. These spiritual lighthouses shine the light of Christ for all to see (cf. Mt 5:14). And the world can only see a light when it is on!

LC

Thursday

YOU ARE KEPT—SO KEEP ON KEEPING ON
Read Jude

But you, beloved, building yourselves up on your most holy faith, praying in the Holy Spirit, keep yourselves in the love of God, waiting anxiously for the mercy of our Lord Jesus Christ to eternal life. (1:20-21)

The Epistle of Jude is a relatively short document, but it packs a powerful punch. In it, Jude commands believers to contend earnestly for the faith in the face of the false teachers who had infiltrated the church (vv. 3-4). These teachers were using God's grace as an excuse to sin (v. 4). They were arrogant, yet ignorant of real spiritual truth (vv. 8-10). They were seeking their own profit, enslaved to their selfish desires (vv. 11, 16, 18-19).

In contrast to these false teachers, who are devoid of the Spirit, Jude reminds believers that they are "beloved" (v. 20), and calls on them to "keep [themselves] in the love of God" (v. 21). The command to "keep" speaks of vigilant care and watchfulness. Jude constructed his sentence to explain how believers are to live out this command—through mutual edification in their most holy faith, through Spirit-led prayer among believers, and through a corporate longing for Christ's return (vv. 20-21).

Notably however, Jude juxtaposes the believer's responsibility with the assurance that God will keep them in His love. Jude opens his book by addressing it to "those who are the called, beloved in God the Father, and kept for Jesus Christ" (v. 1). He closes his epistle with one of Scripture's most glorious doxologies, praising the One who has the power to keep His people from stumbling and cause them to stand in divine glory blameless with great joy (v. 24). God our Savior, through Jesus Christ our Lord, possesses eternal dominion and authority to keep His beloved children (v. 25)!

Believer, rejoice in the glorious truth that you are kept by almighty God. No one can snatch you out of His hand (cf. Jn 10:28). And because you are beloved in this way, keep yourself in the love of God by growing with other believers in the truth of God's Word, by praying together according to God's will, and by focusing on the return of God's Son. You are kept—so keep on keeping on.

RK

Friday

READ AND HEED
Read Revelation 1

Blessed is he who reads and those who hear the words of the prophecy, and heed the things which are written in it; for the time is near. (1:3)

Revelation is the final book in the Bible. It occupies this special place in the canon because of the prophetic nature of the book for both its original audience and modern readers. Written near the end of the first century by the Apostle John while he was in exile on the island of Patmos, it is God's final word of scriptural revelation to His church.

In today's culture, Revelation is often viewed as a source of mystery and fear. A quick look at popular television shows, movies, and books illustrates this confusion. As a result, many Christians avoid reading the book because they misconstrue it as too undecipherable and alarming to be of spiritual value. However, the primary purpose of this letter is to help prepare and encourage its readers for the second coming of Jesus Christ (v. 1). A proper understanding of this book should move its readers from a place of mystery and fear to one of understanding and hope.

Believers ought to find encouragement in the book because it focuses on the Revelation of Jesus Christ (v. 1). It is the written testimony of the Lord and His imminent return—the Second Coming. Saints should take comfort in the words Jesus spoke to the Apostle John—"Do not be afraid" (v. 17). Those who read Revelation and heed its commandments have no reason to fear the Second Coming, for they are blessed (v. 3; cf. 20:6). However, those who ignore the book and its message will experience divine judgment when the Lord returns (v. 18; cf. 20:11-15).

In light of Who the book is about, coupled with the promise of blessing to those who read and heed, the correct response to Revelation is assurance and adoration, not anxiety and apathy. Always remember God's guarantee—"He [Jesus] is coming. ... So it is to be. Amen!" (v. 7).

SB

Monday

THE ONE WHO KNOWS
Read Revelation 2

I know your deeds and your toil and perseverance, and that you cannot tolerate evil men ... and you have perseverance and have endured for My name's sake, and have not grown weary. (2:2-3)

The desire to be known is universal in humans. It is the basis for their need for relationships. And for believers, to be known by God is the ultimate relationship.

This chapter records four of the seven letters that the Lord wrote to various churches located in Asia Minor, i.e., those to Ephesus, Smyrna, Pergamum, and Thyatira. While the letters to these churches have many facets, one pattern that emerges is that Jesus tells these churches He knows them.

Christ knows their "deeds" (vv. 2, 19). He sees their "toil and perseverance" (vv. 2, 19). He sees their "endurance" (v. 3). He sees their hatred of unrighteousness (v. 6). He sees their faithfulness (v. 13). And He sees their "love and faith and service" (v. 19). For their faithfulness, they will be given "authority" to rule over the nations alongside the Son of God (vv. 26-27).

Christ knows their difficulties. He sees their "tribulation" and "poverty" (vv. 9, 10). And He sees their suffering and imprisonment (v. 10). For their faithfulness, they will be given a "crown of life" (v. 10) and "will not be hurt by the second death" (v. 11).

Christ knows their domain. They live in a fallen world (cf. Gn 3). It is a place where Satan reigns (vv. 9, 10, 13; cf. 12:9). It is a place of "blasphemy" (v. 9). It is a place of false teaching (vv. 14, 15). It is a place of "immorality" (vv. 20-22). And it is a place of idolatry (v. 20). For their faithfulness, they will be granted the opportunity to "eat of the tree of life which is in the Paradise of God" (v. 7; cf. 22:2).

Take comfort and rejoice in the fact that the Lord knows us. He knows our deeds, our difficulties, and the domain in which we live. And the One Who Knows will surely reward all those who faithfully live for Him. Amen!

SB

Tuesday

THE ONE WHO EXHORTS
Read Revelation 3

Those whom I love, I reprove and discipline; therefore be zealous and repent. (3:19)

Exhortation is not a commonly used word. The word carries the idea of "vigorously urging" someone to take a prescribed action. It is often used in the sense of correcting bad behavior, but it can also be used to encourage good behavior. In the Bible, God repeatedly exhorts people to live in a manner pleasing to Him. When individuals listen to God's exhortations, they learn wisdom. And when individuals apply God's exhortations, they live wisely.

This chapter records the final three of the seven letters that the Lord wrote to various churches located in Asia Minor, i.e., those to Sardis, Philadelphia, and Laodicea.

In the letter to Sardis, Jesus exhorts the church to "wake up, and strengthen the things that remain" (v. 2) and to "remember what you have received and heard; and keep it, and repent" (v. 3). In other words, the church was encouraged to become spiritually mature through repentance and obedience.

In the letter to Philadelphia, Jesus exhorts the church to "hold fast what [they] have" (v. 11). This church was not in need of correction, they were in need of "perseverance" (v. 10). They had remained faithful, and had not denied the name of the Lord (v. 8).

In the letter to Laodicea, Jesus exhorts the church to "buy from Me gold refined by fire so that you may become rich, and white garments so that you may clothe yourself, … and eye salve to anoint your eyes so that you may see" (v. 18). Essentially, the church was admonished to pursue those things that produce eternal spiritual rewards instead of trusting in their transient material wealth (v. 17).

We usually don't enjoy being told to change our behavior. However, God exhorts us because He loves us (v. 19). The One Who Exhorts wants us to live wisely so that our names might be found in the "book of life" (v. 5), so that we can serve as a "pillar in the temple" in the new Jerusalem (v. 12), and so that we may one day sit with Christ on God's throne (v. 21).

SB

Wednesday

THE ONE WHO REIGNS
Read Revelation 4

... a throne was standing in heaven, and One sitting on the throne. (4:2b)

Have you ever wondered what it will be like to see God and experience the splendor of His throne in heaven? This chapter contains one of the most vivid descriptions of this scene of any of those recorded in Scripture.

The setting of the book moves from earth to heaven as the Apostle John is shown the throne room of God. John saw God the Father sitting on His throne (v. 2). He had the appearance of "jasper", a translucent stone, and "sardius", a red stone (v. 3). His throne was encircled by an emerald green rainbow (v. 3). Around the Father's throne were the thrones of twenty-four elders, who probably represent the raptured church (v. 4). The scene was accentuated by the sight of flashing lightning and the sound of crashing thunder (v. 5). A crystal-like "sea of glass" mirrored the lights and colors, creating an awe-inspiring effect (v. 6). No other King could ever be enthroned in such grandeur!

In the midst of this scene, John saw four "living creatures" (v. 6), who were continuously offering praise to God, saying, "Holy, holy, holy is the Lord God, the Almighty, Who was and Who is and Who is to come" (v. 8). As these living creatures chanted these words, the twenty-four elders bowed before God's throne and worshiped Him (v. 10), saying, "Worthy are You, our Lord and our God, to receive glory and honor and power; for You created all things, and because of Your will they existed, and were created" (v. 11).

Despite the limitations of human language, John's description contains enough detail to teach us that worship in the presence of God will be unlike anything we have ever experienced. Is it any wonder that Isaiah was struck with the reality of his uncleanness in the presence of such a holy God (cf. Is 6:5)? No other King is worthy of our praise. Worship Him today by living a life of holiness and by proclaiming the glory of His name to everyone you meet.

SB

Thursday

THE ONE WHO IS WORTHY
Read Revelation 5

And they sang a new song, saying, "Worthy are You ...." (5:9)

This chapter continues John's vision of the heavenly throne room (cf. 4:1-2). In his vision, John sees God sitting on His throne holding a book with seven seals in His right hand (v. 1). An angel asks a critical question, "Who is worthy to open the book and to break its seals?" (v. 2; cf. 4:11). John begins to weep because "no one was found worthy to open the book or to look into it" (v. 4). In the midst of what seems like a desperate scene, the Lamb appears (v. 6). Jesus, the Lamb of God (cf. Jn 1:29), transforms this hopeless situation into one of hope. There is One Who is worthy!

The Lamb approaches the throne and takes the book "out of the right hand of Him Who sat on the throne" (v. 7). The very fact that Jesus could approach the throne of God and take the book causes the four living creatures and twenty-four elders to fall before the Lamb in worship (v. 8). Their adoration reflects the worthiness of Christ—His blood sacrifice made His followers "a kingdom and priests to our God; and they will reign upon the earth" (v. 10).

As the scene unfolds, John records the worship that erupts in heaven. John's eyes gaze upon the magnificent scene as he hears "the voice of many angels around the throne and the living creatures and the elders" (v. 11). The sheer number of the heavenly worshipers is beyond comparison. John uses the phrase "myriads of myriads" (v. 11), which can be literally translated as "ten-thousands of ten-thousands". This innumerable assembly is appropriate in light of the limitless "power and riches and wisdom and might and honor and glory and blessing" of the Lamb (v. 12).

And the worship was not limited to God's heavenly court—"every created thing which is in heaven and on the earth and under the earth and on the sea, and all things in them" joined in the adulation (v. 13). Given the revelation of Jesus as the One Who is worthy, it is only fitting that all of God's creation worship the Lamb.

Jesus provides hope in hopeless situations. The Lamb is unique—there is no one like Him. Christ alone is worthy. Worship Him!

SB

Friday

THE WRATH OF GOD
Read Revelation 6

For the great day of their wrath has come, and who is able to stand? (6:17)

Though many modern preachers fail to note the fact in their feel-good sermons, God is a God of wrath. He is portrayed as a God of wrath in both the Old (e.g., Ps 21:9; Is 34:2; Ez 36:18; Mi 5:15; Na 1:2, 6; Zep 1:18; Zec 7:12) and New (e.g., Jn 3:36; Rom 1:18; 3:5; 9:22; 12:19; Eph 5:6; Col 3:6) Testaments. And, as one might imagine, He is portrayed as a God of wrath throughout Revelation (vv. 16-17; 11:18; 14:10, 19; 15:1, 7; 16:1, 19; 19:15). Nowhere is the wrath of God more evident than in the book's three series of judgments, consisting of seven seals, seven trumpets, and seven bowls. Collectively, these judgments will inflict catastrophic harm upon not only the human race, but on the entire world.

In the previous chapter, the Lamb approached the throne of God and took the seven-sealed book that was in His right hand (5:7), for He had been found "worthy" to open it (5:9; cf. 5:4-5). As the Lamb opens the first seal, the narration of events shifts from heaven to earth as the Tribulation begins (vv. 1-2).

These seal judgments, the mildest of the three series of judgments, probably take place in the first half of the Tribulation, as can be seen in a comparison of this chapter with Matthew twenty-four. Both passages predict the coming of an antichrist (v. 2; Mt 24:5), war (v. 4; Mt 24:6-7), famine (v. 6; Mt 24:7), death (v. 8; Mt 24:9), martyrdom (vv. 9-11; Mt 24:9), and earthly phenomena (vv. 12-14; Mt 24:7). Assuming Matthew twenty-four is in chronological order, these seals take place prior to the "abomination of desolation" spoken of by Daniel (Mt 24:15). This event will take place "in the middle" of Daniel's seventieth week—i.e., the Tribulation (Dn 9:27). The Tribulation is often divided into two halves in Revelation (cf. 11:2-3; 12:6; 13:5).

Believers of this age need not fear the wrath of God, for we will be "saved" from it because we have been justified by the blood of Christ (Rom 5:9; cf. 1 Thes 5:9). Let us eagerly wait for the coming of the Son, "Who rescues us from the wrath to come" (1 Thes 1:10).

IL

Monday

SEALED AND DELIVERED
Read Revelation 7

For this reason, they are before the throne of God; and they serve Him day and night in His temple. (7:15a)

This chapter serves as a parenthesis in the narrative of the Lamb's opening of the seven-sealed book (cf. 5:1-6:17; 8:1), and is primarily designed to answer the question posed in 6:17, "Who is able to stand?" The chapter is neatly divided into a discussion of the 144,000 Jews who are sealed from harm (vv. 1-8), and the great multitude from all nations who are martyred during the Tribulation (vv. 9-17).

The 144,000 Jews who are sealed are divided into twelve groups of 12,000 from the various tribes of Israel (vv. 5-8). Even though a modern Jew may not be aware of their tribal lineage, God is surely aware of it. This exact list of tribes is unique in Scripture, despite the fact that there are roughly twenty lists of Jacob's sons in the Old Testament. "Joseph" (v. 8) is apparently a reference to the tribe of Ephraim, since Manasseh, the other son of Joseph, is found earlier (v. 6). The tribe of Dan is notably absent from this list, perhaps because of the tribe's history of idolatry (cf. Jgs 18; 1 Kgs 12:29-30). However, the tribe is found in Ezekiel 48:1-2, thus indicating that they will receive a portion of land in the millennium.

While the 144,000 come from one nation, the great multitude is comprised of "every nation" (v. 9). They are pictured standing before God's throne in heaven in the presence of the Lamb (v. 9) and crying out, "Salvation to our God Who sits on the throne, and to the Lamb" (v. 10). These believers have come out of the Tribulation, and have "washed their robes and made them white in the blood of the Lamb" (v. 14)—a reference to the fact that they have been martyred for their faith in Christ. Because of their faithful service, they will no longer suffer (vv. 15-17). Instead, the Lamb will be their shepherd, and will guide them to "springs of the water of life" (v. 17)—an apparent reference to the new heaven and new earth (21:1; cf. 21:6; 22:1).

Just as these groups will be delivered in the age to come, the church will be delivered from the "present evil age" (Gal 1:4). Salvation belongs to the Lord!

IL

Tuesday

SILENCE IN HEAVEN
Read Revelation 8

When the Lamb broke the seventh seal, there was silence in heaven for about half an hour. (8:1)

Have you ever heard the sound of complete silence? A few years ago, my wife and I had the opportunity to take a flight in an airplane equipped with skis that were used to land on the slopes of Mount McKinley in Alaska. After we got out of the plane, the pilot told us to be silent for one minute. The experience was absolutely surreal. As I stood there, I thought about the seventh seal and wondered what it would be like to experience an entire half hour of complete silence.

The chapter begins with the opening of the seventh seal by the Lamb (v. 1; cf. 5:1-6:17). When the Lamb broke the seal, there was silence in heaven for "about half an hour" (v. 1). This is an unusual amount of time and is therefore probably literal—this exact time span occurs nowhere else in Scripture. This period of silence is striking, especially in light of the numerous references to sound in John's vision of the heavenly throne (cf. 4:5, 8, 10-11; 5:9-14).

This period of silence does not appear to be the seventh seal since it takes place in heaven and is not witnessed by anyone on earth. Rather, the seventh seal is probably comprised of the seven trumpets, just as the seventh trumpet is likely made up of the seven bowls. The silence is simply a prelude to the blowing of the trumpets.

Trumpets, which are typically made from the horns of rams, are used throughout Scripture to announce divine action. For example, a trumpet sounded as God arrived at Mount Sinai to speak to the Israelites (Ex 19:16, 19). The Lord established the holy day of trumpets to announce the coming Day of Atonement (Lv 23:24). A trumpet will be blown in Zion to announce the arrival of the Day of the Lord (Jl 2:1). And a trumpet will sound to announce the coming of the Lord (1 Thes 4:16). In a notable parallel to this passage, seven trumpets were used to bring down the walls of Jericho (Jo 6).

As you consider the coming judgments, take a moment to pray the words of Habakkuk, "In wrath remember mercy" (Hb 3:2), knowing that your prayers go directly before the presence of God (vv. 3-4). IL

Wednesday

DIVINE JUDGMENT
Read Revelation 9

The rest of mankind ... did not repent. (9:20a)

This chapter describes the fifth and sixth of the seven trumpet judgments (cf. 8:2, 6-13; 11:15). These judgments increase in severity and intensity as they progress. It is clear that the Apostle John struggles to describe what he sees—there are more than a dozen similes in this chapter.

As the fifth trumpet sounded, a "star" was given the key to the "bottomless pit" (v. 1). This "star" is almost certainly an angel (cf. 1:20; Jb 38:7), whether fallen (i.e., a demon; cf. 12:4; Lk 10:18) or unfallen (cf. 20:1). The "bottomless pit" (literally, "well of the abyss") is the residence of Satan (v. 11), demons (2 Pt 2:4; cf. Jude 6) and the beast (11:7; 17:8). When the angel opened the pit, a swarm of "locusts" poured out (v. 3). These "locusts" could be literal locusts or they could be modern instruments of warfare (e.g., attack helicopters) that John attempts to describe using various elements known to his audience. Locusts are used throughout Scripture to bring divine judgment (e.g., Ex 10:4-6, 12-15; Dt 28:38; 2 Chr 7:13; Jl 1:4).

Although normal locusts have no king (cf. Prv 30:27), these locusts are under the authority of "the angel of the abyss" (v. 11). This angel is further identified by his Hebrew name, Abaddon, and his Greek name, Apollyon, both meaning "destroyer" (v. 11). It seems clear that this angel is Satan. These locust will not be permitted to kill (v. 5; Jb 2:6); they will only be allowed to torment those who do not have "the seal of God on their foreheads" (v. 4; cf. 7:3). These individuals will be tormented for five months (v. 5). Their pain will be so great that they will long for death rather than repent (vv. 6, 20-21).

In a similar situation, the prophet Jonah longed for death when he experienced divine judgment. Refusing to repent, he cried out, "death is better to me than life" (Jnh 4:8). Jonah knew that repentance would lead to divine mercy (cf. Jnh 3:10; 4:2).

Divine judgment is intended to generate repentance (cf. 1 Cor 11:30; Jas 5:14-15). Are you experiencing the judgment of God? Repent and turn from your sin, and you will be forgiven and healed.

IL

Thursday

SWEET AND BITTER
Read Revelation 10

In my mouth it was sweet as honey; and when I had eaten it, my stomach was made bitter. (10:10b)

This chapter begins a series of five chapters of interludes that interrupt the chronological progression of the trumpet and bowl judgments. In this chapter, John doesn't just see and hear what is happening, he becomes an active participant in the unfolding events.

The chapter begins with the appearance of a "strong angel" coming down out of heaven (v. 1). While scholars have tried to identify this angel as Gabriel, Michael, or even Jesus, he appears to be just another of several "strong" angels in Revelation (cf. 5:2; 18:21).

The angel held in his left hand a "little book" (v. 2). This book is probably different from that of 5:1 since a different Greek word is used. The angel stood with one foot on the land and another foot on the sea (v. 2), probably signifying the universal nature of his message. The angel lifted his right hand to heaven and took an oath that there would no longer be any delay, but that the words of the prophets would soon be fulfilled (vv. 5-7; cf. Dn 12:7).

John was then commanded (probably by God Himself) to take the book from the angel and eat it (vv. 8-9). The act of eating is commonly used in Scripture to symbolize the acquisition of knowledge (e.g., Jer 15:16; Ez 3:1-3). In John's mouth, the book tasted as sweet as honey (cf. Ez 3:3), but when he had eaten it, his stomach was made bitter (v. 10). The words of God are routinely portrayed as sweet to the taste (cf. Ps 19:10; 119:103).

The book probably contained the revelation of the rest of the events recorded in Revelation or, at least, those dealing with judgment. This is demonstrated by the command given to John, "You must prophesy again concerning many peoples and nations and tongues and kings" (v. 11). This is why the book made his stomach bitter—because the revelation concerned catastrophic judgments.

Sometimes the words of God are sweet; sometimes they are bitter. But they are always "profitable" (2 Tm 3:16). Meditate on the whole Word of God, not just those passages that make you feel good.

IL

Friday

GOD'S WITNESSES
Read Revelation 11

And those who dwell on the earth will rejoice over them and celebrate; and they will send gifts to one another, because these two prophets tormented those who dwell on the earth. (11:10)

This chapter is the second in a series of five consecutive chapters of interludes that interrupt the chronological progression of the trumpet and bowl judgments. The chapter probably reveals the initial contents of the little book introduced in the previous chapter (cf. 10:2). Once again, John becomes an active participant in his vision (cf. 10:8-10).

The chapter begins with John being told to "measure" the temple of God and the altar (v. 1). This act indicates that God will protect the temple and "those who worship in it" (v. 1). Accordingly, John is specifically told to "leave out the court which is outside the temple" because "it has been given to the nations ... for forty-two months" (v. 3). This forty-two month period is the second half of the Tribulation, i.e., Daniel's seventieth week (cf. Dn 9:27).

During these forty-two months the Lord will "grant authority" to two witnesses to "prophesy" (v. 3). The identity of these two witnesses has been the source of endless speculation. Some identify them as Moses and Elijah; others as Enoch and Elijah; still others as James and Peter. However, there is nothing in the context that demands that these individuals be resurrected saints brought back to earth. It seems best to identify them simply as two individuals living at that time who are specially empowered by God.

These witnesses will endure opposition and persecution until they are finally killed by the Antichrist (v. 7), after which their bodies will lie in the street in Jerusalem (v. 8). People from all nations will rejoice and celebrate the death of these two prophets because they were "tormented" by their messages (v. 10).

Don't be surprised if you experience opposition when serving as a witness, "For the word of the cross is foolishness to those who are perishing" (1 Cor 1:18). Unbelievers often respond to the preaching of the gospel with hostility (cf. Acts 5:17-42). Don't let opposition hinder your ministry—boldly preach the Word (2 Tm 4:2)!   IL

Monday

DIVINE PROTECTION
Read Revelation 12

And they overcame him because of the blood of the Lamb and because of the word of their testimony. (12:11a)

This chapter is the third in a series of five consecutive chapters of interludes that interrupt the chronological progression of the trumpet and bowl judgments. In this chapter, the Apostle John describes what he sees in heaven and what he sees on earth. The chapter focuses on the interactions between a dragon and a woman.

The chapter begins with the appearance of a great sign in heaven (vv. 1-2). This sign is a pregnant woman who is clothed with the sun, moon, and twelve stars. This woman should be identified as the nation of Israel (cf. Gn 37:9).

John then sees a second sign appear in heaven (v. 3). This sign is a great red dragon with seven heads and ten horns. This dragon is later identified as Satan (v. 9). The dragon's tail "swept away a third of the stars from heaven and threw them to the earth" (v. 4), an apparent reference to angels becoming demons when Satan led a rebellion against God (vv. 7-9).

The woman eventually gave birth to the Messiah, "Who is to rule all the nations" (v. 5). This "Child was caught up to God and to His throne" (v. 5), a reference to the Resurrection (cf. Eph 1:20). The woman then fled into the wilderness, "where she had a place prepared by God, so that there she would be nourished for one thousand two hundred and sixty days" (v. 6; cf. v. 14; Mt 24:16; Mk 13:14), a reference to the second half of the Tribulation (cf. 11:2-3).

When the dragon was unable to destroy the woman (vv. 13-16), he focused his attack on the rest of her children, faithful Jews "who keep the commandments of God and hold to the testimony of Jesus" (v. 17). This group probably includes the 144,000 who were specially sealed by God (cf. 7:4-8; 14:1-5).

While there have been many attempts throughout history to exterminate the Jews, they have all failed. No matter how bleak it looks, "relief and deliverance will [always] arise for the Jews" (Est 4:14). God will fulfil His covenant with Abraham (Gn 12:3)!

IL

Tuesday

THE UNHOLY TRINITY
Read Revelation 13

They worshiped the dragon because he gave his authority to the beast; and they worshiped the beast. (13:4a)

This chapter is the fourth in a series of five consecutive chapters of interludes that interrupt the chronological progression of the trumpet and bowl judgments. The chapter describes the actions of two beasts, one coming up out of the sea (vv. 1-10) and one coming up out of the earth (vv. 11-18).

The appearance of the first beast is similar to that of the dragon in 12:3, with an emphasis on heads, horns, and diadems (v. 1). He is further described as having various features of a leopard, bear, and lion (v. 2). These three animals also appear in Daniel's vision of four great beasts (cf. Dn 7:1-28). As a result, this beast probably equates to the fourth beast in Daniel's vision (cf. Dn 7:7-8, 17-26). This beast is given power and authority by the dragon (v. 2). He will be worshiped by "everyone whose name has not been written from the foundation of the world in the book of life of the Lamb Who has been slain" (v. 8; cf. vv. 3-4). This beast will wage war against the saints and will kill many of them (v. 7; cf. 7:9, 14; 20:4). This beast should be identified as the Antichrist.

The second beast operates with the authority of the first beast (v. 12). He essentially functions as the first beast's prophet, performing great signs designed to encourage unbelievers to worship the first beast (vv. 12-15). He then forces these individuals to be given a signifying "mark" on either their right hand or forehead, thus allowing them to buy and sell (vv. 16-17). This mark will bear the first beast's name or number (vv. 17-18). This beast should be identified as the False Prophet.

The dragon and these two beasts basically serve as an unholy trinity, with the dragon seeking to replace God the Father, the first beast seeking to replace the Messiah, God the Son, and the second beast seeking to replace the Holy Spirit. These three will eventually be thrown into the "lake of fire and brimstone" (20:10). "If anyone has an ear, let him hear" (v. 9)!

IL

Wednesday

PERSEVERANCE
Read Revelation 14

Here is the perseverance of the saints who keep the commandments of God and their faith in Jesus. (14:12)

This is the final chapter in a series of five consecutive chapters of interludes that interrupt the chronological progression of the trumpet and bowl judgments. The chapter describes the ultimate victory experienced by the 144,000 (vv. 1-5) along with a contrast between the fate of the rest of faithful believers and the fate of those who follow the beast (vv. 6-20).

In a vision of the end of the Tribulation, John saw the Lamb standing on Mount Zion with the 144,000 who had the seal of God (v. 1; cf. 7:3-8). These 144,000 were honored with a special song that only they could learn (vv. 2-3). They are singled out for special commendation because they have kept themselves chaste, they have faithfully followed the Lamb, they have been purchased as a gift of first fruits to God, and they have been found blameless (vv. 4-5).

John then saw three angels. The first angel had an eternal gospel to preach to those who live on the earth (vv. 6-7). The second angel announced the fall of Babylon (v. 8; cf. 17:1-18:24). The third angel warned those who follow the beast of their future torment in the lake of fire and brimstone (vv. 9-11; cf. 20:10). These individuals are contrasted with those who proved faithful to God (vv. 12-13).

John then describes the results of two sickles that were swung over the earth. The first sickle was wielded by "One like a Son of Man" (v. 14; cf. Dn 7:13), a common messianic title (1:13; cf. e.g., Mt 9:6; 10:23). When He swung His sickle, the earth was reaped, probably indicating a grain harvest (vv. 15-16). The second sickle was wielded by an angel (v. 17). When he swung his sickle, grapes were gathered and thrown into the wine press of the wrath of God, where they were trodden (vv. 18-20). These two reapings seem to be redundant and are probably to be viewed as the same judgment, with two different harvests used to emphasize completeness (cf. Jl 3:13).

Inspired by the example of future saints, let us persevere in keeping the commandments of God and in our faith in Christ (v. 12)!

IL

Thursday

THE SONG OF MOSES
Read Revelation 15

Great and marvelous are Your works, O Lord God, the Almighty; righteous and true are Your ways, King of the nations! (15:3b)

The narrative now returns to the chronological progression of the trumpet and bowl judgments. This chapter serves as a prelude to the pouring out of the seven bowls of wrath (cf. 16:1).

The chapter begins with the appearance of seven angels who had seven plagues (v. 1). These plagues are described as "the last, because in them the wrath of God is finished" (v. 1). These seven plagues are later associated with seven "bowls full of the wrath of God" (v. 7). Collectively, these bowls probably serve as the seventh trumpet judgment. When the seventh trumpet sounded, loud voices announced the arrival of the messianic kingdom, an event that will take place when the seven bowl judgments are completed (cf. 11:15).

John then saw "those who had been victorious over the beast and his image and the number of his name" standing on a "sea of glass mixed with fire" (v. 2). These individuals are probably Tribulation martyrs, having become victorious over the beast because they remained faithful to the Lamb until death (cf. 12:11). The "sea" is probably an allusion to the crossing of the Red Sea by the Israelites (Ex 14:15-31), especially in light of the song that follows.

These individuals sang "the song of Moses, the bond-servant of God" (v. 3; cf. Ex 14:31). This song has remarkable parallels to the song sung by Moses and the Israelites after their crossing of the Red Sea (cf. Ex 15:1-18). Both songs of praise and deliverance use a variety of titles for God (v. 3; cf. Ex 15:1-2, 17), and emphasize the great works of God (vv. 3-4; cf. Ex 15:1, 4-8, 10-13), the fear of those who witness these works (v. 4; cf. Ex 15:14-16), and the holiness of God (vv. 3-4; cf. Ex 15:11, 13).

Have you ever taken the time to compose a song to God highlighting the providence and deliverance He has demonstrated in your life? Follow the example of Moses and Miriam and "sing to the Lord, for He is highly exalted" (Ex 15:1, 21).

IL

Friday

THE BOWLS OF WRATH
Read Revelation 16

Men were scorched with fierce heat; and they blasphemed the name of God Who has the power over these plagues, and they did not repent so as to give Him glory. (16:9)

Nowhere in Scripture is the wrath of God more evident than in this chapter. The chapter describes a series of devastating plagues that will traumatize both those who live on the earth and the earth itself.

The chapter opens with the sound of a loud voice, probably God's, coming from the temple in heaven (v. 1; cf. 15:5-8). The voice commanded the seven angels, "Go and pour out on the earth the seven bowls of the wrath of God" (v. 1).

The first bowl smote those who had the mark of the beast with dreadful sores (v. 2). The second bowl turned the sea to blood and killed all sea creatures (v. 3). The third bowl turned fresh water in rivers and springs to blood (v. 4). The fourth bowl caused the sun to scorch the inhabitants of the earth with fierce heat (vv. 8-9). The fifth bowl allowed darkness to fall upon the earth (vv. 10-11). The sixth bowl dried up the Euphrates River, allowing a massive army to approach Jerusalem from the East (vv. 12-16). The seventh bowl afflicted the earth with a catastrophic earthquake and hundred-pound hailstones (vv. 17-21).

The narrative of the seven bowls is interrupted with a theodicy, i.e., a defense of God's actions (vv. 5-7). An angel cries out, "Righteous are You, Who are and Who were, O Holy One, because You judged these things" (v. 5). The angel's assertion is echoed by voices emanating from an altar, probably from Tribulation martyrs (cf. 6:9), saying, "Yes, O Lord God, the Almighty, true and righteous are Your judgments (v. 7).

In light of the worldwide devastation caused by these plagues, they probably occur in rapid succession at the very end of the Tribulation, likely within the last several weeks. Even though it will be obvious that these plagues have been sent by God, humans will still refuse to repent and will continue to blaspheme His name (vv. 9, 11; cf. Am 4:6-11). O world, "Prepare to meet your God" (Am 4:12)!

IL

Monday

THE BEST INTERPRETER
Read Revelation 17

And on her forehead a name was written, a mystery, "Babylon the great, the mother of harlots and of the abominations of the earth." (17:5)

Revelation 17-18 describe the future destruction of Babylon. The impending doom of this city has already been announced twice in the book (14:8; 16:19). Now, its destruction is described in great detail (10% of the Book of Revelation is devoted to the fate of Babylon).

Perhaps the most common question concerning these chapters is the identity of this city. Those who do not interpret the book literally usually view "Babylon" as a symbol of evil while those who hold to a literal city typically argue for either Rome or a rebuilt Babylon. While the arguments in favor of Rome are certainly substantial, it seems best to view the city as a rebuilt Babylon for the following reasons.

First, it is the most literal view. Second, Babylon is a literal city in all other references in Scripture with the possible exception of 1 Peter 5:13. Third, the term "mother" (v. 5) suggests the religious entity that gave birth to all other religious entities. Many religions predate Catholicism whereas the origins of Babylon can be traced to the time of Nimrod (Gn 10:8-10). Fourth, the "woman sitting on a scarlet beast" is identified as "Babylon" (vv. 3, 5). In Scripture, if a figure can be identified as another figure, then an interpreter can never be sure of his interpretation. Fifth, Babylon has always been opposed to the plans of God (cf. e.g., Gn 11:1-9). Sixth, it is the most natural understanding of Zechariah 5:5-11 since the "land of Shinar" (Zec 5:11) is a rather clear allusion to Babylon (cf. Gn 10:10; 11:2). Seventh, Babylon has a history of antagonism towards Israel (cf. e.g., Jer 52). Eighth, many prophecies concerning Babylon have not yet been fulfilled (cf. e.g., Is 13-14; Jer 50-51).

As you read the Bible, it is imperative that you avoid "newspaper exegesis", that is, interpreting biblical prophecy in light of current events. Even though it is difficult for modern readers to envision the rise of Babylon, it surely would have been equally difficult for medieval readers to envision the restoration of Israel. Always remember, Scripture is the best interpreter of Scripture!

IL

Tuesday

BABYLON THE ~~GREAT~~ GROTESQUE
Read Revelation 18

Fallen, fallen is Babylon the great! She has become a dwelling place of demons and a prison of every unclean spirit, and a prison of every unclean and hateful bird. And in her was found the blood of prophets and of saints and of all who have been slain on the earth. (18:2b; 24)

The previous chapter opened with an announcement of the judgment of the "great harlot" (17:1), the first of four references to Babylon as a "harlot" (17:15, 16; 19:2). Revelation uses the term "immorality" eight times in reference to Babylon (14:8; 17:2, 4; 18:3, 9; 19:2). Throughout Scripture, idolatry is portrayed as spiritual adultery (e.g., Hos 1-3). And there is no sin on earth that God finds more reprehensible than idolatry (cf. Ex 20:3-5; Rom 1:21-27).

Idolatry was the chief sin of the Israelites in the Old Testament. From the earliest days of their existence Israel participated in the worship of foreign gods. While in Egypt, the nation "played the harlot" with the gods of Egypt (Ez 23:3). After leaving Egypt and prior to entering the Promised Land, the Israelites "began to play the harlot with the daughters of Moab" (Nm 25:1). After entering the Promised Land, the children of Israel consistently engaged in the worship of Baal (cf. e.g., 1 Kgs 16:32; 22:53; 2 Kgs 21:3). Ultimately, idolatry is identified as the chief reason for Israel's exile, "They acted treacherously against the God of their fathers and played the harlot after the gods of the peoples of the land" (1 Chr 5:25; cf. 1 Chr 5:26).

During the Tribulation, the nations of the earth will play the harlot with Babylon (vv. 3, 9; cf. 17:2). This city will serve as the center for the idolatrous worship of Satan. This city will "wage war against the Lamb" (17:14) and will become "drunk with the blood of the saints, and with the blood of the witnesses of Jesus" (17:6; cf. v. 24).

But the Lamb will prevail, "because He is Lord of lords and King of kings" (17:14). When the grotesque city is destroyed, there will be a great celebration in heaven, "Hallelujah! Salvation and glory and power belong to our God; because His judgments are true and righteous; for He has judged the great harlot" (19:2).

"Little children, guard yourselves from idols" (1 Jn 5:21)!   IL

Wednesday

HALLELUJAH! WORSHIP GOD!
Read Revelation 19

After these things I heard something like a loud voice of a great multitude in heaven, saying, "Hallelujah! Salvation and glory and power belong to our God." (19:1)

This chapter begins the climax of John's message to the seven churches. It focuses on the heavenly celebrations of God's power, sovereignty, and providence. It is developed in two major sections featuring songs of praise prompted by the judgment and deliverance of God (vv. 1-10), and the sequence of events that constitute the second coming of Christ (vv. 11-21). It therefore functions to conclude the book's section on the defeat and destruction of Babylon (vv. 1-5; cf. Rv 17-18) and to introduce the consummation of God's plan and program for the ages (vv. 6-21; cf. Rv 20-22).

In 18:20, an angel commands heaven, saints, apostles, and prophets to rejoice at the judgment of Babylon. The fulfillment of that command is recorded in verses 1-5, as these groups sing hallelujah praise songs. The term hallelujah, which appears in the New Testament only in verses one, three, four, and six, is the Greek transliteration of the Hebrew phrase *halelu yah*, which means "Praise the Lord" (cf. Ps 150:1). God is to be praised for His righteous judgment of evil Babylon (vv. 1-5), as well as for His deliverance of the saints (vv. 6-10). This echoes the Hallel psalms (i.e., Ps 113-118), which include both judgment (cf. e.g. Ps 115:8; 118:10-12) and deliverance (cf. e.g. Ps 113:7-9; 116:3-8). These psalms were often chanted by the Israelites at national feasts and festivals.

The themes of judgment and deliverance are also found in the climactic vision that concludes the chapter (vv. 11-21). In this vision, Christ is presented as a conquering King who comes to deliver the righteous by destroying the wicked.

Like John, all Christians should be overwhelmed by the awesome wonder of the revelation of God's majesty and might. Let us sing songs of praise to Him. Let us carry out the command of the angel and "worship God" (v. 10)!

FB

Thursday

THY KINGDOM COME, THY WILL BE DONE
Read Revelation 20

They came to life and reigned with Christ for a thousand years. They will be priests of God and of Christ and will reign with Him for a thousand years. Then I saw a great white throne and Him Who sat upon it. And I saw the dead, the great and the small, standing before the throne. (20:4b, 6b, 11a, 12a)

This chapter serves as the culmination of several of the major themes of Revelation, including the defeat of the wicked, the judgment of the unrighteous, the deliverance of the Tribulation saints, and the vindication of the divine nature of God as it relates to the marauding presence of evil. As this chapter narrates the close of human history, at least on this earth (21:1; cf. 2 Pt 3:10-13), it focuses on the prophetic events of the millennial kingdom (vv. 1-10) and the great white throne judgement (vv. 11-15).

The millennial kingdom refers to the literal thousand-year reign of Jesus Christ on earth that takes place after His second coming and before the creation of the new heaven and the new earth (vv. 4, 6; 21:1). During this period, Christ will serve as the world's governing ruler, spiritual leader, and focus of worship (cf. Ps 2:8-12; Is 11; Zec 14:9, 16). This kingdom is promised to all those who receive eternal life, and is characterized by peace, justice, and righteousness (cf. Is 11; Mi 4:2-4).

After the millennium, at the great white throne, the unsaved dead of all ages are resurrected, judged, and sentenced to eternal torment in the lake of fire (vv. 5, 11-15). This judgment is not arbitrary—individuals are judged "according to their deeds" (vv. 12-13), as well as their rejection of Christ (cf. Jn 12:48). The names of these unbelievers will not be found in the "book of life" (vv. 12, 15). This book contains only the names of those who are declared righteous by God through faith in Christ (cf. Ps 69:28; Rom 4:5).

This chapter encourages its readers to believe in Jesus Christ by describing the future reward for the righteous and judgment for the unrighteous. Do you know anyone whose name is not written in the book of life? If you do, share the gospel of Christ with them. Time is running out. Christ's kingdom is coming soon (cf. 22:20).   FB

Friday

ALL THINGS WILL BECOME NEW
Read Revelation 21

Then I saw a new heaven and a new earth; for the first heaven and the first earth passed away, and there is no longer any sea. And I saw the holy city, new Jerusalem, coming down out of heaven from God, made ready as a bride adorned for her husband. (21:1-2)

In this chapter, the Apostle John presents the climax of human history—the final resting place of the redeemed people of God. In the future, the righteous will eternally enjoy the Lord's promised presence, peace, power, and provision while the wicked will suffer His eternal punishment.

In his vision, John saw a "new" heaven and a "new" earth, for the first heaven and the first earth had passed away (v. 1; cf. 2 Pt 3:10, 12). The term translated "new" connotes a better or superior replacement of the obsolete (vv. 1, 2, 5; cf. Is 65:17; 2 Cor 5:17). The new creation is better in part because it is absent of seven evils that plague the present age: the sea, death, mourning, crying, pain, the curse, and night (vv. 1, 4; 22:3, 5). The centerpiece of the new creation is a new Jerusalem (v. 2).

John provides several characteristics of this new Jerusalem. It will be holy (vv. 2, 10; cf. v. 27), it originates from God (vv. 2, 10), it serves as the "wife of the Lamb" (v. 9; cf. v. 2), and it reflects the glory of God (v. 11). The city has a great and high wall (v. 12), thus providing security, and it has twelve gates (v. 13), thus providing access to God (cf. v. 25). The city has no need of a temple, for the Lord God and the Lamb serve as its temple (v. 22). The city also has no need of a sun or moon, for it is illumined by divine presence (v. 23). The city will be filled with the glory and honor of the nations (vv. 24, 26). The city will only be visited by the righteous—"those whose names are written in the Lamb's book of life" (v. 27).

The measuring of the city (vv. 15-17) suggests its stability as well as its preservation for blessing and protection from defilement. The materials of the city (vv. 18-21) demonstrate its majesty, grandeur, and splendor.

Praise and worship God today for His promise of a new creation!

FB

Monday

HE IS COMING SOON
Read Revelation 22

Behold, I am coming quickly, and My reward is with Me, to render to every man according to what he has done. He who testifies to these things says, "Yes, I am coming quickly." Amen. Come, Lord Jesus. (22:12, 20)

The Apostle John closes Revelation, and the entire Bible, with words designed to comfort and challenge his readers. In this chapter, five subjects are stressed: additional characteristics of the new Jerusalem (vv. 1-5; cf. 21:10-27), validation of the authenticity of the prophecy (vv. 6-7, 8, 16, 18-20), the imminence of Christ's return (vv. 6-7, 10, 12, 20), commendation for those who heed the words of the book (vv. 7, 9, 11-12, 14, 17), and condemnation for those who reject the call of salvation (vv. 11-12, 15, 17-19).

The final description of the new Jerusalem focuses on the inner conditions of the city that bring nourishment and richness to the lives of God's people: the river of the water of life (v. 1), the tree of life (v. 2), the presence of God and the Lamb (v. 3), intimate fellowship with God (v. 4), and the illuminating light of God's presence (v. 5).

The epilogue emphasizes the fact that all who read this book have a choice to make. They can either continue in sin or practice righteousness (v. 11). When the Lord returns, He will render eternal judgement on the righteous and the unrighteous based on each person's actions (v. 12). Those who "wash their robes" (i.e., become righteous by means of the blood of Christ) have the right to enter the city and partake of the tree of life (v. 14). Those who love sin will be kept outside (v. 15). Therefore, the book calls on its readers to immediately trust Christ for deliverance since His return is near, and after which there will be no opportunity for repentance.

As you consider the imminent return of Jesus Christ, urgently seek out opportunities to share the gospel with unbelievers. If you have close friends or family members who are not saved, plead with them to accept the free gift of salvation—the water of life is without cost (v. 17; cf. 21:6). Don't give up on them—it is truly a matter of life and death. Time is of the essence. He is coming soon!   FB

SCRIPTURE INDEX

Scripture Index

Genesis
1:26-27	179, 181
1:27	19
2:17	180
2:20-24	217
2:24	19
3	240
3:1-7	170
3:4	233
6:8-9	229
7	229
10:8-10	255
10:10	255
11:1-9	255
11:2	255
12:1-3	165
12:3	250
13:1-11	229
13:12, 13	229
14:1-12	229
14:12	229
14:13-16	229
14:18-20	209
14:20	211
15:5-6	165
15:6	165, 229
17:5	165
19:1, 14	229
19:24-25	229
19:31-38	229
25:23	201
28:15	17
33:14	208
37:9	250
38	1
45:5, 7	125
50:20	125

Exodus
3:6	22, 40
3:12	107
10:4-6, 12-15	247
12	66
14:15-31	253
14:22	4
14:31	253
15:1-2, 17	253
15:1-18	253
15:14-16	253
15:21	253
17:2	4
19:16, 19	246
20:3-5	256
20:12	195
23:1	162
32	4

Leviticus
5:11	213
11:44	164
12:8	34
17:11	165
19:2	164
19:16	162
23:24	246

Numbers
3:6-10	209, 211
15:32-36	206
25:1	256

Deuteronomy
6:13, 16	4
8:1-3	48
8:3	4

Scripture Index

Deuteronomy (cont.)
10:20	4
12:9-10	208
12:10	208
17:6	162
19:15	112, 162
21:23	165
23:3	1
28:13	208
28:34	247
30:19	235

Joshua
1:5	107
6	246

Judges
15:15	42
18	245

1 Samuel
1:26	85
16:7	35

2 Samuel
7:12-16	208

1 Kings
8:54	85
12:29-30	245
16:32	256
18:46	42
22:53	256

2 Kings
21:3	256

1 Chronicles
5:25, 26	256

2 Chronicles
7:13	247

Ezra
10:1	85

Esther
4:14	250

Job
2:6	247
38:7	247

Psalms
2:8	166
2:8-12	258
8:2	21
16:11	122
19:10	248
21:9	244
34:5	175
51:12	223
69:28	258
78:52	4
95:7-11	207
113-118	257
113:7-9	257
116:3-8	257
118	21
118:26	39
119:103	248
145:8	182
150:1	257

Scripture Index

Proverbs
3:11-12	216
6:6-8	169
16:4	125
16:33	221
18:21	220
19:11	120
22:15	194
27:5	162
27:5-6a	132
27:5-6	138
30:27	247

Ecclesiastes
1:2, 14	122
2:24	194
5:18-20	194

Isaiah
4:4	210
6:5	242
6:8	133
6:9-10	117
9:1-2	76
11	258
13-14	255
29:18-19	9, 10
34:2	244
35:5-6	9, 10
49:2	174
52:7	127
53:3	63
59:2	179
62:1-2	34
62:4-5	212
65:17	259

Jeremiah
1:5	201
1:8	107
9:24	181
15:16	248
31:31-34	212
31:38-40	212
50-51	255
52	255

Lamentations
3:18-23	265

Ezekiel
3:1-3	248
3:3	248
13:8-16	112
18:23	230
23:3	256
36:18	244
48:1-2	245

Daniel
7:13	17, 77, 252
7:1-28	251
7:7-8, 17-26	251
9:27	244, 249
11:36-37	189
12:7	248

Hosea
1-3	120, 256
6:6	9

Joel
1:4	247
2:1	246

Scripture Index

Joel (cont.)
2:28-32	91
3:13	252

Amos
4:6-11	254
4:12	254

Jonah
3:10	247
4:2, 8	247

Micah
4:2-4	258
5:15	244

Nahum
1:2, 6	244

Habakkuk
2:4	14
3:2	246

Zephaniah
1:18	244

Haggai
2:9	63

Zechariah
5:5-11	255
5:11	255
7:12	244
9:9	21, 39
13:7	42
14:21	1

Malachi
2:10-16	217
3:1	11

Matthew
1:20-21	201
1:21	3
1:23	3, 69
3:3	15
3:17	76
4:17	5
5-7	8
5:3-10	13
5:11	162
5:14	6, 237
5:20	12
5:28	217
6:11	171
6:30	14
7:15	109
7:28-39	8
8:10	15
8:26	14
9:3	15
9:6	252
9:9	53
10:5	25
10:6	15
10:17-23	11
10:23	252
10:34	63
11:5	90
12:14	15, 16, 21
12:22-24	13
12:23	15
12:24	15, 16
12:33	13

Scripture Index

Matthew (cont.)
12:36-37	182
12:40	27
12:46	87
12:46-50	87
12:49-50	166
12:51	63
13:55	34
14:31	15
14:20	14
14:33	16
16:8	14
16:15	16
16:18	66
16:21, 22, 28	17
16:21-23	89
19:28-29	20
19:30	20
20:16	20
20:17-19	20
20:20-21	17
22:26-40	193
24	244
24-25	24
24:5, 6, 7, 9	244
24:15	244
24:16	250
25:1-13	232
26:33-35	89
26:36	86
26:36-39	49
26:39, 42, 53	86
27:56	87
27:62-66	43
28:18	163, 166
28:18-20	1, 127, 198
28:19	15, 90, 163
28:20	81, 107

Mark
1:45	30
3:39	179
5:7	34
6:3	179
6:34-44	36
6:37	36
13:14	250
13:21-22	44
14:14-15	196
14:62	37
16:1	88

Luke
1:3	68
1:12-13	46
1:13-17	201
1:15	201
1:29-30	46
1:37	43
2:9-10	46
2:11	46
2:13-14	63
2:14	63
2:24	34
2:32	46
2:41-43	66
2:49	67
2:50	68
3:14	162
3:21	49
4:16-30	34
6:12	49
6:13-16	61
6:27-28	146

Scripture Index

Luke (cont.)
6:38	158
7:1-10	61
7:11-15	61
8:27-33	61
8:41-56	61
9:23	70, 103
9:29	49
9:45	68
9:46-48	61
9:51-19:27	53, 63
10:18	247
10:39-42	193
11:1-4	49
11:5-8	49
11:9-13	49
12:18	169
12:42	137
12:42-48	60
12:48	193
12:54-59	60
13:33-35	59
15	18
17:3-4	151
18:1	49
18:32	67
18:34	68
19:43-44	64
21:3-4	157
21:36	49
21:40, 46	49
22:24	81
22:31-32	89
22:41-42	49
22:42	75, 86
23:34	85
23:50	43
24:5	88

John
1:1	164, 179, 233
1:12-13	166
1:14	34, 164, 179, 186, 236
1:18	179, 181
1:34, 41	16
1:46	34
1:49, 51	77
2:18-22	88
3:3-6	12
3:16	130
3:36	244
4:6	69
4:25-26	16
5:18	75
6:14-15	16
6:38	75
6:51-56	236
7:5	87
7:57	76
8:12	6, 77
8:44	166
8:45	186
8:59	86
9:39	84
10:27-29	210
10:28	238
10:30	69
11:19-30	101
12:31	84
12:48	257
13-16	84, 85
13:1	86
13:8	89

Scripture Index

John (cont.)

13:21-27	86
13:27	26
13:33, 36	82
13:37-38	86
13:38	93
14:2	84
14:2-3	84, 186
14:6	179, 186
14:9	179, 205
14:16, 26	91
14:16-17	167
14:26-27	84
15:13	89
15:26	91
16:8	167
16:13	68
16:33	223
17:3	179
17:4	86
17:3	181
18:2-11	87
18:10	26
18:12	87
18:12-14	87
18:17	89, 93
18:19-24	87
18:25-27	89, 93
19:26-27	195
18:28-40	87
19:28	69
19:38-40	43
20:19	93
20:28	163
21:18-19	29, 42

Acts

1:1	68
1:3	68
1:8	102, 106, 113
1:15	57, 68
1:45	91
2:1-7:60	97
2:2-4	189
2:10	117
2:32	163
3:1-4:31	235
3:2-8	93
3:12-22	93
4:3	110
4:12	179
5:17-42	235, 249
5:18-19	101
5:18	110
5:32	235
5:34	111
5:40	110
5:40-41	235
6:5	97
6:11	96
7:53	206
7:55	95
9:1-2	163
9:4	25
9:15	114, 115
9:16	110
9:3	153
11:19-20	99
11:26	204
12:2	29
12:1-4	110
13-14	126
13:14-52	103

Scripture Index

Acts (cont.)
14:1-6	103
14:19	150, 161
14:27	104
15:1	164
15:11	133
15:40-41	105
15:40-18:22	105
16:6	108
16:6-10	110
17:1-14	183
17:22-31	106
18:23-21:17	108
19:21	110
20:23	110
20:31	108
21:30-32	150, 161
22:6	153
22:25	112
22:25-30	112
23:11	114
23:13-14	113
25:11-12	112
25:12	116
26:13	153
26:24-25	31
26:32	116

Romans
1-2	193
1:1	133
1:7	163
1:9, 15	133
1:16	102, 133
1:18	120, 244
1:18-32	119
1:21-27	256
1:23	64
1:31	130
2:11	47
3:1-3	134
3:5	244
3:21-28	38
3:25	180
3:28	121
4:5	258
5:9	244
5:12	170
5:14-18	170
6:6	124
6:23	180
7-8	124
7:12	164
7:14-25	161
8:3-4	124
8:11	154
8:15, 17	156
8:26-39	210
8:28	175
8:29	64, 166, 181
8:34	66
9:11-12	201
9:22	244
10:4	211
10:17	102
12:2	152, 181
12:4, 7	134
12:4-8	145
12:14	155
12:18	58, 172
12:19	244
14:12	134
15:16	167
15:26	157

Scripture Index

1 Corinthians
1:2	137, 150
1:3	163
1:18	249
2:6-13	139
2:13	136
3:12-13	167
4:4	
4:16	173, 204
4:19-21	158
5:1, 11	156
6:15-20	141, 156
6:19	181
6:20	120
9:24	168
10:7, 14	156
10:13	227
10:31	122
11:1	173
11:30	247
12:7, 7-11	167
12:13	167
13:4-8	130
15	28
15:3-4	133
15:6	68
15:7-8	142
15:35-53	154
15:51-54	199
16:1-2	157

2 Corinthians
3:4-6	127
3:18	122, 181
4:4	197
4:4-6	4
4:7-18	154
5:8	40
5:14-15	5
5:17	170, 259
5:18-19	151, 180
5:20	127
5:21	121
6:14-7:1	156
6:15	156
7:14	150
8-9	157
11:10	150
13:14	163

Galatians
1:4	245
1:6-9	164
1:10	137
1:11-12	133
1:13-14	164
2:7-9	133
2:16	219
2:20	181
3:13	126
3:19	206
4:4	168, 179
4:6	163
4:13-15	161
5:22-23	50, 83, 131, 234
6:1	132, 138, 162
6:2, 5	30

Ephesians
1:1-14	163
1:2	163
1:5	166
1:11	125
1:11-14	210

Scripture Index

Ephesians (cont.)

1:13	150, 174
1:15	172
1:15-23	171
1:19	171
1:20	250
1:20-22	166
2:1, 2, 4-5	166
2:4	172, 180
2:6	180
2:8	104, 174
2:8-9	38
2:10	164, 202
2:13	180
2:15-17	172
3:1	180
3:5	172
3:6	99
3:16	168
4:7-13	145
4:11-12	145
4:14	189
4:15, 22, 24	174
5:6	244
5:18	167
6:10-11	205
6:11-17	187
6:18	167
6:24	172

Philippians

1:9-10	132
1:21	96
2:1-4	139
2:3-4	18
2:3-8	225
2:4	178

2:5-8	69
2:10	205
2:10-11	163
2:20-22	105
2:22-25	178
2:27	178
3:2	84
3:7-10	178
3:17	204
3:20	178, 223
4:6	171
4:6-7	6

Colossians

1:5	150
1:15	64, 181, 205
1:15-17	69
1:17	221
1:27-28	181
1:28	132
2:2-3	132
2:6-7	181
2:9	179
2:10	228
3:2	196
3:6	244
3:8	182
3:10	64
4:3, 10, 18	179

1 Thessalonians

1:6	172
1:10	244
2:1-20	185
2:7-12	126
2:8-11	188
2:14	172

Scripture Index

1 Thessalonians (cont.)
3:6-12	188
4:7	150
4:9	130
4:14-16	40
4:16	246
4:16-17	82, 187, 189
4:17	199
5:9	244
5:14	132
5:19	167, 181
5:24	201

2 Thessalonians
1:1, 2	190
2:1-12	188
2:13-3:15	188
3:1-3	112

1 Timothy
1:3-7	109
1:19-20	109
2:1	85
2:5	166
2:11-12	193
3:1	194
3:8-13	95
4:1-3	189
4:6	189
5:17-18	193
5:19	162
6:20	197
6:20-21	109

2 Timothy
1:6	194
1:9	201
1:14	181, 194
2:2	105
2:10	201
3:3	130
3:15	194
3:16	248
4:2	249
4:3-4	189
4:6-8	150
4:7	160, 168

Titus
1:5-9	202
1:9	189
1:10-16	202
1:16	202
2:11-12	199
2:12	203
3:5	38

Hebrews
1:2	69, 166
1:3	179, 221
1:14	206
2:1	209
2:6-8	179
2:9	210
2:14	205
2:18	236
3:1	210
3:2-19	208
3:18-19	208
3:13	209
4:14	208, 209
4:15-16	236
5:11-6:20	211
5:12	210

Scripture Index

Hebrews (cont.)
6:12	173
6:19	206
7:25	85
8:13	213, 214
9:11-28	214
10:32, 34	210
10:32-37	215
10:36-37	216
11:40	216
12:1	168
12:2	228
12:5-11	83
12:15	125, 161
13:1	130
13:20-21	114

James
1:2-4	83
1:3-5	225
1:5-6	22
1:6	14
1:8	143
1:19	182
1:23	224
1:27	195
2:10-11	164
2:13-3:7	224
2:13-14	225
2:15-16	203
2:18	225
2:17, 20	164
2:21-25	225
3:2-12	182
3:8, 9, 10	182
3:13-18	218
4:1-4	219
4:6-10	219
4:8	219
5:14	171
5:14-15	247

1 Peter
1:3-5	210
1:15-16	156
1:16	164, 234
1:19-20	201
1:21	234
3:16	113
4:10	198
4:14	113
5:7	116
5:8	160
5:10	223
5:12	226
5:13	255

2 Peter
1:1	179
1:16-18	17
1:21	167, 174
2:4	247
2:10	259
3:1	228
3:10-13	258

1 John
1:1	234, 235, 236
1:6-7	140
2:18, 22	189
3:2	200
3:11, 23	232
4:4	108
4:2	236

Scripture Index

1 John (cont.)

4:7, 11, 12	232
5:4-5	4
5:21	256

Jude

1:6	247

Revelation

1-3	231
1:13	252
1:11	231
1:16	17
1:20	247
2:2	109
3:10	189
4:1-2	243
4:5, 8, 10-11	246
4:11	243
5:1-6:17	245, 246
5:4-5	244
5:7	244
5:9	244
5:9-14	246
7:3	247
7:3-8	252
7:4-8	250
7:9, 14	251
8:1	245
8:2, 6-13	247
10:2, 8-10	249
11:2-3	244, 250
11:7	247
11:15	247, 253
11:18	244
12:4	247
12:6	244
12:9	240
12:11	253
13:15	244
14:1-5	250
14:8	255, 256
14:10, 19	244
15:1, 7	244
15:5-8	254
16:1	244, 253
16:19	244, 255
17-18	255, 257
17:1	256
17:1-18:24	252
17:2, 4, 6	256
17:14	256
17:15, 16	256
17:8	247
18:3, 9	256
18:21	248
19:2	256
19:15	244
20-22	257
20:1	247
20:4	251
20:6	239
20:10	252
20:10-15	154
20:11-15	239
21:1	258
22:3, 5	259
21:4	84
21:1	245
21:6	245, 260
21:10-27	260
22:1	245
22:2	240
22:20	258

SUBJECT INDEX

Subject Index

Abrahamic Covenant 1
Accountability 162
Adoption 166
Affliction 161, 188
Angels 205, 206
Anxiety, Worry 6, 11, 14, 82
Authority 159
Baptism of Jesus 3, 4
Calling 150
Christ, Authority of 8, 21, 205
Christ, Person of 1, 34, 69, 73, 76, 179, 205, 208, 211, 231, 235, 236
Christ, Responses to 2
Christ, Return of 24, 65, 187, 239, 260
Christian Liberty 131, 141
Christmas 2
Comfort 125, 154, 185, 186, 188
Communion/Lord's Supper 144
Conflict Resolution 134, 136, 139, 172, 204
Confrontation 138, 151, 162
Demon/Demonic 9, 33
Devil/Satan 4, 13, 16, 227
Discipleship 8, 11, 17, 19, 20, 28, 29, 31, 38, 53, 58, 64, 68, 70, 78, 86, 90, 163, 198
Discipline 216
Divorce 19
Edification 147
Eternal life 40, 238
Evangelism 7, 26, 46, 54, 90, 91, 94, 99, 102, 106, 115, 117, 118, 126, 127, 132, 153, 225, 249
Example/Reputation 183, 237

Faith/Trust/Belief 12, 14, 15, 16, 22, 27, 36, 42, 61, 66, 72, 79, 82, 88, 96, 128, 176, 215, 219, 221, 235
Faithfulness 105, 110, 129, 137, 143, 149, 155, 195, 200, 240
Fellowship 91, 98
False Teaching 189, 191, 194, 234
Forgiveness 9, 51, 66, 138, 151, 180, 204, 213, 231
Fruitfulness 32, 52, 83, 167, 203, 228
Genealogy 1
Giving/Stewardship 149, 157, 158, 195, 196
Godliness 35, 192, 202, 203, 228, 237
Grace 121, 164, 202, 214, 229, 236, 238
Gratitude 178
Great Tribulation 25
Growth, Spiritual 48, 61, 132, 152, 181, 209, 214, 224, 230, 238
Heaven 245, 246, 259, 260
Holiness see Sanctification
Holy Spirit 3, 4, 5, 167
Hope 27, 43, 122, 154, 186, 188
Humility 18, 20, 22, 23, 37, 81
Hypocrisy 23, 143
Illumination 62, 68
Judgment 188, 229, 230, 244, 247, 251, 254, 256, 259
Kingdom 5, 6, 9, 10, 13, 17, 24, 57, 89
Lawsuits 139
Leadership 20, 96, 105, 109, 136, 184, 191, 193, 194, 195
Legalism 11, 35, 152
Lordship 163

Subject Index

Love 5, 50, 59, 130, 141, 142, 146, 151, 173, 233, 234
Magi 2
Marriage 19, 140, 217, 225
Ministry 153, 155, 168
Miracles 8, 11, 13, 74, 77, 79, 92
New Covenant, Superiority of 212, 213
Obedience 8, 32, 39, 114, 233
Parables 13, 20, 25, 59
Peace 11, 84, 208, 221
Persecution 25, 56, 84, 94, 96, 97, 103, 104, 107, 108, 112, 113, 160, 175, 199, 249
Perseverance 31, 57, 66, 148, 149, 160, 168, 201, 206, 223, 238, 241, 252
Prayer 7, 10, 45, 49, 54, 55, 85, 101, 171, 192, 222, 246
Priorities 6, 58, 195
Prophecy 24, 25, 41
Providence 116
Provision 36
Red Sea 4
Redemption 120, 165, 180
Relationship 87, 185
Repentance 5, 11, 12, 13, 47, 63, 89, 207, 254
Responsibility 190
Rest 11, 208
Resurrection 22, 27, 28, 40, 88, 148, 177
Reverence 67
Reward 38, 200, 210, 259
Righteousness 5, 119, 177, 232
Salvation 1, 3, 12, 13, 26, 33, 34, 46, 71, 111, 119, 120, 123, 164, 169, 170, 177, 180, 203, 228, 244, 245, 250, 256
Sanctification 14, 123, 124, 133, 152, 156, 181
Self-examination 144
Sermon on the Mount 5, 6, 7, 8
Service 25, 37, 81, 95, 136, 137, 176, 184
Sin 1, 9, 170, 180, 231
Singleness 140
Sinlessness of Jesus 2, 3
Sovereignty 75
Speech 182, 220
Spiritual Gifts 145, 226
Spiritual Warfare 174
Suffering 17, 161, 175, 218, 223, 226
Teamwork 30
Temptation 4, 143, 227
Testimony 80
Testing 4
Transfiguration 17
Unity 100, 134
Watchfulness 41, 65
Wealth, Money 5, 6, 195, 196
Wilderness 4
Wisdom/Discernment 7, 22, 44, 60, 135, 150, 218
Word of God 197, 248, 255
Worship 2, 21, 205, 206, 242, 243, 253, 257, 258, 259

CONTRIBUTING AUTHORS

AH   **Alex Hernandez,** Th.M., Assistant Professor

AL   **Artis Lovelady, III,** M.A.C.E., Director of Library Services; Assistant Professor

BBH   **Brittany Burnette Hansen,** D.Min., Distance Education Associate Dean; Professor

BH   **Bryce Hantla,** Ed.D., Academic Dean; Professor

FB   **France Brown, Jr.,** Th.M., Ernest L. Mays Assistant Professor

HF   **Harold Fisher,** Ed.D., Professor

IL   **Israel Loken,** Ph.D., Chair, Bible and Theology Departments; Professor

JDB   **John Bechtle,** D.Min., Professor

JTB   **Joel Badal,** Ph.D., Dean of Institutional Effectiveness; Professor

JP   **Joseph Parle,** Ph.D., Provost; Professor

KB   **Kirk Barger,** D.Min., Associate Professor

LC   **Luzmar Cobos,** M.L.S., Assistant Librarian; Instructor

MA   **Mike Ayers,** Ph.D., Professor

MM   **Marvin R. McNeese Jr.,** Ph.D., Chair, General Education Department; Professor

MS   **Marcus Schrader,** M.Div., Dean of College of Biblical Studies, Indianapolis Campus; Professor

NE   **Nicolas Ellen,** D.Min., Senior Professor

PN   **J. Paul Nyquist,** Ph.D., Vice President of Discipleship, Special Assistant to the President

CONTRIBUTING AUTHORS

RC   **Richard M. Cozart**, Ph.D., Professor

RK   **Eric (Rick) Kress**, M.Div., Assistant to the President

SB   **Shane Boothe**, M.A.C.E., Distance Education Associate Dean; Assistant Professor

SE   **Sergio Estrada**, Ph.D., Professor

SS   **Steve Sullivan**, Ph.D., Chair, Ministry Skills Department; Senior Professor

VE   **Venessa Ellen**, Ph.D., Chair, Women's Ministry Department; Associate Professor

WB   **William "Bill" Blocker**, D.Min., President, Professor

ZB   **Zelda Blocker**, M.B.T.S., Associate Dean of Women's Discipleship, Instructor

www.ingramcontent.com/pod-product-compliance
Lightning Source LLC
Chambersburg PA
CBHW071944110426
42744CB00030B/282